VICIOUS

JON T. COLEMAN

Vicious

WOLVES AND MEN IN AMERICA

YALE UNIVERSITY PRESS   NEW HAVEN & LONDON

Published with assistance from the income of the Frederick John Kingsbury Memorial Fund.

Designed by Rebecca Gibb. Set in FontShop Scala and Scala Sans by Duke & Company, Devon, Pennsylvania. Printed in the United States of America by R. R. Donnelley & Sons.

Library of Congress Cataloging-in-Publication Data
Coleman, Jon T., 1970–
Vicious : wolves and men in America / Jon T. Coleman.
    p.   cm.—(Western Americana series)
Includes bibliographical references (p.   ).
ISBN 0-300-10390-5 (cloth : alk. paper)
1. Wolves—United States—History. I. Title. II. Yale Western Americana series.
QL737.C22C62 2004
599.773′0973—dc22
2004000176

A catalogue record for this book is available from the British Library.

The paper in this book meets the guidelines for permanence and durability of the Committee on Production Guidelines for Book Longevity of the Council on Library Resources.

10 9 8 7 6 5 4 3 2 1

To Annie

CONTENTS

Preface   ix

Acknowledgments   xiii

Introduction   1

PART ONE: SOUTHERN NEW ENGLAND

1 Howls, Snarls, and Musket Shots: Saying "This Is Mine" in
Colonial New England   19

2 Beasts of Lore: How Stories Turned Fearsome Monsters into
Skulking Criminals   37

3 Wolf Bullets with Adders' Tongues: How to Kill a Wolf in
Colonial New England   52

PART TWO: THE NORTHEASTERN WOODLANDS

4 Predator to Prey: Wolves' Journey Through the Northeastern
Woodlands   69

5 Surrounded: Fear and Retribution in the Northeastern
Forests   102

6 Metaphors of Slaughter: Two Wolf Hunts   123

PART THREE: THE AMERICAN WEST

7 A Wealth of Canines: Mormon Americans on the
Great Plains   147

8 Call It a Coyote: How to Exterminate Wolves in
Colonial Utah   173

PART FOUR: THE FEDERAL GOVERNMENT

9 Annihilation and Enlightenment: The Cultural Extinction
of North American Wolves   191

Reintroduction   225

Notes   237

Index   267

I WISH I could trace my fascination with wolves to an event worthy of a good story. Perhaps a tale about a bite from a beast on a moonlit forest path, followed by years of feverish research and writing as the canine obsession grew in my blood. Alas, this book emerged from a mundane insight, not rabid inspiration. One day, sitting at my computer, I looked away from the screen and realized that I was surrounded by animals. A whale swam on my coffee mug, a monkey waved from a birthday card, and a cat figurine lounged atop the computer monitor. A quick count of the animal images and effigies in the apartment yielded 113 beasts. The place was a representational ark, and I had barely noticed as the menagerie filed in.

I began to look for animals in other places. As a history graduate student with my eyes fixed on books, documents, and microfiche most of my waking hours, I tried to spot animals in the mountains of text. I found them everywhere. Real and imagined beasts surrounded the Euro- and Native American humans at the center of my research. The history of the colonization of North America was an animal history, and no creature prompted as much discussion or fired as many imaginations as wolves.

Wolves popped up in town records, legislative journals, personal correspondence, and local histories. The evidence was fragmentary—a reference here, a quip there—but as the snippets piled up, a story took shape far bigger and more interesting than even I, an animal fancier, could have anticipated.

The wolf documents betrayed the historical circumstances of their production. When I read in a wolf bounty certificate from colonial New England that Ezekiel turned in a severed wolf's head to his town selectman for a promissory note worth three pounds, the Old Testament name and the payment scheme indicated the transaction's antiquity. And when the selectman nailed the canine's bloody skull to the side of the town's meetinghouse for the residents to ponder and admire, the fissure separating the dead Puritans' worldview from my own opened like a gaping maw. Yet, while rooted in the eras of their making, the wolf documents also migrated across time periods. The same wolf legends and wolf hunting rituals appeared in diverse locales and epochs. Wolves seemed both embedded in time and free to roam through it.

Tracking wolves through the documents of their eradication brought me to paths that led both into and out of history. Wolves raised questions whose answers opened new routes into well-mapped times and places. Why did colonial New Englanders fasten wolf heads to the structures that embodied their civic and religious communities? Gory and flamboyant, these decorations challenged the Puritans' reputation for somberness. Yet even as wolves tempted me to delve deeper into a particular historical situation, the animals pulled me away from the study of the past as I knew it. Beasts steeped in myth and symbol, wolves existed in the realm of folklore as well as that of history. While a disciplinary cousin, folklore worked on scales of time and space far broader than those of history. Folklorists possess different evidentiary standards, and they operate according to a different set of assumptions. Historians, for example, seek to explain change, while folklorists try to understand why some cultural artifacts—stories, songs, jokes, and dances—resist change. Wolves connected history and folklore, revealing how timeframes and disciplines interact, and the complementary ways that history and folklore track change.

And the wolves' trail carried me still farther from my academic home. A history of animals demands some reckoning with biology—a subject I had successfully avoided since sophomore year in high school. Comprehending wolves' behaviors, social structures, communication systems, and ecological relationships forced me to wrestle with the language and epistemology of the life sciences. Wolf howls, for example, chilled the spines of Euro-American colonists from Maine to Montana. Colonists proclaimed the yowls haunting, devilish, foreboding. Engrossed in the projects of livestock raising and territorial conquest, Euro-American settlers were poor listeners. In post–

World War II United States and Canada, better listeners asked new questions about wolf howls. Instead of trying to determine what the howls meant to them, wildlife biologists wondered what the songs meant to wolves. It turned out that the species' talent for long-distance communication was critical to the maintenance of pack territories. Their songs acted as an early warning system, keeping rival groups from needless confrontations as they moved through overlapping territories in search of food. Instead of fiendish messages from the heart of darkness, wolf howls were a brilliant solution to a predator's dilemma. They helped packs concentrate their energies on the acquisition of more energy rather than the elimination of each other.

Listening to wolf howls through history alone distorts the past. It allows humans to hold tight to the fallacy that the universe revolves around them. Wolves had their own reasons for singing. Euro-American livestock owners overheard a conversation intended for furrier ears and used the misinformation they gathered to persecute the howlers. The story of wolves combines biology, folklore, and history, and this story can be told only by melding the techniques, the concerns, the triumphs, and the shortcomings of several disciplines. The result is still history, but history altered in structure and portent by its exposure to biology and folklore—an interdisciplinary mutant.

Human beings have never been fond of mutants. Throughout history, people labeled creatures that crossed boundaries, mixed classes, and bewildered categories unclean and dangerous. Yet mutants represent one of the most creative biological forces on earth. A mutation occurs when the copying of genetic material from one generation to another goes awry. The imperfect copy may wind up crippled or disfigured, but she may also acquire a physical attribute that enhances her life and the lives of her offspring. Mutation can be a blessing as well as a curse. Genetic accidents help drive evolution, adding to the spectacular diversity of living beings on this planet.

Including animals as equal partners in American history triggers a mutation. History becomes something else, a story in which perspectives, disciplines, timeframes, and types of evidence mingle. The result may be a freak, but I am convinced it is a blessed one.

ACKNOWLEDGMENTS

I WROTE this book in the dark mostly. Hauling myself out of bed at five every morning to lay down a few sentences before more important duties—changing diapers, grading papers, folding laundry—seized my attention. I live in Indiana and writing in the morning is easy here in the summer. However, as the leaves fall and the ground freezes, an enfolding gloom turns the wee hours grim. Most of Indiana is in the same time zone as Maine, but it gets the sun about an hour later; in winter the morning darkness lingers like a drunk uncle after Thanksgiving dinner. I endured these black hours, with a little help from Abe, my basset hound, whose thimble-sized bladder roused him and me every morning, because I enjoy what I do. I like writing history, and I have a lot of people to thank for helping me discover and nourish an affinity strong enough to defeat the call of a warm bed on cold mornings.

This book sprung from a doctoral thesis directed by John Mack Faragher at Yale University. Without Johnny the book would have been a nice little study about wolves in colonial New England. He encouraged me to think big and gave me the freedom to wander off into the intellectual bushes. I could not have wished for a better adviser. I first delved into animal history in John Demos's research seminar. Over the years, his enthusiasm for the wolf project kept mine from wavering. Steven Stoll, Stephen R. Kellert, David Waldstriecher, and Virginia Anderson read all or portions of the book in its various incarnations, improving it greatly with their comments.

I have had a string of amazing teachers. Philip Deloria, Fred Anderson, Gloria Main, Julia Green, Nancy Cott, and David Montgomery taught me much more than history, prying open a world of ideas and inquiry I scarcely knew existed growing up. To all of them, I am grateful. Patricia Nelson Limerick has been an inspiration for a number of years. She set a literary standard of clarity, humor, and relevance I try to live up to with every word I write. I owe Patty a mountainous debt that can be repaid only by giving my students the same good-natured working over she gave me.

Yale and the University of Colorado are brimming with smart, funny, and politically engaged graduate students. I was lucky to call dozens of them friends. David Sanders, Carlos Aramayo, Dan Lanpher, Gerry Ronning, Bob Vance, Rob Campbell, Kieko Matteson, Joelle Olcott, Lis Pimentel, Stephen Vella, Kristie Starr, Michelle Nickerson, Ben Johnson, Scott Saul, Wendi Walsh, Antony Dugdale, Brendan Walsh, Rachel Sulkes, Michelle Stephens, and Joseph Entin taught me that scholarship and activism both proceed better with stellar conspirators.

Kevin Cramer, Linda Santoro, Stephen Heathorn, Weitse DeBoer, Rene Berenstein, Michael Snodgrass, Monroe Little, and the entire history department at IUPUI have made life and work in the Midwest both enjoyable and enlightening.

Research for this book could not have been completed without the assistance of timely grants and helpful archivists. A Mellon research grant got the project off the ground, while a Beveridge Research Grant from the American History Association kept it going at a critical juncture. A monthlong stay at the John Nicolas Brown Center at Brown University helped me complete the New England research for the book. Archivists and librarians at the Denver Public Library, the Vermont Historical Society, the Vermont State Library, the Massachusetts Historical Society, the New England History and Genealogical Society, the Western Reserve Historical Society, the Ohio Historical Society, the Utah State Archives, and the archives at Utah State University answered questions, offered advice, and rounded up texts. I appreciate all their work. I would like to especially thank Stephen Sturgeon at Utah State for helping me do a lot of research in a short amount of time. I would also like to express my gratitude to Elliot West for sharing his research on the Great Plains canines with me.

Many thanks to Lara Heimert, Dan Heaton, and the editors at Yale University Press who shepherded the manuscript to publication. The project benefited greatly from the insightful comments of Andrew Cayton, Alan Taylor, Louis Warren, and several anonymous readers. Their encouragement and criticism helped me find the book lurking in my early drafts.

My parents, Barb and Tom Coleman, read every chapter and helped me track down photographs in Colorado. In many ways, this book was written to them. They were representatives from the nonacademic audience I hoped to reach. They are also model parents, so I could imagine not only a curious, engaged, and witty audience but a loving and generous one as well. John Gilbert read the manuscript and helped me with the biological concepts. He is an extraordinary scientist and an even better friend. Cally Gilbert's heartfelt support for the project and roast chicken during my Vermont research trips kept my spirits and waistline from dissipating.

Finally, I am fortunate to be the member of a loving home pack. I am grateful to my son Harry for asking why and answering cause and my daughter Louise for blessing us with her smile; Abe, Oscar, and Bug, the group's animal constituency, deserve credit for the walks and wake-up barks; and, most of all, I want to express my love and gratitude for our fearless leader, Annie Gilbert Coleman. Annie listened to every word of this book, and her comments improved the manuscript immeasurably. She also made the life surrounding the text a merry adventure. Her contributions warrant a tattoo, not a mere mention in a set of acknowledgments. Nonetheless, I am eternally grateful.

Introduction

ON A SNOWY winter morning in 1814, the wildlife painter, hunter, and naturalist John James Audubon watched a livestock owner torture a family of wolves. The farmer had captured the animals in pit traps dug along the parameter of his Ohio River Valley land. Every night he set hunks of venison on platforms of interwoven twigs balanced over four eight-foot-deep craters. When a wolf seized the bait, the platform swung on a hidden axis, dumping the animal into the hole.[1]

On the morning Audubon accompanied him, the farmer caught three wolves in one pit. The predators "lay flat on the earth, their ears laid close over their head, their eyes indicating fear more than anger." The farmer surprised Audubon by leaping into the hole armed only with a knife. The wolves astonished Audubon further by cowering before the farmer. They did nothing as the blade "cut the principal tendon above [their] joint[s]." After hamstringing his prey, the farmer hoisted the animals out of the trap one by one with a rope and set his hounds on them. The first wolf, a female, fought the dogs. She "scuffled along" at a "surprising rate," legs dangling behind her, and managed to remove a patch of skin from one of her tormenters before the farmer shot her. The she-wolf's packmates crouched in silence. Audubon and the farmer hauled up one black-pelted male who was "motionless with fright, as if dead, its disabled legs swinging to and fro, its jaws wide open, and the gurgle in its throat alone indicating that it was alive." The hounds then "worried him to death."[2]

The scene was horrid, but neither the farmer nor the naturalist felt the least bit queasy about the carcasses slumped in the snow. The farmer mutilated the animals to exact revenge. During the fall, a pack of wolves had robbed him of "nearly the whole of his sheep and one of his colts." For him, it made sense to devote his winter labor to digging pits, weaving platforms, hunting bait, and setting and checking his traps twice daily. The animals had injured him, and "he was now 'paying them off in full.'" Audubon's reaction to the slaying of the wolves is less understandable. The naturalist was astounded many times during the episode. The ingenious pit traps amazed him, as did the fearsome predators' meek behavior and the childlike glee the farmer took in his work. The violence Audubon witnessed, however, did not shock him. Watching a pack of dogs rip apart terrified and defenseless animals was a "sport" both he and the farmer found normal and enjoyable.[3]

In this book I seek to understand wolf killing in American history. I shall ask three questions: Why did European-Americans hate and destroy wolves for centuries? Why did they treat the animals so cruelly? And, given the ferocity of their emotions and conduct, why have Americans recently tried to protect and restore the predators?

Audubon's encounter with the Indiana wolves suggests the monumentality of this attitude shift. Audubon and the farmer shared a conviction that wolves not only deserved death but deserved to be punished for living. Wolves had no place in a society and an environment organized to produce marketable plants and animals. This cultural consensus no longer exists. As a whole, Americans at the turn of the twenty-first century have a splintered opinion of wolves. Younger, college-educated Americans living in cities tend to view wolves favorably, while older and rural Americans tend to see wolves in a harsher light. Americans' attitudes have traveled from unanimity to ambiguity, and this is a remarkable cultural journey considering the brutal treatment of wolves in the past. To fully measure the scope and significance of this transformation, however, it is crucial to understand the fear, antipathy, and ugliness that fueled wolf killing.[4]

Naturalists, scientists, journalists, wildlife activists, policy analysts, government bureaucrats, and historians have examined the motives behind wolf killing. In his influential *Of Wolves and Men,* the nature writer Barry Lopez offers several theories. Humans, of course, destroyed predators of all kinds to safeguard livestock. But the persecution of wolves was "fundamentally different because the history of killing wolves shows far less restraint and far more perversity." Ultimately, Lopez attributes this perversity to "theriophobia," an irrational and deep-seated fear of "the beast." In his pivotal study of wolf behavior and ecology, L. David Mech blames the ecological "blindness" of "antiwolf people" for excessive wolf killing. Oblivious to the actual behavior of wolves, antiwolf people based their hatred on "myths, tales, and legends."[5]

Dispelling the myths that led to the near extinction of a species has been a central goal of the authors of books dedicated to uplifting people's opinions of wolves. Building on the ecological and behavioral studies performed by wolf biologists, these popular works depict wolves as complex and sympathetic creatures. Wolves hunt, play, travel, establish pecking orders, create affective bonds, educate pups, demarcate territories, and converse in a language of howls, scents, and gestures. Wolves rarely attack humans, and they do not howl at the moon. (There is no record of a nonrabid wolf killing a human in North America since the arrival of Europeans.) They are neither innate cowards nor wanton killers. "Wolves are wolves," explains Lopez, "not men." With Lopez's book in the forefront, wolf studies have gone a long way toward understanding wolves as wolves rather than as figments of human imaginations.[6]

A remarkable role reversal has accompanied this new, enlightened vision. As wolves have become more comprehensible, reasonable, and sympathetic, human beings have become less so. In the wolf books, people are the irrational wasters and despoilers. They poison wolves with strychnine, hunt them with eagles, and drag them to death behind horses. Humans hide mackerel hooks in balls of tallow, leaving the lethal tidbits along forest paths for random wolves to ingest. They set wolves on fire, kill them with dogs, and capture them alive only to release them with their mouths or, perhaps, their penises wired shut. (This last trick was popular amongst nineteenth- and twentieth-century bounty hunters and government trappers, who collected wolf urine to use as a lure.) The scale and sadism of the violence has prompted some authors to compare predator control campaigns to pogroms, and has tempted others to search for innate flaws in the human psyche that could explain such fiendish behavior. Wicked and unfathomable, humans have assumed the villain's role, a part once reserved for wolves.[7]

Despite their attempts to challenge the way readers think about wolves, wolf studies have preserved the rigid dichotomy of good and evil that always characterized people's opinions of the animals. They simply flip-flop the villains and the victims. Stripped of the dark legends that surrounded them, wolves emerge as sensible predators. People, on the other hand, descend into madness, butchering a species and taking pleasure in the bloodbath. With the best of intentions, wolf books have refurbished a mythology instead of dismantling it. The shadow these studies cast on the human heart cancels out the light they shed on the nature of wolves.

Animals and humans are neither intrinsically sinister nor essentially angelic. Both deserve to be understood on their own terms. Indeed, the inscrutability of wolf killing makes it a perfect candidate for historical analysis. Historians, argues Robert Darnton, should seek out the unfamiliar in order to capture the "otherness" of the past, thereby avoiding the pitfalls of anachronism. Rituals, jokes, practices, and beliefs that appear opaque and bizarre to us, the living, may "lead into a strange and wonderful world view." Learning to decipher the culture that simultaneously persecuted and mythologized wolves for more than three hundred years begins with the acts of cruelty we scarcely understand. The investigation of wolves in American history may not lead to a wonderful worldview, but it promises insight into how people in the past understood their world and acted on those perceptions.[8]

Why did European-Americans hate wolves for centuries and then begin to change their minds? The answer to this question can be found in that special preoccupation of historians—time.

The violent interaction of three timeframes—historical, folkloric, and biological—explains the longevity of wolf hatred and the brutality of wolf killing, as well as the rise of wolf popularity. Over three hundred years, the concerns of history—territorial conquest, agricultural settlement, and livestock protection—mixed with wolf legends and hunting rituals that stretched far into Euro-Americans' cultural past. These cultural traditions and historical circumstances, in turn, met a third timeframe, the slow-moving processes of biological change and evolutionary adaptation.[9]

John James Audubon watched these timeframes collide in 1814. The Ohio Valley farmer destroyed wolves to pacify a rural landscape, transforming an ecosystem that nourished wolves into a habitat that grew and protected marketable plants and animals. A set of historical circumstances, including the United States' military conquest of the Ohio River Valley and the expansion of a market economy into the region, prompted the farmer to excavate his holes. The farmer's cruelty signaled the presence of folklore in the pits. Wolf baiting was a Euro-American hunting ritual, and these rituals turned pragmatic acts of predator eradication into gruesome expressions of revenge, anger, and dominion.

And biology? In the grand scheme of natural history, the death of a pack of wolves was a puny event. Yet biological change and evolutionary adaptation did intrude on that snowy day. The wolves' passive reaction to their capture and torment reflected their sociality. Group hunters, wolves developed an intricate social hierarchy to bond and organize their packs. Subordinate wolves bowed before their superiors. Stuck in a hole and attacked by an aggressive predator, the wolves ducked and cringed in an attempt to communicate their willingness to trade submission for mercy.

Wolves and Euro-Americans battled across the frontiers of time and space, and they fought for a common goal: transcendence. Both struggled to pass down genetic, cultural, and material legacies to their offspring, and this conquest of time, played out over history, culture, and biology, explained the longevity and intensity of the species' conflict.

For three centuries, an antiwolf consensus pushed the animals toward oblivion despite the political upheavals, economic disruptions, and cultural revolutions that transformed the rest of American society. The consensus survived because Americans embedded their hatred of wolves in stories, rituals, and institutions built to withstand historical change. Families, governments, legal systems, private property, churches, folklore, and literature preserved the possessions and beliefs people valued most. They sometimes failed to safeguard the sacred items and ideas humans placed under their care: governments were overturned, farms were condemned, laws were rewritten, and legends were forgotten. Yet, while hardly impervious to change, these stories, rituals, and institutions could and often did reach across generations and continents.

The story of wolf killing illustrates the tenacity of two Euro-American conquering devices—folklore and property. Folklore fueled wolf hatred through rituals and legends codified into motifs and transmitted by word of mouth. Wolf lore survived by being remembered and retold, while property in the form of livestock also traveled across landscapes and lifetimes. Domestic beasts sauntered, hopped, galloped, and clip-clopped through space. As creatures that sexually reproduced, domestic beasts also broadcast a genetic legacy through time. Farmer Jones not only owned the heifer and bull grazing in the back pasture, he owned their offspring. Even more, Jones's children possessed the offspring's offspring. The lives of individual animals were brief, but the herd lived forever as long as new calves replaced slaughtered cows.

Cattle and tall tales may seem unlikely co-instigators in humans' battles with wolves, but the ability of property and stories to travel brought them in direct conflict with the wild animals. Reproduction lay at the heart of this struggle. Humanity's quest to reproduce ideas and possessions clashed with wolves' mission to survive as a species through sexual reproduction. Wolves were formidable biological competitors. One of the world's most adaptable species, they thrived in an amazing range of climates and ecosystems. Individual wolves were resilient, and so were wolf populations, which could lose as many as a third of their numbers each year and survive. Had the conflict remained an ecological contest between two top predators trying to fill the same niche, wolves might have stood a chance. But wolves faced a biological competitor with expansive goals. Like wolves, human beings participated in the Darwinian struggle to transmit a genetic legacy to future generations. Unlike wolves, people also sought to pass on their possessions and ideas. Progeny, property, and folklore offered three pathways to transgenerational immortality. The skirmish between wolves and humans was a minor battle in the grand war all living creatures wage against death, and their fight revealed the common thread that unites history, culture, and biology: the struggle for transcendence.[10]

An unpleasant fact of existence on this planet is that death far outstrips life. All living creatures "produce more offspring than can possibly survive." Dandelions launch thousands of seeds into a summer breeze, but only a few take root and even fewer grow to launch their own seeds. Salmon release thousands of eggs, but only a fraction of these become adults capable of re-production. Unlike weeds or fish, mammals dedicate their resources to a few young, hedging their bets that a couple well-fed and well-tended progeny have a better chance of survival than a thousand cast to the wind or the water. Yet even this cautious reproductive strategy tends toward the same result: mammals produce more offspring than can possibly survive. They do so for good reasons. Floods, famines, fires, droughts, diseases, and predators make the world a dangerous place for youngsters. Only those best adapted to the contingencies of their environment can hope to stay alive. No parent can predict which children will thrive or perish. Therefore they generate many, and natural selection determines the fittest. This long-term process drives evolution. Over millions of years, the lives and deaths of countless individuals shape the development of entire species. Some species change color, while others take flight. Some grow fur; others sprout opposable thumbs. The earth owes its spectacular diversity of living creatures to evolution by natural selection.[11]

Wolves evolved over millions of years from ancestral carnivores that chased their dinner. Wolves distinguished themselves from other meat eaters by chasing in groups. Packs enabled wolves to hunt the largest and fiercest animals around, securing their niche as top predators. In order to keep their packs together, they developed social hierarchies as well as affective relationships. To protect their food supply from rival packs, they marked and defended territories. To communicate across their territories, they cultivated a repertoire of howls. Wolves accomplished all these nifty adaptations as a species, not as individuals. Wolves that formed packs, established territories, and employed long-distance communication tended over millennia to reproduce more successfully than those that did not. Evolution works at a glacial pace, and individual lives matter little in such a grand timeframe.[12]

Humans, of course, have their own evolutionary history. Like wolves, humans hunted in groups. They developed complex social relations, territories, and communication systems. Most significantly, humans acquired large brains in proportion to the size of their bodies. All the characteristics that supposedly separate humans from their animal ancestors—culture, language, agriculture, and technology—arose from this biological adaptation. The story of the evolution of the human brain is too long and involved to delve into here. The key points to remember are these: First, humans acquired nimble brains as a species, not individuals. Ancestral humans with larger brains tended to reproduce more successfully than those with smaller brains. Second, human evolution took a very, very long time. Third, human beings do not represent the apex of evolution. Evolution works toward no end and for no one, it just works.[13]

Given the evolutionary histories of humans and wolves, a conflict seems imminent and an outcome seems assured. Both species established and defended territories to protect their food supply from rivals, and humans' large brains ensured their ascendancy over lesser-endowed foes. But this classic Darwinian scenario of tooth-and-claw competition contradicts both science and history. Evolution tends to reduce rather than inspire interspecific annihilation. Species avoid competition by spacing themselves out and specializing in the foods they eat. When animal A confronts animal B, B will move or acquire a new diet before waging a war of extermination with A. Neither wolves nor humans would have survived for millennia at each other's throats, and history shows that they did indeed coexist for thousands of years. Wolves and humans clashed, but the two species had enough space and food to side-step a battle to extinction. This long, uneasy stalemate ended around 1500, when a rowdy assembly of people calling themselves the English managed to destroy all the wolves residing in their island nation.[14]

Wolf extermination dates pockmarked the next five hundred years: Scot-land in 1684, Ireland in 1770, Denmark in 1772, Bavaria in 1847, Poland in 1900, France in 1927, the United States (outside Alaska and sections of Min-nesota and Michigan) in 1950, and Mexico in 1960. Humans and wolves co-existed for millennia; then, in a scant five centuries, humans drove wolves to the edge of worldwide extinction. What happened to break down the eons-old stalemate between the two species?

European humans tried to conquer the globe. The year 1500 represented the midpoint of western Europe's recovery from the Black Death, a plague that killed a third of the region's people in 1348–49. From 1460 to 1620 the population of western Europe doubled. England's demographic expansion hit full stride in the sixteenth century. The country entered the century with 2.5 million people and exited with 5 million. One of the ways Europeans coped with their reproductive bonanza was to pack up their progeny and leave. Population growth fueled European colonization, and colonization re-arranged biological communities throughout the world.[15]

The European conquest of North America could be described as a mas-sive intrusion of biology into history. For centuries, plants, animals, and people living on the Eurasian landmass swapped goods, livestock, and pathogens. Species grew opportunistic and aggressive through eons of bio-logical infighting. Set loose in the New World, the weedy European species quickly overran the more isolated North American plants, animals, and people. Dandelions, pigs, and humans with immunities to smallpox, tuber-culosis, and measles replaced grama grass, passenger pigeons, and humans with more attenuated immune systems. The accidents of biogeography— the east-to-west orientation of the broadly plained Eurasian continent, as op-posed to the north-to-south configuration of the frequently bottlenecked Western Hemisphere, which eased the movement and exchange of diseases and technology—underwrote the amazing success of the European conquests.[16]

Unfortunately, the power of biology to determine and explain the human past declines rapidly when we factor in the wildly divergent concerns of natural and human history. Evolution cares nothing for peoples, races, cultures, nations, or religions. Indeed, it cares for nothing at all. Evolution is a selection process with no preference for the beings it selects. The organisms best suited to their environment live and reproduce, while organisms ill-suited to their environment die. No species, however tough or smart, is guaranteed survival, because environments change all the time. Temperatures drop, water holes dry up, fires transform habitats. The evolutionary struggle is not a battle for supremacy among organisms so much as a war all living beings wage to outlast the contingencies of their worlds.

The European colonization of North America introduced a new set of contingencies to a continent that already had plenty. Both the invading organisms and the native scrambled to pass down legacies in an increasingly chaotic environment. This struggle proved especially taxing for European and Amerindian humans. The mere genetic conquest of time satisfied neither group. They hoped to pass along their cherished ideas and possessions as well as genes. This desire not only to survive but to create and safeguard the institutions, the belief systems, and the lines of property that gave meaning to survival distinguished human and natural history. Humans set conditions on life while biology set none.

And wolves, cows, and folk legends? Where do they fit in the humans' conquests? Livestock and folklore mediated the encounter between wolves and humans. Wolves had a ghostly presence in colonial landscapes. Settlers heard howls, but they rarely spotted their serenaders. The fearsome beasts avoided humans. People frightened them, and colonists knew this: "They are fearfull Curres," reported Thomas Morton in 1637, "and will runne away from a man (that meeteth them by chance at a banke end) as fast as any fearefull dogge." Humans and wolves scared one another, and their mutual unease kept the species apart. This situation made evolutionary sense. Fear creates space, and competing species need distance to sidestep ruinous brawls. Instead of inciting bloodshed, strong emotions prevented violence. Livestock, however, thwarted wolves' emotional rescue.[17]

Domestic animals moseyed into the buffer zone between the species. As mobile property, domestic beasts transported the fortunes of invading humans on their backs and their bones. Without livestock the European conquest of North America would have gone nowhere. Animal muscle energized colonization, hauling possessions and filling stomachs. Domestic beasts, however, did not always carry their owners into the places and the situations the humans wished to go. Livestock continually wandered into trouble, and they dragged their caretakers with them.

The same attributes that endeared animal property to colonists sparked conflicts with indigenous people and predators. Whether disembarking from a ship in Boston harbor or climbing down from a Conestoga wagon on the shores of the Great Salt Lake, Euro-American colonists faced a herding dilemma. With few adult workers to spare, infant colonies either allowed their livestock to fend for themselves or assigned the task of oversight to children. Both solutions offered ample opportunities for livestock to roam. The blessing of animal property—self-propulsion—turned into a nuisance. Pigs wandered into Indian cornfields; calves met wolf packs; and sheep nibbled poisonous forbs. Domestic animals picked fights and courted dangers, increasing the havoc of colonization. To save their beasts, Euro-Americans attacked the people, plants, and wildlife that threatened their property. Thus livestock both eased the conquest of North America and raised the level of contention.

Domestic beasts nourished colonists' anxieties as well as their bodies, revealing one of the chief ironies of the European invasion of North America: colonization often left the conquerors feeling as besieged, as bewildered, and as enraged as the conquered. In the course of becoming the most dominant predator on the continent, Euro-Americans often conceived of themselves as prey.[18]

From the perspective of a pack of slaughtered wolves or a family of enslaved Amerindians, the frustrations and disappointments of Euro-Americans were a ridiculous consideration. Who cares how the conquerors felt? Yet however delusional and convenient, the colonists' sense of themselves as beleaguered, and in some cases victimized, is pivotal to understanding the cruelty of wolf killing as well as the role of folklore in colonization. From the invaders' point of view, their territorial remove should have preserved, increased, and improved the institutions, the possessions, and the ideas the colonists valued most. Families should blossom, purses should overflow, and communities should flourish. Euro-American colonists exposed their bodies, their fortunes, and their belief systems to the dangers of an unknown place in the hopes of securing better lives for themselves and their offspring.[19]

Given these aspirations, the disenchantments that followed were hardly surprising. Instead of safeguarding cherished items and ideas, colonization often threatened them. Take livestock, for example. Cows and pigs found the New World delicious. They thrived in the grassy marshlands and the oyster beds of coastal North America, and grew fat and plentiful without much supervision. From the colonists' perspective, this was how the conquest should work. By undertaking the cost and risk of transporting livestock across an ocean, they hoped not only to reproduce the animals they owned but expand the herd for their children's benefit as well. Wolves disrupted these plans. They ate free-ranging herbivores and came to symbolize the maddening tendency of colonization to both surpass expectations and dash them.

Killing wolves represented one way to synchronize the conquests of space and time. But Euro-Americans never merely killed wolves. They embroidered the pragmatic act of destroying livestock-devouring predators with a series of dramatic and bloody symbols, legends, rituals, celebrations, and competitions. The citizens of New England towns nailed wolves' heads to the clapboards of their meetinghouses. In Vermont storytellers spun legends in which wolf packs surrounded unwary trekkers in the woods. In Ohio communities organized grand "circle hunts" in order to rid entire counties of wolves and other wildlife. In Utah, Mormon wolf killers divided themselves into teams and staged monthlong competitions to see who could gather the most wolf skins. The public display of heads, traveler legends, circle hunts, and hunting competitions pushed the utilitarian defense of livestock into the realm of folklore. This lore included wolf legends and hunting rituals passed down from generation to generation that explained not only how to rid an agricultural landscape of predators but also how to feel about their riddance. Americans killed wolves to safeguard domestic animals; folklore gave these killings cultural and social meanings. As folk villains, wolves symbolized the frustrations and anxieties of colonization, and the canines paid in blood for their utility as metaphors.

Why did Americans hate wolves for hundreds of years and then begin to change their minds? Livestock, folklore, and sex underpinned the longevity of wolf hatred. Humans designed property and folklore to endure. As biological reproduction created new generations, cultural reproduction passed them the motives and meanings that drove wolf eradication. Property, folklore, and genes made continuity possible, but these conquering devices also contained the impetus for change.

In the early twentieth century, livestock owners, professional hunters, and federal bureaucrats divvied up the labor of wolf killing in the American

West, and this bureaucratization of wolf control severed the link between livestock protection and folklore production. Livestock owners lost their monopoly on wolf stories and hunting rituals. The bureaucratization of predator eradication created a new folk group with its own lore. Like the farmer-colonists before them, the government wolf hunters told stories about their work. These narratives both influenced and reflected enormous changes in Americans' relationship to animals. Government scientists and trappers replaced livestock owners as the central producers of wolf folklore at the same time that American society grew more urban and industrial. Wage earners living in apartments own goldfish, not cows, and as the sting of livestock depredation faded from many Americans' lives, so did their hatred of wolves. The antiwolf consensus fractured, and the severing of the historical link between folklore production and property ownership underwrote this monumental shift.

The federal government entered the wolf-killing business in 1906 at the behest of national livestock associations. The scientists and trappers of the Bureau of the Biological Survey were lethal and efficient. By the end of the 1940s, they had purged wolves from most of the continental United States. The bureau's hunters owed their deadliness to outrageous amounts of strychnine and new insights into wolf behavior. In order to destroy more wolves, government biologists began collecting information about the animals. They published manuals for killing wolves based on observations made in the field. Many of their conclusions were faulty. Early researchers gathered much of their evidence from a biased set of informants, professional wolf hunters. Yet the curiosity that bureau scientists showed in the actual behavior of wolves paved the way for a sympathetic view of the animals.[20]

As wildlife biologists inched toward an ecological understanding of wolves, professional hunters transformed wolf folklore. They introduced the doomed yet heroic "last wolves" into the lexicon of wolf legends. The last wolves differed from the legendary wolves of the past. First, they had names. By naming their quarry, professional hunters gave the Custer wolf, Three Toes, Lefty, Phantom, Bigfoot, and Rags the Digger the individuality and personality earlier storytellers had denied wolves. Second, the last wolves were respected foes. Their penchant for swallowing livestock made them outlaws, but the last wolves' flair for survival earned them the admiration of human hunters. The last wolves killed prodigiously without the assistance of packs; they escaped the best-laid traps; and, when spotted, they carefully stayed beyond the range of high-powered rifles. The wolves' cunning overmatched the skills of amateur hunters. Livestock owners had to hire professionals. These men eventually brought the animal outlaws down, but their triumph was bittersweet. The deaths of last wolves evoked mixed emotions. The animals were vermin, but they were exquisite vermin. The last wolves embodied intelligence, ferocity, and wildness. Standing over the corpses of legendary predators, humans mourned the passing of ideals they despised in living wolves but revered in dead ones.

The mythology of the last wolves engendered feelings of loss and longing at the same time that scientific observation of wolves generated evidence that contradicted the darkest vision of wolves as irredeemable murderers. This combination of nostalgia and insight proved crucial to improving people's opinions of the animals. For nearly three centuries, folklore and property had worked together to sustain wolf hatred. The federal takeover of predator control disrupted this dynamic. A government bureaucracy with its own wolf legends and hunting rituals introduced a new wolf to an American population becoming ever more urban and industrial. In one sense, the scientific wolf killers fulfilled livestock owners' wildest fantasies: they reduced a wolf population that once had numbered in the hundreds of thousands to a couple remnant packs. Yet in the process, the biologists and trappers gathered evidence and created legends that set the stage for wolves to return under government protection.

In 1973 the Department of Fish and Wildlife placed the wolves still living in the United States outside of Alaska on the list of animals protected by the Endangered Species Act. The act required the federal government to not only forestall the extermination of species but also work to promote their recovery. Scientists and bureaucrats began plotting the reintroduction of wolves to New England, the northern Rockies, and the Southwest in the 1970s. These plans went nowhere. It was easy to imagine hauling packs of Canadian wolves (thousands of wolves survived in the North) and setting them loose in sanctuaries like Yellowstone National Park. But the politics of such an adventure kept the Canadians at home. The federal government would not import livestock-eating predators as long as Ronald Reagan, an actor-president who liked to play rancher on his California spread on the weekends, held power. As livestock owners and environmentalists argued over recovery plans and federal mandates, the wolves took matters into their own paws. Dispersers traveled across the border into Idaho and Montana.

These colonizers spurred action. Wolves were coming back, and they had the full protection of the Endangered Species Act. Ranchers faced jail and fines if they killed the animals. Even worse, they might lose grazing rights or even the control of their own land if scientists deemed it critical wolf habitat. The nightmare scenario of federal agents ordering livestock owners to allow wolves to congregate on the pastures led to a deal. Beginning in 1990 wolf reintroduction moved forward, but the translocated animals would be an "experimental non-essential population," not an endangered species. Under the right circumstances—for example, if a rancher actually saw a wolf attack a calf—the animals could be shot with impunity. In 1995 the Fish and Wildlife Service set fourteen wolves from Alberta, Canada, loose in Yellowstone. Nine years later the population had grown to 148 predators, and packs of "non-essential" gray and Mexican wolves loped in Idaho, Arizona, and New Mexico. If wolves could smell human irony as well as they detect bison musk or deer sweat, the odor of the United States at the turn of the twenty-first century would knock them silly. The same people who once poisoned their whelps, dragged them to death behind horses, and pierced their intestines with mackerel hooks now spent millions of dollars and waged political wars to bring them back. The world had turned for the predators.[21]

Wolves and people remain cotravelers in American history, and this lingering partnership reminds us humans that our concerns and aspirations exist alongside others. People never monopolized the creation of history. Indeed, including wolves in history splinters the very notion of a coherent American past. Wolves' story included time periods, actors, regions, and processes familiar to American historians. They howled in colonial New England, bled before John James Audubon, and endured the European conquest of North America. Yet wolf history also included cultural phenomena and biological transformations that operated on timescales in which events like colonization, or identities like American, had little meaning. Three timeframes collided when Euro-Americans met wolves, and, by watching biology, folklore, and history interact, humans can better understand their place in the incessant struggle of living beings to transcend death by casting bits of themselves to the future.

Time is a squirrelly concept, and telling a story that tries to weave together three temporal existences is a recipe for mind-numbing abstraction. The history of wolf killing in America oozed blood and passion, items rarely found in an academic treatise. To keep this history visceral, I have limited its scope. The story follows a single Euro-American immigration path. Starting in southern New England in the 1620s, it moves to Vermont and New Hampshire during the Revolutionary period, northern Ohio in the early national period, the Mormon settlements in Nauvoo, Illinois, and Utah's Salt Lake Valley in the nineteenth century, and the U.S. Biological Survey's western Colorado predator eradication efforts in the early twentieth century.

Focusing mainly on the area that would become the United States and the slim strata of people encompassing New Englanders and their offspring ignores wolf killing in the American South, Canada, and Alaska, as well as the multitude of Native American and African-American experiences with the animals. The New Englanders' story was neither exceptional nor universal. A southern route across the continent, perhaps tracing the movement of wolf-hating livestock owners from Virginia to Kentucky to Missouri to Texas, would have been equally valid and enlightening. I hope other scholars, making different choices, will visit the times and places I could not.

PART ONE SOUTHERN NEW ENGLAND

Howls, Snarls, and Musket Shots

SAYING "THIS IS MINE" IN COLONIAL NEW ENGLAND

Woath woach ha ha hach woath. The great and hideous cry jerked the landing party awake. "Arm, arm," yelled a sentinel. Muskets boomed and fell silent. Men traded whispers in the dark. One, a sailor, had heard the cry before. Companies of wolves, he reported, often sung to him and his mates on the cod fishing boats off the coast of Newfoundland. Convinced that wolves "or such like wild beasts" had made the noise, the men slept, rousing themselves in the morning to pack their shallop (the small boat sent from the *Mayflower* to search for a settlement site) and eat. A group hauled the party's armor down to the boat. The tide was low. They would have to wait to launch the craft until the shallow waters surrounding Cape Cod rose. The armor bearers headed back to break their fast. Near the encampment, they heard the sound again: *woath woach ha ha hach woath*. "They are men, Indians, Indians." Arrows flew. Miles Standish fired his snaphance. More blasts followed. The Indians' captain stepped from behind a tree and shot three arrows. He uttered "an extraordinary shriek," and the Indians slipped away.[1]

Sound and fear permeated the Plymouth colonists' first encounters with New England's "wild beasts and wild men." Lacking a common language, the English and the Indians communicated their unease by making a ruckus. Fear underlay the shots and shouts. The midnight howl alarmed the landing party. The colonists answered the cry with musket shots intended to scare the beasts that had scared them. Again, in the morning, a hideous

sound frightened the English, and, again, they answered with their most potent noisemakers. (Cumbersome and inaccurate, the English guns were
more loud than lethal.) The Indian leader ended the conversation with a yell.
His shriek epitomized the double meaning of all the shots and shouts. He
screamed after a musket ball hit a tree next to his head, making "the bark or
splinters . . . fly about his ears." The cry registered the Indian's fright at nearly
being decapitated. The shriek expressed terror; but it also induced terror.
The "great and strange" noise filled the English with "dread." *Woath woach
ha ha hach woath* was the sound of a colonial encounter. It captured the confusion, violence, and shared apprehension of two peoples that could not
speak to one another but could scare the hell out of each other.[2]

Animals, including human ones, squeak and bellow for reasons, and
their outbursts carry numerous messages. Chirps beckon mates, roars an-
nounce physical vigor, and bleats help mothers locate wayward young. Noises
strengthen group cohesion; they coordinate hunting and travel; and they express emotions. Birdsongs, elk bugles, rhinoceros snorts, and leopard purrs
fill the air with affection, lust, anger, and elation. Animals also use sound to
create and maintain territories. A territory consists of the area an animal or
group of animals occupies exclusively by repelling interlopers. Territory is
space with teeth, and the promise of violence arranges spatial relations among
similar species. The key word here is *promise.* Most species try to avoid fights
to the death, turning instead to ritualized displays of dominance, vocal signaling, and scent marking to keep competitors at a proper distance. Animals
need space to survive, and they acquire this space through communication
as well as bloodshed.[3]

Human beings claim a mastery over communication not shared by their
nonbipedal brethren. Animals make noise; people manipulate language.
The human song of plosives, nasals, fricatives, and vowels carries sophisticated
data no grunt, cluck, or moo could articulate. Yet while a pig may never grasp
the nuances of Shakespeare, people have overestimated their prowess as
communicators. When comparing ourselves to other creatures, we continually
mistake difference for superiority. Human language differs from, say, the
chirps and whistles of chipmunks by being flexible, interchangeable, and
infinite. Like many nonhuman animals, chipmunks communicate through
a limited set of signals. The meanings of their sounds and gestures are ge-
netically fixed. An aggressive posture that warns "stay away from my acorns"
always means "stay away from my acorns." By contrast, human beings monkey

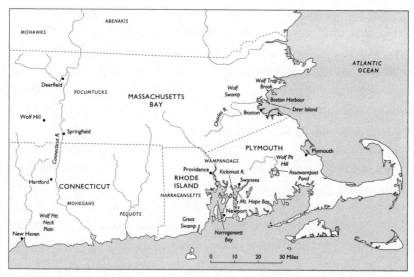

FIGURE 1 Southern New England.

with meaning. They rearrange sentences, invent words, and concoct metaphors, puns, and double entendres. The astonishing elasticity of language
allows humans to express complex ideas, but all this creativity comes at a
price. Over thousands of years, people have mixed and matched sounds and
symbols to generate thousands of languages. Alone among the earth's animals,
human beings have fashioned a communication system that can make members of the same species incomprehensible to one another.

The 1620 fight between the Plymouth colonists and the Cape Cod natives
illustrated the advantages and the pitfalls of linguistic creativity. Indians and
colonists possessed the amazing ability to learn and devise new languages,
but they still managed to ignore, misread, and remain oblivious to each
other's signals. The English-speaking colonists and Algonquian-speaking
natives yelled, blasted, and wailed across a cultural chasm. The humans' inventive communication system generated confusion when they needed clarity most. The European invasion of New England not only rearranged the
spaces humans and animals claimed as their own, it disrupted the flow of
information that created and maintained peaceful distances between ecological
rivals. The Cape Cod episode demonstrated just how frightening, haphazard,
and violent establishing new lines of communication and territory would be
for the region's top predators—Indians, colonists, and wolves.[4]

Wolves participated in the Cape Cod skirmish, if only as figments of overheated imaginations. Even disembodied, their presence was telling. To bridge their cultural differences, New England's humans often borrowed other animals' signals. These signals included noises and gestures that communicated a simple yet crucial idea. Howls, growls, and yelps expressed territoriality on an emotional level both natives and newcomers could understand. Animal noises and postures inspired dread, and dread was an effective space-creating emotion. All the shrieks and shots of early colonial encounters represented humans' attempts to use the clarity of other beasts' vocalizations and dominance displays to extricate themselves from the muddle in which their language had trapped them.

As the 1620 fight exposed the downside of the humans' flexible communication system, it also confirmed the resilience of language. The meanings of words may break down over long distances, but a record of the Cape Cod incident managed to travel across several centuries intact. The English wrote the episode down, verbalizing a confrontation notable for its inarticulateness. The written record was the last act in the clash. Equally engrossed in fear and befuddlement at the time, the invaders reclaimed their mastery of the situation later, describing it in print. Their history made the skirmish intelligible—from their perspective. The English emerged from the incident with a document that by its continued existence proclaimed them the region's dominant communicators.

It is hard to argue with this assessment. The colonists left a written record whereas New England's other top predators—Native Americans and wolves—scribbled little or not at all. Writing secured the invaders' conquest, filling archives with scripts that enshrined their vision of territorial expansion as the prime interpretation of the experience. Or did it? Writing is not the only form of communication that withstands time; it is merely the form with which historians feel most comfortable. Europeans dominated the transcribed record of the past, but other timeframes impinged on history. Both European and Native American humans preserved narratives and rituals in folklore, and wolves exchanged information through gestures, scents, and sounds that adhered to a time regime far slower than those of folklore or history. Wolf communication was simple, rigid, and slow to change, and, while these qualities may tempt some to see the animals' exchanges as inferior, their system accomplished goals similar to humans' nimble language. Like people, wolves colonized, and their unpretentious signals proved an effective aid to their adventures in territorial acquisition.

Like humans, wolves traveled long distances in search of fresh territories to inhabit. They colonized, and, while their conquests differed in sophistication and purpose from human voyages of aggression, wolves shared a dilemma with imperialist people: to avoid bloodshed, they had to communicate territoriality (that is yours, this is mine) with native inhabitants who neither agreed with nor fully comprehended their notions of property. Wolves developed a set of communications that minimized bewilderment and violence. Unlike humans, they colonized with little confusion, and a close look at wolf dispersal reveals an alternative history of colonialism in which animals traveled long distances and expressed territoriality with the help of a simple, rigid, and slow-changing collection of signals.

Wolves were born to lope. With long legs and narrow, "keel-like" chests, wolves move in a fluid stride, hind and forelegs swinging in line like pendulums. This trot carries the animals far. Wolves may trek between ten and twenty miles a day within their territories searching for and hunting down prey, and every so often lone wolves leave their home range and set off on extended journeys. Wildlife biologists call these wolves dispersers, and their travels demonstrate the effectiveness of wolf communication.[5]

Dispersal remains one of the more mysterious wolf activities. Scientists noted the phenomenon only after radio collars allowed long-distance monitoring of individual animals. The number of miles covered by these trekkers surprised their human observers. In one famous instance, the biologist L. David Mech lost track of a female wolf in a Minnesota study area. The wolf turned up five hundred miles away, shot dead by a Saskatchewan farmer. A recent study of wolves in the Rocky Mountains straddling the American and Canadian border followed the movements of forty-two wolves. Seventeen (40 percent) left their home range, and fourteen of these traveled a hundred miles or more. One, a young female, roamed 840 miles, a journey that took her from Banff National Park, Canada, across the international boundary through northwest Montana and into Idaho. A pack of scientists trailed this radio-collared pup via ground triangulation, aircraft, and orbiting satellites. The female, however, kept her motivations hidden. Researchers suspect that competition and aggression prompt dispersal. Wolf packs grow each breeding season through the addition of new pups. Disease, rival packs, and food scarcity encircle the inflating family unit like barbs surrounding a balloon. Lack of meat is by far the sharpest threat, and wolves feel the stab in their stomachs and social relationships. As hunger increases, so do the numbers of fights and dominance showdowns. At some point, the pressure becomes unbearable, and individuals leave, reducing the stress on the group.[6]

Whatever triggers the urge to ramble, the decision to disperse has serious consequences. Territories and packs benefit wolves, so much so that the abandonment of familiar hunting grounds as well as familiar hunting partners borders on lunacy. Unlike most predators, wolves subsist on animals larger than themselves. Wolves kill with numbers, and they depend on each other to procure a daily calorie allowance equal to four pounds of flesh. (Wolves dine irregularly. They may go for days without a meal, then bolt down twenty pounds of meat, marrow, gristle, and hide at one sitting.) Dispersers may snack on the occasional beaver or rummage through the leftovers of another pack's kill, but they will enjoy fewer engorgements. Without feasts to break their famines, the travelers risk malnutrition, if not starvation. Even with hunger gnawing at their guts, dispersers must outrun the bite of another lethal adversary: the prime enemy of lone wolves is other wolves.[7]

Lone wolves must pass through a landscape organized on wolf principles, not human ones. Wolf territories would flummox a real estate agent. They shrink and advance, blossom and collapse in accord with the seasons, the size of packs, and the migrations of prey. Wolves mark their territory, but, unlike cartographers, they do so without parameters. They neither own, control, nor care about land. Wolves' territorial obsession is spacing, not space. Neighbors howl, fight, snarl, stick up their tails, raise their back fur, and secrete a cornucopia of bodily fluids in order to create and maintain a socially acceptable distance between one another. "Territorial behavior," writes the ecologist Paul Colinvaux, "is explained as a process of 'keep away from me' not of 'this dirt is mine.'" Actually, wolf territories function on a "keep away from us" basis. Packs organize wolf landscapes through violence, scent-marking, vocalization, and dominance displays. As packs change over time, so do territories. Social fluidity begets spatial flux, and dispersing wolves must navigate a territorial map under constant revision.[8]

Communication plays such an essential role in dispersal because of the behavior's paradoxical goals. The survival of long-distance travelers depends on avoiding wolves as well as on finding them. Dispersers continually weigh their need for hunting partners, sexual mates, and social companions against their desire to escape the snapping teeth of hostile packs. The stakes of this balancing act are incredibly high. In a recent study of wolves in Alaska's Denali National Park, scientists found "that widespread intraspecific strife . . . is a normal consequence of wolf territoriality in the absence of extensive human interference." In other words, free from the ravages of human traps and bullets, wolves ravage one another. In Denali neighboring packs killed 52 percent of the thirty-one radio-collared wolves in the study group. Approach or run? Long-distance travelers confront a tough choice when they encounter strangers. Wolves are fierce creatures, but dispersers must rely on social grace to save them, not brute force. They gather and interpret social cues, betting their lives on their skill at discerning friend from foe.[9]

Wolves have evolved into formidable communicators. From nose to tail, their bodies have become complex signaling devices. Take the animal's charismatic grin, for instance. Americans have grown to love this smile. Today, wolf faces grace calendars, greeting cards, magazine covers, coffee cups, place mats, and print ads. The popularity of wolf images is due in part to the species importance as a symbol of endangered wildness. But wolves have achieved supermodel status for another reason: humans find the predator's mug attractive. Many wolves appear to be wearing makeup. Their eyes, mouth, and ears are outlined in black. Their muzzles are often a lighter color than the rest of their faces, making their dark lips stand out further. (Wolves come in a wide spectrum of colors. However, the images in popular culture tend to overrepresent gray wolves, which have the most distinctive facial markings.) The color contrasts, slightly upturned mouths, and overall fuzziness of wolf faces communicate nobility, friendliness, and intelligence. The consumers of wolf kitsch react to the expressiveness of wolf faces, but they misread the animals' markings. Wolves use their faces to signal each other, and this dialog, while intelligent, has little to do with nobility or friendliness. Snarls, furrowed brows, squints, stares, and drawn-back ears indicate social rank. The dark outlines around wolf eyes, ears, and mouths enhance facial gestures that advertise dominance and submission. Within packs, dominant members appear more relaxed and confident than submissive ones. Dominant wolves may look gallant, but a snapshot of the behavior their regal stare inspires would sell few calendars. A full-blown display of submission contorts wolves into ghoulish postures. Submissive wolves bare their teeth and lick their lips obsessively while dropping their eyes, ears, tails, and buttocks. They crouch, whimper, and roll on their backs in order to urinate on themselves. The markings and expressions human consumers find so attractive belong to a social world most of them would find bizarre and repulsive.[10]

The social order of wolves revolves around an endless contest over food, space, and sex. Wolf packs are hierarchical, and a pack's dominant male and female (wildlife biologists have labeled this ruling couple the "alpha pair") eat the choicest morsels, slumber in the comfiest spaces, and copulate with the sexiest partners. Dominant wolves take the initiative during group activities. They confront strangers, lead attacks on prey, defecate first on scent posts, and decide the day's travel itinerary. The dominance system of wolf packs resembles the cutthroat politics of a junior high school gym class: the strong bully; the weak cower. Yet while aggression and humiliation remain bedrock realities of wolf life, the species would not have survived for as long as it has with a social order based solely on bluster and cringing. Dominance and submission arrange social relations within groups, but affection keeps wolf packs together.[11]

Wolves establish affective relationships with packmates first as pups and then again as sexual partners. Puppies are exempt from the adult dominance system. They can nip, growl, and stare down their elders with impunity. During most years, packs rear one litter, and every member helps care for the whelps. The young therefore form bonds with all the adults in a pack. All this changes as the pups mature. Around the age of three months, juvenile wolves become wary of strangers. They stop forming social attachments to new individuals, and their world hardens into a circle of intimates surrounded by a host of dangerous outsiders. Adults rarely make new friends. In studies of captive wolves, scientists have clocked the slow thaw of wolf xenophobia. The socialization of strangers takes at least six months. While stingy with their affection toward outsiders, adult wolves do have another opportunity to create and renew emotional bonds after puppyhood. Like all canines, wolves experience a "copulatory tie" during sexual intercourse. Swelling at the base of the male's penis, combined with the constriction of the sphincter muscles in the female's vagina, stops sexual partners from uncoupling after ejaculation. This tie can last as long as thirty minutes. While the ultimate purpose of this phenomenon remains a mystery, Mech has a theory. The tie, he suggests, "may be important in completing the psychological bond between two newly mated animals." If Mech's surmise is true, then the copulatory tie works as a form of biologically enforced cuddling. The tie bonds the mating pair, ensuring that pups have at least two adults to care for them. The pups, in turn, bond with their parents and other pack members. The copulatory tie may be crucial to the emotional reproduction of the pack.[12]

Long-distance dispersers live on the fringe of a social world that rivals human societies in dynamism and complexity. Dispersers leave behind the emotional attachments of their natal packs. There is no need to romanticize this break. Cruelty and affection intermingle in wolf packs. A subordinate position in the pecking order may be the reason some wolves migrate. Whatever prompts their departure, once dispersers abandon their packs they must deal with other wolves' aversion to outsiders. In order to find a mate or enter another pack, a disperser needs to socialize with other adults. As we have seen, socialization among adult wolves is a long and tortuous process involving months of cautious advances and retreats. The fact that traveling wolves may be killed if they encounter a hostile pack makes the business of establishing affective bonds even trickier.

Dispersing wolves survive on the fringe of wolf society by gathering and interpreting signals. Long-range and long-term information help long-distance travelers avoid unfriendly groups, while short-range gestures, postures, and vocalizations help them negotiate a socialization process that can turn strangers into sexual partners and wanderers into packmates.

Wolves emit long-range and long-term signals from the orifices located at their bodies' polar extremes. Currently in the United States, people pay fees to enter captive-wolf parks or trek hundreds of miles into roadless wilderness to hear the sonorous howls that pass through wolves' mouths, but no one opens a wallet or laces a hiking boot to watch the animals spray urine on a twig or deposit feces on a rock. For dispersing wolves, however, critical information flows equally from both ends. Wolves advertise territory through scent marking. They defecate, urinate, and rub themselves on familiar landmarks, creating scent posts. These stations receive careful attention and repeated dousings. Packs check and refresh them as they travel along the paths they have worn in their territories. Biologists can only speculate at the messages contained in a whiff of wolf excrement, but they know the olfactory prowess of canines. Dogs can distinguish identical twins by their scent, and they can detect a human fingerprint on a glass slide six weeks after the initial smudge. Scent posts give wolves a way to deposit long-term signals. With territories of many square miles to maintain, wolves need warning signs that transmit data long after the departure. Smells linger, guarding space, while the scentmakers go about wresting a livelihood from that space.[13]

Scent posts alert dispersing wolves to the presence, the activity, and, perhaps, the strength of unknown packs. The information gleaned from these fragrant landmarks, however, has a drawback: the news is all past tense. Scent posts indicate that a pack exists, considers a space its territory, and travels past a spot from time to time. The freshness of the scent records the interval since a group last visited a landmark. While helpful, this is not the information a dispersing wolf needs most. Its health depends on knowing where hostile wolves are, not where they were. Howling reveals the current location of packs.

Wolves howl for several reasons. Within groups, howls help locate and call together pack members spread across a territory. At times, packs howl in chorus. These communal outbursts may refresh social attachments in the same way drinking songs bond saloon mates. Howling also functions as an early-warning system. Packs communicate their strength and proximity to rival groups through strategic wails. The wolf expert Fred H. Harrington has studied the role of howling in territory maintenance. Over two years in the early 1970s, Harrington and his colleagues monitored the response rates of wolf packs in Minnesota's Superior National Forest. The scientists hiked into the woods, let loose with their best imitation wolf howl, and recorded the reaction. The wolves answered only 29 percent of the time. The low response rate underscored the major findings of the study. The researchers discovered that the Minnesota wolves howled from a position of strength. Alpha males howled more than their beta companions; larger packs howled more than smaller ones; and lone wolves howled rarely, if ever. The presence of food and puppies also affected response rates. Faux howls elicited more replies from packs near kills and rendezvous sites (temporary summer headquarters of packs whose pups remain too young to travel). Howling, the scientists concluded, was a calculated behavior that balanced the risks of exposure to attack against the benefits of keeping rivals away from a critical, and relatively immobile, group resource. The haunting cries that have fired human imaginations throughout American history may actually be songs intended to protect infants and carcasses.[14]

Howls and scent posts guide dispersing wolves through social spaces where trespassers court death. Violence organizes wolf landscapes. Howling and scent posts work as signals because they inspire anxiety. Humans have cloaked these markers in the language of science and fantasy. But wolves neither perform a cost-and-benefit analysis nor express a dreamy longing when they howl. Like all forms of nonhuman communication, wolf signals are simple, clear, and rigid. Wolves communicate through basic dichotomies: present or absent, approach or retreat, fight or flee, trust or fear. They have no talent for nuance or novelty. Wolves' minimal vocabulary exposes the fallacy of some people's Doolittleian yearning to talk to the animals. If wolves could speak, they would say next to nothing.

Yet while the predators would kill the banter at a cocktail party, their signals and marks suit long-distance migration better than human language. Wolves' communication system minimizes confusion, distortion, and misinterpretation over distances. A scat in Manitoba confers the same type of information as a scat in Colorado. Dispersing wolves communicate with an ease dispersing people could never achieve. As we shall see, language could be an irritant as well as a balm. When long-distance travelers entered a rival's territory in colonial New England, the resulting confusion, distortion, and misinterpretation damaged both humans and wolves.

Human language may dwarf animal communication in sophistication and ingenuity, but for nearly a century the level of discourse between Algonquians and Europeans in southern New England rarely surpassed the eloquence of a yowl, chirp, or squeal. The 1620 fight between the Cape Cod natives and the Plymouth colonists demonstrated the problems the humans faced. Unable to communicate with words, the combatants shrieked and blasted at one another. This episode was extraordinary for two reasons: first, it showed people communicating like beasts, and, second, the incident took place ninety-six years after the Algonquians first spotted Europeans. Decades before the English dispersers beached their shallop on Cape Cod, Europeans and natives traded along New England's coast. Brief and sporadic, these early encounters featured humans borrowing animal noises and gestures to communicate ideas their disparate languages could not. The Plymouth colonists entered an ongoing dialog about territory and power conducted without words.

In 1524 Giovanni de Verrazano, a Tuscan sailing for the French, entered Narragansett Bay. After spying fires on an island "about the bignesse of the Ilande of Rodes," Verrazano weighed anchor, hoping to trade and replenish his supplies. Twenty small boats met the vessel. The Indians halted fifty paces from the larger craft and screamed at the crew. Verrazano interpreted their "divers cries" as signs of wonder and gratitude: "They stayed and behelde the artificialnesse of our ship, our shape and apparel, they al made a loud showte together declaring that they rejoiced." The French sailors encouraged the natives to move closer by mimicking their gestures. When they came within throwing distance, the sailors tossed "bells and glasses and many toys" to the canoes. The gifts broke the impasse. The Indians "lookte on them with laughing and came without feare aborde our ship."[15]

Verrazano's sojourn with the Narragansett Bay Indians marked the first recorded encounter between Europeans and Algonquians in southern New England. It was a happy beginning. The humans exchanged gifts, traded information, and seemed genuinely bemused by each other. The natives shared their food and pointed out safe harbors. The Europeans welcomed Indian representatives aboard their ship. Both sides communicated through gestures and signs. Smiles and laughter were especially prominent signals. In his report to the French King, Verrazano noted the "great pleasure" the Indians took "in beholding our apparel and tasting our meates." A "King" of a small island in the bay entertained the sailors by "drawing his bowe and running up and downe with his gentlemen." The Indians arrived at the ship with their faces "all bepainted with divers colours," explaining through gestures "that it was a signe of joy." While Verrazano emphasized the congenial aspects of his two-week visit, his report also captured an undercurrent of suspicion below the grins and chuckles. The Indian men kept their wives and daughters away from the ship. The women either stayed in the canoes or were dropped off on nearby islands while the men explored the French vessel. Despite "all the intreatie we could make, offering to give them divers things, we could never obtaine that they would suffer them to come aborde our ship." Verrazano interpreted the Indians' smiles and laughter as symptoms of their innate jolliness. They were "the goodliest people" he had met. But their cheer had limits. The Indian men drew the line at sailors fraternizing with Indian women. Verrazano and his crew enjoyed their visit because they never tested their hosts' good humor.[16]

Nobody growled during Verrazano's stay. The absence of animal noises and gestures was due to the absence of discord. Over time, the meetings between European traders and Southern Algonquians became less pleasurable, and as the friction rose so did the human barking. The source of the tensions was hair. The Europeans wanted beaver hides, and the animal's coat grew long and luxurious in the North's cold winters. The traders refused to swap their best goods (guns) for the South's beavers. For the Southern Algonquians, the fur trade brought political dishonor as well as economic frustration. The Europeans not only withheld items the Southern Algonquians desired, the traders insulted them with low-quality gifts.

In 1606 Jean Biencourt de Poutrincourt led a French expedition to establish relations with the Indians living on the shores of Massachusetts Bay and Cape Cod. The mood had changed among the Southern Algonquians since Verrazano's visit. Smiles and laughter gave way to anger and violence. The French stopped in Gloucester harbor, only to cast off in the face of a sizable group of riled-up warriors. Next they sailed to Monomy, an Algonquian village near Pleasant Bay. Again the presence of hundreds of Indians rattled Poutrincourt's nerves. He ordered a display of power. The French fired their guns, waved their sabers, and planted a man-sized wooden cross on the beach. The Indians responded by dismantling the village and moving back into the woods, an action Poutrincourt correctly read as a precursor to an attack. The French retreated to their ship, but five stragglers missed the boats. The Indians hit them at dawn, killing one and injuring three. A rescue party chased the attackers back. The French buried their comrade and left. Sailing out of the harbor, Poutrincourt watched the Indians dig up the body and tear down the cross. They also performed their own dominance display. The warriors turned their backs to the ship, bent over, and proceeded to take "sand in their two hands" and cast "it between their buttocks, yelping all the while like wolves."[17]

Conflict summoned the beast in the humans. At a loss for words, Europeans and Indians tried to communicate through a medley of dominance signals. The presence of so many warriors made Poutrincourt anxious. He fought fear with fear, directing his men to signal the group's martial and spiritual power. The natives, however, did not prostrate themselves before the French cross or guns. They fled. An experienced trader, Poutrincourt recognized the retreat as a sign of aggression, not submission. He fled, leaving the unlucky dawdlers behind. The Indians displayed their strength by attacking the stragglers; the French displayed their strength by chasing the attackers back into the woods. The yelping warriors on the beach continued the exchange by defiling a cross, a corpse, and the Europeans' dignity.

By comparing the warriors to wolves, Poutrincourt added a final round to the dominance showdown. As the author of the report, he controlled the depiction of the Algonquians' behavior. He used print to insult those who had denigrated him in person, calling them beasts. European colonists loved this slur. They repeatedly contrasted their humanity with the Indians' animality. William Bradford wrote of "the vast and unpeopled countries of America . . . where there are only savage and brutish men which range up and down, little otherwise than the wild beasts of the same." "They run up and down as roaring lions," wrote John Underhill, "compassing all corners of the country for a prey, seeking whom they might devour." Reversing the predator metaphor, William Hubbard described the final days of King Philip, the famous Wampanoag leader: "Philip, like a salvage and wild Beast, having been hunted by the English forces through the woods . . . at last was driven to his own den." Mary Rowlandson, a war captive of the Narragansetts, likened her kidnappers to "hell-hounds," "ravenous bears," and "wolves." Like Poutrincourt, these authors wielded animal metaphors like machetes. They cut their adversaries down to level of brutes, while reassuring themselves of their superiority as humans.[18]

Europeans wrote endlessly about Indians. They filled sheave after sheave with portraits, ruminations, observations, compliments, and slanders. Arrogance runs through most of these texts, even the friendly ones. As Christians and civilized persons, the authors felt superior to pagan savages. Colonization, however, was more than a linguistic exercise. Ascendancy on the page did not mean power on the ground. Europeans and Indians struggled for supremacy. Words were critical factors in these contests, not as marks on paper but as wellsprings of confusion. Neither side could convince the other of its dominance through language, so they employed dominance signals and gestures. European observers interpreted the natives' yelling and sand flinging as signs of their animal nature. But the enlightened Christians also used animal communication to get their ideas across. They may have resisted the urge to utter howls and growls themselves, but they commanded animals that had no such modesty.

European crews often sailed with very large, very mean dogs. Mastiffs were the choice of many expeditions, and the English displayed a special affinity for the breed. Today's mastiffs are jowly, barrel-chested giants. A full-grown male can weigh 230 pounds, the size of a linebacker in the National Football League. The animals accompanying the European traders may have looked different. In the seventeenth century, dogs were defined by their work, not their appearance. A bulldog, for example, was a dog that fought bulls.

The size, shape, or color of the canine did not matter as long as he could sink his teeth into a bovine's nostrils and hang on. Mastiffs fought bulls as well as bears and lions, but their primary occupation was biting people. They labored as guard animals and dogs of war. In England nobles raised mastiffs to protect their estates, and Henry VIII presented four hundred mastiffs to the Spanish King Charles V to deploy in battle. In America the dogs served as emissaries of terror. "Good Mastiffs are singular defenses to plantations," wrote William Morrell, "in terrifying or pursuing the light-footed Natives."[19]

In 1603 two English ships under the command of Martin Pring sailed into Provincetown harbor near the tip of Cape Cod with two mastiffs on board. Financed by Bristol merchants, the Pring expedition sought a fortune not in precious minerals but rather in prized vegetables. The explorers constructed a shack to protect them at night and spent their days searching for and cutting sassafras. The plant gatherers soon drew the attention of the local Nausets. The two groups exchanged gifts, and a sailor entertained the Indians with a guitar. Long trading and get-to-know-you sessions, however, frustrated Pring, who wanted the sassafras harvested quickly. When the Nausets loitered at the shack, he unleashed Fool and Gallant, the expedition's mastiffs. Pring described the animals as "great and fearefull," and they were an awesome sight, especially Fool. He had acquired the habit of lugging around a half-pike in his mouth like a ham bone. "When we would be rid of the Savages company," Pring wrote, "wee would let loose the Mastives, and suddenly with out-cryes they would flee away."[20]

One afternoon, seventy Nauset warriors armed with bows and arrows approached the shack. Most of the English men were hunting sassafras, and they had taken the dogs with them for protection in the woods. Inside, the four sentries guarding the barricado "utterly refused" when the Indians asked to "come downe unto them." Watching the action from the harbor, the shipmaster ordered a volley fired in hopes of frightening the warriors away. But no one budged. A second volley thumped overhead. Then, off in the distance, the Indians spied the pickers running toward the beach led by Fool. Confronted with "the Mastiff which they most feared," the Nausets "turned all to a jest and sport, and departed away in a friendly manner." A giant dog clutching a spear in his jaws could inspire more congeniality than a fusillade of cannon. At least, according to Martin Pring.[21]

English traders, explorers, and colonists tested Pring's claims, and found them mostly true. George Waymouth sailed with two mastiffs in 1605. His

Indian trading partners so feared the animals that they demanded the brutes be shackled "whensoever any of them came aboard us." The Indians may have never met canines as daunting as Waymouth's, but they were familiar with dogs. Both Indians and Europeans raised the animals. Indeed, dogs were the only domesticated beasts common to both cultures. Dogs, therefore, provided a cross-cultural bridge. Both sides understood the species' sounds and postures, and it appears that both sides exploited these signals. During a trading visit to Pemaquid, Waymouth encountered a Micmac war party that included "two hundred eighty three Savages, every one with his bow and arrows, with their dogges, and wolves which they keepe tame at command." The inclusion of canines in Waymouth's list of Micmac weaponry suggested that he saw the animals as markers of the Indians' power. Dogs and wolves added to the Micmacs' ferocity just as mastiffs enhanced the might of Waymouth's expedition.[22]

A question lingers after these dog tales: did the Indians truly fear mastiffs to the extent Europeans asserted? The natives, after all, lived with dogs, and they tangled with dangerous beasts on a regular basis. Young warriors proved their valor by jumping on the backs of bears and drowning them as the animals swam to coastal islands in search of deer.[23] Would bear wrestlers fall apart at the sight of a large canine? The perspective of the sources makes gauging the Indians' reaction impossible. Pring and his associates did not conduct exit interviews with their foes after a tussle. They based their reports on appearance, not understanding. The reports tell us more about the Europeans' biases and assumptions than about the Indians' thoughts and feelings. Yet even benighted sources can be educational, and Pring's account demonstrates how animals could break through cross-cultural bewilderment. From Pring's vantage point, the mastiffs expressed his group's dominance more forcefully and clearly than words or gunpowder. Fool and Gallant created space when confusion threatened to explode into violence. Whether the Nausets truly feared the dogs or not, they retreated in the animals' presence, and that was all the cultural awareness Pring desired.

The European conquest of North America began with territorial contests more like animal brawls than human battles. European explorers and traders planted crosses and flags, claiming vast regions for God and country. But these were fantasy empires. The humans conducted the actual work of claiming territories through the exchange of gifts, smiles, shouts, insults, and cannon blasts. In southern New England, these early encounters ran

the gamut from Verrazano's pleasant sojourn to Poutrincourt's angry stopover.
Whether happy or violent, these episodes shared a key ingredient: miscommunication. The humans' language foundered on its own complexity.
During congenial encounters, grins and laughter muted linguistic differences.
During conflicts, however, both the Indians and the Europeans expressed
their dominance through noises and gestures rather than words. Their repertoire of signals included sounds (gunshots and howls), pantomimes (saber
waving and sand flinging), and proxies (slobbery mastiffs and tame wolves).
These noises and gestures carried a clear and simple message. In moments
of crisis, howls and blasts exclaimed: "Keep away from us." Vocalizations
and dominance displays inspired fear and fear created space. Thus the humans established territories a wolf could appreciate.

But these territories satisfied neither the Algonquians nor the Europeans.
Unlike wolves, the humans based their territoriality on social custom as well
as physical dominance. Both Indians and Europeans shared an assumption
that rules backed by forces, not sporadic outbursts of anxiety, should organize territories. As soon as the Europeans and the Indians learned more of
each other's languages, they began contesting these rules. They battled for
the right to determine whose customs would govern the demarcation, ownership, and transference of territory. These battles differed from wolves' territorial
conflicts. Whereas wolves growled, howled, and squirted to keep rivals at a
distance, people fought over a set of abstract principles as well as parcels of
land. Laws, customary or codified, may seem a more dignified approach to
territory maintenance, but the humans splattered as much blood over their
laws as wolves spilled over their buffer zones. In fact, the violence of human
territorial conflicts engulfed other species.

Wolves became casualties in a struggle beyond their comprehension.
With time, colonists and natives cobbled together enough linguistic com-
monality to converse, trade, argue, evangelize, and negotiate. Unlike the
creatures they mimicked, human animals could expand their repertoire of
signals with startling speed. Yet even as colonists and Indians talked more
and howled less, wild animals continued to facilitate human communication
in colonial New England. The region's humans transformed animals into
cultural symbols, and no species better served the quarreling bipeds' need
for shared symbols than wolves.

Perched atop the food chain, wolves competed with humans for space and calories. Although blessed with jaws that cracked moose femurs, wolves' weapon of choice in this competition was information. The fearsome predators used their keen senses to locate their enemies and run away from them. Wolves' shy behavior highlighted the critical role of communication in territorial creation and maintenance. In a perfect world, ecological rivals acquired living space through advertisement first, violence second. Colonial New England, however, was not a perfect world; it was a communication disaster. Wolves had enough sensibility to retreat from people, but they had no way of knowing that some humans' notion of territoriality extended to the exotic beasts they imported. When they sank their teeth into cows, goats, pigs, and sheep, wolves committed sins unimaginable to them.

Wolves attacked livestock and people attacked wolves with such enthusiasm in colonial New England that a battle to extinction would seem as predictable as the tides. Yet enamored as the English colonists were of the idea of predestination, the annihilation of wolves was not inevitable. All the region's top predators exhibited a talent for conflict avoidance. Wolves had coexisted with the Algonquians for centuries despite hunting the same prey. Even after the English invasion, wolves and colonists generated enough mutual trepidation to keep the species apart. Why, then, did humans and wolves fight, and what explained the conflict's savage violence?

The English colonists' concept of territory—the idea that land, animals, and even people were property—ambushed wolves. The English colonists marked their territory, but wolves could not imagine the significance of the notches and half-moons the humans cut into their beasts' ears to indicate their ownership. Humans killed wolves to safeguard animal property, but another territorial conflict endowed wolves' trespasses with a second, more sinister meaning. Wolves became symbolic participants in the humans' escalating conflict over land and political ascendancy. The English and the Algonquians used wolves to communicate. The Algonquians modeled their war cries on wolf howls; colonists and natives employed wolves as metaphors in diplomatic negotiations; and finally, the severed heads of Indians and wolves decorated English towns, serving as the ultimate markers of territory. Wolves died by the thousands for their inability to understand humans any better than humans understood each other.

CHAPTER TWO

Beasts of Lore

HOW STORIES TURNED FEARSOME MONSTERS

INTO SKULKING CRIMINALS

IN THE WINTER of 1621 the wolves of southern New England chased their first domesticated European, the Plymouth colony's spaniel. The colony had two dogs, the spaniel and a mastiff bitch. When not frightening Indians, the dogs flushed geese and deer for the settlement's hunters, and the canines were unruly workers. They frequently took off after game and refused to come back. On one occasion two gunners, Masters Goodman and Jones, became lost in the woods while searching for the dogs. The men "passed an unhappy night . . . terrified at the howling of wolves, which they mistook for lions." Ten days later Goodman met the howlers in the flesh. He rescued the spaniel from two wolves by smacking the predators with a stick. Still later, Jones happened upon a pack munching on the carcass of a deer caught in an Indian's trap. He shooed away the thieves and stole the meat for himself.[1]

In 1621 Goodman and Jones encountered a creature of legend. Born decades after the animals' extermination in England, the Plymouth colonists had never seen, heard, or destroyed a wolf. Short on experience, they possessed a wealth of myths, stories, and cultural associations, and this wolf lore shaped their perceptions of New England's packs. European folklore was replete with toothy monstrosities. Werewolves laid siege to villages; mad wolves bit the noses off fair maidens; rampaging wolf squads chased down peasant families in the snow; and sexually charged lone wolves drooled over red-clad pubescent girls.[2] Given the deep, horrible power of these cultural images, one might expect an attack of jelly-kneed horror when European voyagers met the New World's wild canines. Instead, Masters Jones and Goodman beat the animals with tree branches and pilfered their dinner, and the men's blasé courage requires some explanation.

The full force of European wolf folk traditions did not hit the beaches of Massachusetts Bay like a tsunami with the arrival of English colonists. Only a few legends, rituals, metaphors, and symbols dribbled ashore. Werewolves, for example, missed the boat to New England, victims of a cultural winnowing process difficult to trace and hard to explain. How much of the vast and ancient European wolf lore was familiar and available to the colonists who settled southern New England? Did they discard the bits of lore that no longer applied to their lives? If so, why did they choose some legends over others, and what was the meaning of their selections?

These are the kinds of questions that drive historians out of archives and into bars.

Infectious as ad jingles or pop songs, folklore was designed by humans to be repeated without the assistance of written texts. Historians catch glimpses of wolf stories and hunting rituals in documents written years, decades, even centuries after their telling and enactment. These publications create their own contexts for the lore. The particularities of time and place—the storytellers' social strata and gender, for instance, or the listeners' economic condition and political station—are often missing. Plucked from the circumstances of their production and repetition, the folk traditions that made it into print violate many of the restrictions of evidence and argument historians place on themselves. Historians, for example, would never use a modernized version of an old wolf tale, like the origin myth of the Roman Empire featuring Romulus and Remus being suckled by a she-wolf, as evidence for the attitudes of the seventeenth-century Protestant separatists who journeyed to New England. But a folklorist might.

Folklorists recognize that some cultural forms slip through historical contexts like piglets through a rundown fence. They study the journey of stories, songs, jokes, customs, and artifacts; they collect legends, trace their geographic diffusion, and chronicle their evolution. Armed with tape recorders and motif indexes, they can capture the latest version of a folktale and follow its trail back across centuries and continents. Yet even with their finely honed research techniques, folklorists struggle with the same questions of meaning that badger historians. Why do some legends survive while others fade away?

What prompts some individuals to alter stories while others repeat them? What do these narratives signify to the people who tell and listen to them?[3]

Both historians and folklorists search for meaning in remnants from the past, but the assumptions of their disciplines pull them in opposing directions. Historians respect the limits of time and place, while folklorists honor the ability of some cultural forms to transcend these limitations. In 1621 Masters Jones and Goodman stood at the juncture of folklore and history. They fantasized about howling monsters, and then snatched a meal from one of them. The men indulged in storytelling and at the same time responded to the exigencies of their situation: the Plymouth colonists needed the wolves' food; they were starving that winter. Masters Jones and Goodman tied the wolves of southern New England to a string of stories, legends, songs, and rituals that spun out into the distant past.

European humans could dream up a truly astounding wolf. A fourteenth-century bench-end carving from Hadleigh church in Suffolk, England, depicting the legend of Saint Edmund hints at the bizarre and frightening animals that lurked in their fantasies.[4] An Anglo-Saxon king who lost his skull battling heathen Danes in 870, Edmund became a saint through the miraculous intercession of a gray wolf. According to the legend, the Danes promised to spare Edmund's life if he renounced Christianity. When he refused, they tied him to a tree and filled his body with so many spears that the king appeared to have grown "hedgehog's bristles." They then lopped off his head and hid it in a thicket of brambles. After the Danes left, the townspeople of Hoxne, the village near the battle site, searched for the head. They found Edmund's skull between the paws of a gray wolf. The animal had protected the head from other wild animals, and his howls—sounding like "here, here, here"—called the villagers to the sacred remains. The wolf allowed the humans to carry the head back to Hoxne for burial. He followed the procession "as if he had been tame," and returned to the woods only after "seeing the head to safety."[5]

In the bench-end carving, a wolflike animal holds Saint Edmund's head in its mouth. The wolf has neither ears nor fur. The teeth clutching the skull are human, not canine. The beast's eye sockets are also human. The wolf's paws, however, are cloven, like a sheep's hooves. While the legend of Saint Edmund depicted the wolf as a spiritual ally of Christians, the biological allegiance of the carved wolf is mysterious. Perhaps the figure's human features symbolize the coming together of man and wolf through religion. But the effect of this amalgamation is creepy, not harmonious. The creature defies easy characterization, and because of this complexity, the bench end serves as a fitting symbol for Europeans' understanding of wolves. Their cultural vision of the animals was old and multifaceted, overwhelmingly negative but never simple.

The bench-end wolf can also serve as a token of the interpretive quagmire that surrounds folklore. Whittled from a church pew in East Anglia, the region of origin for most New England immigrants, the wolf thing inhabited a time and a place close to actual colonists. But no direct evidence links the carving, or the legend it represented, to the mental lives of the long voyagers who met wolves in North America. At best, the Saint Edmund's wolf belonged to the collection of shared symbols, narratives, icons, and artifacts that made up the travelers' culture. Yet if we admit the bench-end creature into the English migrants' cerebral universe, do we also have to admit lore from times and places even farther away? The answer is yes, maybe.

Scholars have fished the depths of European wolf lore and come back with examples as plentiful as they are strange. A wolf's tail buried beneath a village road kept the predators from entering. A pregnant mare that kicked a wolf would miscarry. Wolves' fangs rubbed against a baby's gums relieved the pain of teething, and the predators' steamy breath cooked the meat they devoured as it entered their gullet. Wolves bore their young in stands of acorn trees because she-wolves ate the blossoms to open their wombs. Wolves despised music and hated stones. Their spines contained only a single vertebra, making it impossible for the animals to look behind them. (You could drown a wolf in a stream while holding onto his tail.) Some wolves ate marjoram before a hunt, while others gorged on heavy mud, transforming their bodies into wrecking balls that when flung leveled oxen and horses. Peasants looked for wolves through "loupholes" cut in their front doors, while young women who lost their virginity were said to have "seen the wolf." Sex and death, diseases and cures, herbs and livestock, science and mysticism, language and dung—wolves touched every aspect of the human experience.[6]

Collected from documents spread across centuries—Aristotle reported the stiffness in wolves' spines in 1000 B.C.; Albertus Magnus noted their mud-eating habits in A.D. 1300—these snippets of lore suggest the vastness of European wolf beliefs and practices.[7] Oral and interpersonal, folk traditions moved through informal and thus largely invisible channels. The bits that surfaced in print represented a mere sampling of a reservoir of wolf associations whose true size and age can only be guessed. Alas, even if every scrap of European wolf lore could be gathered into an oceanic pool, the immensity would be stunning but somewhat meaningless. The significance of all these legends, sayings, and curatives lay at the moments where they intersected with people's lives. Surveys of wolf traditions reveal the ease with which the legends traveled across historical circumstances, but people locked in particular times and places gave these traditions meaning.

The challenge, then, is to discover the instances when folklore entered history, to pinpoint where the ocean of European wolf lore met the shore of southern New England experience. At one such juncture stood the immigrants' Bible. This book featured animals of all sorts. Heroes escaped lions' dens and slew multitudes with jackass mandibles. Jonah explored the gut of a leviathan, while Eve succumbed to the hiss of a serpent. Domestic beasts flocked through its pages. The Bible was unmistakably pastoral, and the symbolism of shepherds, lambs, and wolves gave English colonists a readily available template for interpreting their encounters with predators.

The Bible was a fountainhead of wolf lore. It taught colonists to beware of wolves dressed in sheep's clothing. Jesus sent his twelve apostles to preach to hostile nonbelievers with a wolf simile: "Behold, I send you forth as sheep in the midst of wolves: be ye therefore wise as serpents, and harmless as doves." A favorite activity of biblical wolves was "ravening." False prophets corrupted the souls of the followers like "wolves ravening the prey." In the book of Genesis, Jacob condemned his son Benjamin to "ravin as a wolf: in the mourning [you] shall devour the prey, and at night [you] shall divide the spoil." Wolves were ravenous—hungry. But ravening also meant corrupting and despoiling. The two meanings came together in the Bible's descriptions of wolves' feeding habits. "Evening wolves" fed on putrid (or regurgitated) flesh killed during the day.[8] That was the gist of Jacob's prophecy. Benjamin would fill his stomach in the morning and nourish his family with disgorged tidbits in the evening.

The Bible offered English colonists a host of negative wolf images and metaphors. In paradise predacious canines may slumber with lambs, but in colonial New England, Christian flocks needed to guard against a throng of "ravening wolves." In addition to the teeth-and-tail variety, the colonists had to watch out for humans with wolfish intentions—false prophets, sinners, and heathens. A series of shepherds protected the faithful from these predators.

Christ was the "good shepherd." Another guardian, the disciple Paul, warned the Jews of Ephesus that "after my departing shall grievous wolves enter among you, not sparing the flock."[9] In America town ministers served as metaphoric shepherds.[10] Edward Johnson employed this imagery in a poem about the founding of Concord, Massachusetts. "In Desert's depth where Wolves and Beares abide, there [Rev.] Jones sits down a wary watch to keepe o're Christs deare flock, who now are wandered wide."[11] In 1691 Cotton Mather, minister of Boston's First Church, assumed the shepherd role in his anti-Quaker pamphlet *Little Flocks Guarded Against Grievous Wolves.*[12]

The 1691 publication date of Mather's warning against grievous Quakers indicates that the colonists' encounters with real wolves did little to change their perception of the beasts. After seventy years of contact and countless instances of the animals' shying away from humans, wolves remained despicable creatures; flocks and shepherds lived on as potent metaphors; and calling a person a wolf continued to be an insult. The biblical vision of wolves with its focus on greed, corruption, and theft flourished in New England while other European traditions seemed to decline. The colonists outran werewolves, and they left behind the Old World's miraculous and magical wolves as well. Neither very frightening nor mysterious, New England wolves were skulking criminals.

The colonists' depiction of wolves as robbers is hardly surprising given the beasts' fondness for pork loins and muttonchops. The predation of livestock played into the travelers' religious wolf lore. As members of a spiritual flock, they identified with the animals wolves assaulted. The Bible turned English conquerors into innocent lambs. Livestock supplied European voyagers a metaphor to disparage adversaries of many species, nations, religions, and cultures. Dutch traders, French Catholics, Quakers, and Indians harassed the English as wolves persecuted their domestic beasts. The interplay between wolves as predators and wolves as metaphors explained the animals' criminalization in New England. The colonists arrived in their New World with ancient and complex wolf lore, and the experience of colonization winnowed this cultural legacy to a handful of useful symbols and metaphors. At the juncture of folklore and history, ravening thieves of all kinds besieged real and symbolic flocks.

Cotton Mather turned Quakers into wolves, but in colonial New England nobody endured more transmogrifications than Native Americans. From the colonists' perspective, Indians sang, talked, prayed, fought, and traveled like wolves. The English missionary John Eliot theorized that the over-abundance of "oo" sounds in the Algonquian language came from its origins in the lowest sorts of "sounds and tones uttered by Mankind": "Ululation, Howling, Yelling, or Mourning." English men and women spoke and sang in tones of "Elation and Joy," while Indians bellowed like animals.[13] Indians, wrote Solomon Stoddard, "doe acts of hostility, without proclaiming war, they do not appeare openly in the field to bid us battle, they use those cruelly that fall into their hands . . . they act like wolves and are to be dealt withal as wolves."[14] In 1665 the Boston Court admonished a Mohawk raiding party for "killing people in a base and ignoble manner." Instead of meeting their Algon-quian enemies out in the open, the Mohawks preferred "lying in ambushment, thickets, and swamps by the way side." Their surprise attacks were "inhuman and barbarous," and the entire practice of Iroquois warriors traveling south to raid their Algonquian foes struck the Boston judges as wolfish. "It was inhumanity," they lectured, "and more like wolves than men, to travel and wander so far from home, merely to kill and destroy men, women, and children."[15]

The 1665 incident with the Mohawk raiding party exposed the English colonists' penchant for conflating Indians and wolves. But the episode revealed more than that. By 1665 likening Indians to wolves had become more than a derisive metaphor Europeans slung at natives. Comparing a person to a wolf remained a slander, but in 1665 it was a metaphor both Indians and colonists used.

The appearance of the Mohawks alarmed the residents of Boston. Armed with firelock muskets, pistols, hatchets, and long knives, the warriors em-bodied the colonists' worst nightmares. Apprehending them outside John Taylor's house, the sheriff escorted the Mohawks to the Boston jail, where they received the court's lecture on their ignoble methods of warfare. The tongue-lashing was their only punishment because looking scary was their only crime. They had no intention of harming the colonists. They had traveled to Massachusetts from their northern homes in order to "avenge themselves of the Indians, their enemies," the Algonquians living around Boston.[16]

Hearing of the Mohawks' imprisonment, the neighboring Algonquians "flocked into Boston in great numbers." The contrast between these "praying Indians" and the Mohawk raiders was striking. The Algonquians dressed in "English fashioned apparel" and kept their hair trimmed short. They spoke

English and many had converted to Christianity. To the colonists, the praying Indians appeared harmless enough. (The court described them as "very poor.") But the Mohawks saw them as rivals, part of a larger confederation of Algonquians with whom they had been fighting for control of hunting grounds in western Massachusetts for most of the 1660s. The English authorities knew of this struggle and hoped to stay out of it. They armed the praying Indians so that they could protect themselves and asked each side to stop raiding and ambushing the other and settle the dispute on a battlefield. The Boston Court even challenged the Mohawks to "fight . . . openly and in plain field," conditions they were certain "our Indians would gladly accept." Knowing the thoughts of their Indians, however, was not the English authorities' strong suit. Set-piece battles did not interest the Algonquians any more than the Mohawks. The praying Indians wanted the raiders put to death, and they pleaded their case with a wolf metaphor.[17]

In order to persuade the English to kill the Mohawks (or release them for the Algonquians to execute), the praying Indians donned sheep's clothing and outfitted their enemies in wolf skins. "These Mohawks," they proclaimed, "are unto us as wolves are to your sheep. They secretly seize upon us and our children, wherever they meet us, and destroy us." Killing these sneaky and brutal men was the court's obligation, just as slaughtering sneaky and brutal predators was the Algonquians' duty. Letting the Mohawks escape would be like "if we had taken five wolves alive, and should let them go again, and not destroy them, you Englishmen would be greatly offended with us for such an act: and surely, the lives of men are of more worth than beasts." The members of the court mulled over the argument, and after long deliberations they forbade the Mohawks to "kill and destroy" any Algonquian wearing short hair and English trousers within a forty-mile radius of Boston. With that, they let the raiders go. Perhaps the court had an epiphany, realizing in the final analysis that men were not beasts. More likely, they saw a wolfishness in both parties. They could accept the Mohawks as vicious predators, but the Algonquians' self-portrayal as helpless lambs was a stretch.[18]

The trading of wolf metaphors during the 1665 Mohawk episode illustrated the predicament of New England's live wolves. In order to protect their livestock, the English colonists enlisted the help of their Algonquian neighbors. Wolf killing facilitated communication across cultures, supplying Indians and Europeans with shared symbols and common metaphors. Since the humans used these symbols and metaphors to mark their territories and advertise their power, wolves became embroiled in wars that had nothing to do with their predation of livestock. The Indians, for example, signed treaties that required them to present an annual tribute of wolves' heads to colonial authorities. These tributes rid the country of a few predators, but the true reason the English demanded the heads was symbolic. For them the skulls represented the Indians' submission to colonial rule. By the end of the seventeenth century, wolves' role as a symbol endangered them as much as did their enthusiasm for domesticated meat. Colonists displayed the heads of wolves and Indians to proclaim their dominance over "beasts and beast-like men."

Yet wolf metaphors and symbols were unruly tools of conquest. The English may have wanted their Algonquian neighbors to understand wolves as they did, but the natives had their own wolf lore. The 1665 Mohawk incident is so extraordinary because it recorded the coming together of two folklores in one historical setting. The colonists' ravening wolves met their Algonquian counterparts, and, surprisingly enough, the Indians' legendary creatures shared a trait with their European brethren. They were criminals too.

During the winter of 1621 southern New England wolves first encountered Englishmen and English dogs in the woods surrounding New Plymouth. For the people and, no doubt, the dogs, it was an extraordinary moment: a legendary animal came to life before their eyes. But for the wolves the encounter was ordinary. They had been running into humans and dogs in the forests of southern New England for a long time. The Algonquian natives trapped wolves and exchanged wolf skins, and while the nuances of their predator-and-prey relationship are beyond recovery, the writings of English colonists provide some clues to how Indians and wolves lived and died with one another.

Native Americans, of course, possessed wolf lore equal to Europeans' in age and complexity. Navajo witches transformed into werewolves, and a person wanting protection against these supernatural horrors kept a sample of wolf gall in his or her pockets.[19] The Skidi Pawnee dressed in wolf skin cloaks, and their neighbors on the Great Plains called them the Wolf People.[20] In the Pacific Northwest, the Nootka held a wolf ceremony in early winter, initiating young men into adulthood through the reenactment of a legend in which a wolf pack stole a boy.[21] Pregnant Hidatsa women rubbed wolf skin on their bellies during grueling births to acquire the animal's stamina and power.[22] Indians across the continent named children Wolf Man, Wolf Eyes, Mad Wolf, High Wolf, Little Wolf, and Wolf Lying Down; Nez Perce fighters jammed wolf fangs through the cartilage in their noses to display their toughness.[23] Native Americans imitated, wore, studied, revered, and killed wolves. The animal was a lodestar in many tribes' mental universes.

Yet while folklore's ability to slip across miles and generations deserves respect, Native American narratives and rituals, like their European counterparts, made sense in their historical contexts. Piling up North American wolf traditions illustrates the vitality and variety of the Indians' lore, but the heap explains little about the role wolf traditions played in actual lives. The best source for southern Algonquians' conceptions of wolves is not other native groups' folklore—very little of the southern New England Indians' wolf lore has survived—but descriptions of their hunting practices made by English colonists. These documents are slippery to read: the men who wrote them disliked wolves and misunderstood Indians.

In *A Key into the Language of America*, Roger Williams mentioned the wolf-hunting practices of the Narragansetts, an Algonquian speaking people living near his home in Providence, Rhode Island. Filled with antiwolf sentiments, the passage articulates Williams's outlook nicely. The challenge is pinpointing where his opinions stopped and the Narragansetts' began:

> When a Deere is caught by the leg in a Trap, sometimes there it lies a day together before the Indian come, and so lies a pray to the ranging Wolfe . . . who seaseth upon the Deere and robs the Indian (at his first devouring) of neere halfe his prey, and if the Indian come not sooner, hee makes a second greedie Meale, and leaves him nothing but the bones, and the torne Deereskins, especially if he call some of his greedy Companions to his bloody banquet.
>
> Upon this the Indian makes a falling trap called *Sunnuchig*, (with a great weight of stones) and so sometimes knocks the Wolfe on the head, with a gainefull Revenge, especially if it bee a blacke Wolfe, whose Skins they greatly prize.

The language of theft, greed, and revenge advertise Williams's biases. He viewed wild animals as allegorical "emblems." Mild and meek, the deer are stand-ins for "God's persecuted," while wolves symbolize the "fierce blood-sucking persecutor." "The Wildernesse," he wrote, "is a cleere resemblance of the world, where greedie and furious men persecute and devoure the harmlesse and innocent as the wilde beasts pursue and devoure the Hinds and Roes." The Narragansetts' hunting practices interested Williams less for the story they told about wolves' place in the Indians' wilderness than for the lessons they taught about greed in his world. Understanding wolves from the Indians' perspective begins where Williams's passage ends: the skins of black wolves.[24]

The Algonquians coveted these hides as ceremonial gifts. "When there ariseth any difference betweene prince and prince," wrote Thomas Morton, "the prince that desires to be reconciled to his neighboring prince does endeavor to purchase it by sending him a black wolf's skin for a present, and the acceptance of such a present is an assurance of reconciliation between them." Why black wolves? A shadowy predator seems an odd symbol for social harmony. Morton could have asked his Algonquian neighbors to explain the animals' cultural significance, but such questions did not interest the fur trader. The forty beaver skins the Indians would pay for the hides of black wolves piqued Morton's curiosity. That high price turned a worthless beast (in Morton's words, a "discommodity" throughout the "Countries of Christendom") into a commodity.[25] Morton was tipping his readers off to a business opportunity by mentioning the role of black wolves in Indian diplomacy.

Wolves and Indians intrigued Morton and Williams for reasons that had little to do with the Indians' relationship with wolves. Profits captivated Morton; allegories enthralled Williams. Neither explicitly compared the Algonquians' perception of wolves with their own. They implied differences and similarities, but their curiosity dwindled on the brink of revelation. Again, the black wolves help root out the differences and similarities between the humans' understanding and treatment of the animals.

As a species, wolves are a multicolored lot. Gray-haired animals predominate, but they also come in white, rust, black, buff, tawny, and cream.[26] The reason for this wide range of pelage is simple: in most environments, color does not matter. A pastel wolf would have trouble sneaking up on prey, but earth-toned hunters have few problems with camouflage. In midlatitude environments similar to southern New England, genetic mixing ensures that most wolves grow coats with hairs of several muted colors, making them look gray. Most likely, then, black wolves were oddities in colonial New England; part of their cultural significance arose from their scarcity; and their value as diplomatic gifts made them scarcer still. The Algonquians were culling the black animals from the region's wolf population. Over time, fewer monocolored wolves reproduced, further enhancing the shade of gray.

Their rarity, however, only partially explains black wolves' significance. Black wolves were scarce in southern New England, but so were albino otters and two-headed deer. The Algonquians did not bestow gift status on every genetic misadventure in their midst. A black wolf's wolfness was as important as its blackness. A fellow predator, the wolf's relationship to Indians differed from those of other animals. Scholars have chronicled the Algonquians' spiritual conception of the animals they hunted.[27] Taboos instructed the killing and consumption of game. Believing divine forces guided the success or failure of hunts, the Algonquians adhered to rituals that displayed their respect and gratitude for the gift of meat. Hunters gave thanks, not to a god on high, but to a spirit—a Manitou—that manifested itself in the animals they stalked and trapped. According to Roger Williams, the Narragansetts believed "a Divine power" resided in deer.[28] Did spiritual forces motivate wolves as well? Ethnohistorians and anthropologists have little to say on the subject of animals that took meat instead of giving it. However, the hunting practices and diplomatic rituals described by Morton and Williams indicate that the Algonquians extracted a payment from wolves for excessive and disrespectful killing the same way Manitous made human hunters pay for their transgressions.

The Indians did not hunt wolves indiscriminately. Wolf trapping was a by-product of deer trapping. The Algonquians snared deer after the harvest. The Narragansetts moved their families into the woods each fall and erected "hunting houses." The trappers marked off territories, "each man tak[ing] his bounds of two, three, or foure miles, where hee sets thirty, forty, or fiftie Traps." The Narragansetts, reported Williams, constructed their wolf-killing engines following the predators' ingestion of ensnared deer. They smashed the animals' skulls only after the wolves' actions warranted their destruction. Williams understood the wolves' behavior as thievery. He was right, but he imagined the wrong victim. The wolves robbed the deer, not the humans. Trapping was a spiritual as well as a meat-taking activity. "They are very tender of their traps," Williams wrote, "where they lie, and what comes at them; for they say, the Deere (whom they conceive have a Divine power in them) will soone smell and be gone." Trappers had to address their quarries' divinity. Subterfuge, hiding snares and masking scents, mattered less than following rituals and displaying respect. Ultimately, the deer trapped themselves. They gave their bodies to humans, who showed them honor and gratitude. Wolves stole this gift, and they paid for it with their hides.[29]

Wolf trapping was about justice, but not the retributive justice familiar to Europeans like Roger Williams or Thomas Morton. Wolves donated their skins to the cause of reciprocal justice. They became gifts, taking the place of the animals they had consumed. Williams noted this reciprocity in another context. He described how Indian "states" dealt with theft. Following a robbery, the victims asked the sachem of the offender's tribe to "grant Justice." If this failed, the aggrieved "take satisfaction themselves, yet they are carefull not to exceed in taking from others, beyond the Proportion of their owne losse." Repairing the damage done by the crime rather than punishing the criminal was the core idea of reciprocal justice. Narragansett trappers did not punish wolves as much as exact restitution comparable to the animal's offense. A wolf skin signified atonement. That was why black wolves' skins worked so well as peace offerings. They were rare gifts that signaled the giver's desire to expiate past misdeeds.[30]

Both Indians and Europeans killed wolves in response to predation they found displeasing. In both cases, a common prey species—an animal eaten by humans and wolves—sparked the conflict. Wolves and people were not natural enemies. The humans' relationship with other animals established their rivalry with wolves. Indians and Europeans killed wolves on behalf of deer and livestock, and both understood these slayings as just rewards for bad acts. At this juncture, the humans swerved apart. The locus of the conflict between Indians and wolves was the trapping field. Season and place limited the Algonquians' wolf killing. Wolves hunted deer all year long, but Indians hunted wolves in the fall, when the animals pilfered divine gifts. The Algonquians' sense of justice demanded that the wolves atone for the deer they stole. The animals repaired the breach in reciprocity with their skins. The price wolves paid for mouthfuls of English livestock would be considerably higher. The Indians destroyed individual wrongdoers; the English punished an entire species.

Wolves' criminality made them effective cross-cultural metaphors. They helped groups of stymied humans, floundering in the complexity of their language, discuss and administer justice. The 1665 Mohawk affair, however, showed that bicultural metaphors often cloaked deeper misunderstandings. The praying Indians wanted the Mohawks destroyed as an act of reciprocity.

Their deaths would avenge the losses the Algonquians had sustained during past raids, bringing parity to the Indians' exchanges of violence. By using a wolf metaphor, the Algonquians also signaled the English that killing the Mohawks was important to preserving their reciprocal relationship with the colonists. When the Boston Court refused to kill the raiders, the magistrates assumed the symbolic position of negligent wolf hunters. They let a pack of murderers go free, injuring their diplomatic ties to the Algonquian "shepherds." To repair the breach, the English should have offered a gift, perhaps a black wolf's skin. Because of the colonists' own cultural assumptions about wolves and justice, however, no presents exchanged hands.

The English would never associate a wolf skin with reciprocity. To them, the notion that a wolf could atone for past misdeeds by giving up her skin would seem absurd. Wolves' badness was indelible. It could not be hidden, absolved, or negotiated. In colonial New England, sheep could become wolves, but wolves could never become sheep. In his *History of New-England,* Edward Johnson explained this one-way transformation in a set of cryptic instructions to church leaders: "Feed the flock of Christ, and not for lucre to admit mostly of such sheepe; whose faire fleece allure much: nor yet filling the flocks to crowd in infectious sheep, or rather wolves in sheepes cloathing."[31] Minister to the poor as well as the rich, preached Johnson, and take care whom you admit into church membership. Haste may bring into the flock sheep infected with wolfishness, a contagion no good shepherd wanted to encourage. In Christian mythology, wolves might try to disguise their base nature, but they could never erase the stain of corruption and evil. Unlike the Algonquians' robber wolves, the English colonists' ravening wolves remained steadfast criminals.

The 1665 episode demonstrated how quickly linguistic common grounds could devolve into actual battlegrounds. The Algonquians used wolf and sheep metaphors to warn the English: freeing the Mohawks would injure their diplomatic relations. The Boston magistrates did not have to stretch their imaginations far to see the Mohawks as wolves. They agreed that the raiders fought like animals, but the court rebuffed the praying Indians' extension of the metaphor. The English declined the invitation to play the good shepherd and, in doing so, gave the Algonquians some subtle advice: be careful with wolf analogies. The praying Indians wielded a set of symbols as hazardous to them as Mohawk warriors. If they ever acted to punish the colonists for their violations of diplomatic reciprocity, the Algonquians, with their English attire and haircuts, would look like predators in borrowed cloth-ing. Instead of "poor" harmless lambs, they could become infectious sheep and suffer a criminal's fate. In colonial New England, wolf lore endangered men and beasts.

CHAPTER THREE

Wolf Bullets with Adders' Tongues

HOW TO KILL A WOLF IN COLONIAL NEW ENGLAND

IN THE NORTHEAST corner of Middleboro, Massachusetts, John and James Soule farmed side-by-side parcels in the shadow of Wolf-Trap Hill. A family folktale explained mound's name. At dawn each day, one of the brothers hiked the hill to check the pit trap they had dug to catch poultry-stealing wolves. One morning, the inspector peered into the trench and discovered a wolf balled up at one end and an Indian shivering at the other; both had crashed through the boughs that covered the ditch in the night. The farmer killed the wolf, and "after an examination he found that the Indian was on his way from Nemasket to Plymouth upon legitimate business, so he was released and allowed to continue his journey." The promontory overlooking the Soule's neighborhood became Wolf-Trap Hill to honor the pit that swallowed a thieving canine and a suspicious human in one gulp.[1]

Wolf killing in colonial New England created landscapes of frustration and distrust. English colonists imported domestic beasts that ranged beyond the humans' ability to safeguard them, and, to prevent wolves from gutting their investments, they dug traps, offered bounties, erected fences, and experimented with exotic technologies like mackerel hooks and "wolf bullets with adder's tongues." Towns urged residents to purchase hounds and mastiffs and train them to hunt wolves. Governments asked and, when they could, forced Native Americans to help slaughter the predators. All these efforts failed to eliminate the menace at a pace satisfactory to livestock owners.

Wolves continued to eat property, and farmers continued to kill wolves well into the eighteenth century. European colonists did not march across New England from east to west driving wolves before them. Instead, humans and wolves coexisted belligerently for more than a hundred years in a patchwork landscape of agricultural strongholds and feral woods.[2]

The region's lupine place names documented this landscape. English colonists affixed wolf names to fields, meadows, brooks, hillocks, swamps, and forests. In Hopkinton, New Hampshire, for example, there was a local spot called Wolf Meadow, for "the frequency with which wolves were once observed in the vicinity." Some New England wolf sites, then, were actual wolf places; the names indicated that the animals traveled through or lived there. This was especially true of the region's many Wolf Swamps, pockets of undrained wildness famous as predator hideouts. Other wolf places received their designation for a more practical reason. Colonists fashioned wolf landmarks to notify each other of the location of their pit traps. Indians might survive in a hole with a wolf, but no farmer wanted to see whether his neighbor's daughter could overnight with a ravenous beast. Place names like Wolf-Pitt Brook, Wolf Pit Neck Plain, Wolfe-Pit Meadow, Wolf Hole, and Wolf Trap Neck served as seventeenth- and eighteenth-century versions of flashing yellow construction lights: visitors to these wolf locales needed to watch their steps.[3]

Wolf traps lined the border between the wild and the pastoral, danger and safety, loss and profit. The trenches marked a cultural divide as well. The conflict between wolves and livestock gave New England's humans the chance to unite as a species against an ecological rival. The Algonquians destroyed wolves and exchanged black wolf skins as ceremonial gifts, and the English seemed prepared to enter and expand this trade, offering native hunters cloth, corn, and ammunition in return for wolf heads. But in the end predator eradication drove the humans apart rather than together. Both colonists and natives misconstrued the meaning of the wolf skulls. The Algonquians saw the heads as symbols of partnership, alliance, and equality, while the English understood them as tokens of fealty, submission, and pacification. As the Soule episode demonstrated, suspicion and wolves strode the woods of New England together. The Indian who fell into the pit on Wolf Trap Hill had to prove his legitimacy in order to continue his journey. Unsure of their Indian neighbors' true loyalties, the English tried to make wolf heads icons of certainty and reassurance. Instead, the detached craniums became mementos of the humans' failure to understand and trust one another.

* * *

The English needed Indian allies to fight wolves because they let their livestock wander beyond their ability to protect them. Turned loose, large domestic
animals thrived in coastal New England. They rummaged through coastal
ecosystems, gorging on salt grasses and muddy bivalves. Animal bodies and
animal herds grew without a large investment of human labor, a blessing
since the colonists lacked the manpower to replicate the meticulous herding
practices they had left behind. In England, drovers and shepherds tended
domestic beasts, moving them from pasture to pasture to forestall overgrazing
and to spread manure on tired fields. In America the supervision of livestock was a low priority. Towns collected their animals into common herds
and appointed teenage boys to look after them. This freed the men to labor
in the fields, but the arrangement also freed the animals. Livestock frequently
escaped pubescent keepers short in stature and attention spans. Horses invaded cornfields; cows wandered into swamps; and pigs assaulted people
on village streets. Town councils across New England passed laws aimed at
taming unruly beasts, but free-ranging livestock was a fact of life. So much
so that the colonists reversed the English fencing laws: they erected fences
to keep domestic animals out of their fields rather than in.[4]

The effect of these lax herding practices was the extension of the colonists'
territory. It may seem strange to think of a cow as a mobile chunk of territory.
An animal, after all, is a living being, not a locale. Yet living beings take up
space. Skin envelops area as well as organs, and all creatures defend their
bodies against trespass. Throughout their eons of association, the human
caretakers of domesticated beasts have dedicated their time, labor, and wealth
to policing the boundaries of their animals' bodies. They monitored the food
that came in; they controlled reproduction, overseeing the exchange of genetic
material between bodies; and they even collected and redistributed the scat
that exited. All this work and worry, however, meant nothing if livestock owners allowed the teeth of wild canines to tear into their animals' skin.

A shortage of herders forced the English colonists to loosen their supervision of their animals' bodies. The beasts sauntered away, ingesting novel
delectables and exchanging genes with whomever they pleased. Their independent travels exposed them to wolves, and the predators ate them.
Humans had undermined their animals' ability to defend their own flesh.
When choosing traits, livestock owners favored slow and peaceful over
fleet and bellicose. Therefore domesticated beasts needed people to guard

them, and the colonists endeavored to protect their territories, wherever they roamed.

In 1634 the Massachusetts Bay Colony received a shipment of weapons to protect human and animal bodies. The arms molded in barrels at Boston's fort for two years until the court ordered their disbursal to the colony's settlements. William Pincheon oversaw the task. He inventoried the arsenal before divvying it up among the nine towns. Pincheon's inventory listed such obvious examples of seventeenth-century weaponry as swords, muskets, and bandoleers, as well as now obscure implements like linstocks, ladles, demi-culverins, and sakers. The strangest ordinance in the colony's arsenal, however, was the supply of two hundred wolf hooks, twenty wolf hooks to hang, and six wolf bullets with adders' tongues. The derivation and design of wolf bullets with adders' tongues were mysteries that died with William Pincheon, but other colonial sources referred to wolf hooks. John Josselyn, an English traveler and writer who visited New England twice in the seventeenth century, described them. He reported that livestock owners often tied two mackerel hooks together, dipped them in tallow, and left the balls of fat out for wolves to swallow. In 1634 John Winthrop Jr. wrote Edward Howes asking for "devices to kill wolves." Howes suggested two: hunks of sponges hidden in carrion and "pieces of stronge wyer twisted together, ether 4, or 3, or 2 pieces, and the ends to be bowed and filed sharpe, and beards cutt in them like fish hookes; and them put within theire meate." Among the colonists' experiments in wolf control, hooks represented the pinnacle of their inventiveness and the depth of their cruelty.[5]

The residents of colonial New England auditioned a number of wolf-killing techniques. They assaulted the animals' guts with sponges and metal hooks. They chased wolves with mastiffs, greyhounds, spaniels, and beagles. They dug pits, erected pens, and rigged guns to blast passersby. They appointed hunters, granted monopolies, and offered bounties. They built fences across the necks of isthmuses and let the ocean protect their livestock on three sides. They organized community hunts that cleared entire islands of predators. Given names like Hog, Goat, and Calf, New England's coastal islands became havens for domestic creatures. The range of wolf-killing ideas and techniques signaled the colonists' predicament. With neither the time nor the workforce to oversee their property, livestock owners tried to replace shepherds with devices, schemes, and rewards.[6]

The records of Ipswich, Massachusetts, document one town's search for a method of wolf killing that worked. In 1635 Ipswich received twenty-five wolf hooks from Mr. Wilson, an English merchant. In 1642 the town ordered householders with estates valued above five hundred pounds to buy and keep mastiffs for wolf hunting. Households worth less than five hundred pounds but more than one hundred were to "provide a sufficient hound or beagle." The next year, the town sweetened the bounty for people hunting wolves with dogs. It paid a twenty-shilling bounty for wolves destroyed with the aid of a dog and five shillings for those killed in traps. In 1668 Ipswich increased the bounty to forty shillings with no provisions except that the wolf be slain within two miles of the town center and that the hunter bring the head to the meetinghouse and nail it to the side. Yet even after all these experiments with techniques and incentives, wolves continued to harass the residents of Ipswich. In 1723 the town advised parents to accompany their children to worship. A pack of wolves had been seen lurking near the meeting-house at the center of town.[7]

The Ipswich experience was not unusual. Colonists and wolves lived to-gether as unhappy neighbors in many parts of New England for more than a century. The immigrants cleared wolves out of their population centers, but the predators survived for long periods of time in the areas between En-glish strongholds. Philip Curtis killed Boston's last wolf in 1657. Thomas Smith collected the final wolf bounty from Watertown, Massachusetts, in 1658. The New Haven Colony paid its last wolf bounty in 1659, while in the Connecticut River Valley, the town of Springfield granted its last bounty in 1682. Towns west of the Connecticut River battled wolves well into the eigh-teenth century. In 1775 Williamstown's Samuel Kellog received twenty pounds for slaughtering ten wolves. Located in the far northwest corner of Massa-chusetts, Williamstown would seem a likely spot for a final showdown between colonists and wolves. But according to local wolf lore, George Braley shot Massachusetts's last wolf in 1837, and he performed the deed in the Sandwich Woods of Cape Cod. The Braley episode was an extreme, nearly unbelievable, case of a New England wolf dying in an unexpected time and place. But there were others. Gloucester on Cape Ann paid John Lane a pound and ten shil-lings for a wolf's head in 1713. In 1745 the town voted to increase the wolf bounty to four pounds. Dedham granted John Draper a bounty for killing a wolf in 1716, eighty years after the town's founding. In 1787 Amherst's Isaac Hubbard destroyed a wolf and collected a bounty.[8]

Coastal Boston exterminated wolves in 1657, while seaside Gloucester continued to battle the animals in 1745. Three factors explain how this could happen. First, wolves and humans avoided one another. Fear separated the species, creating buffer zones between them. Second, when European animals wandered into these zones and wolves attacked them, the colonists limited their response. Bounty laws required wolf killers to swear that the head in their hands came from an animal slain within that town's boundaries. Authorities refused to pay for other towns' wolves. Nor would they grant bounties for predators destroyed in the spaces between towns. Of course, hunters could lie and collect bounties for wolves killed in the wilderness beyond the English settlements. But a third factor made this scenario unlikely.[9]

Most English colonists possessed neither the aptitude nor the desire to chase wolves into unfamiliar territories. As hunters, they excelled at ending the lives of waterfowl. They waited on the banks of ponds and marshes and fired muskets loaded with shot into flocks of ducks, geese, and simplicities (small, "simple" birds gunners slaughtered in "heaps"). Tracking a wolf into a strange forest or swamp in the hopes of killing it with a bullet was beyond consideration for most. An average hunter would get lost before glimpsing his quarry. Wolves troubled Gloucester nearly a century after they disappeared from Boston because the colonists' hunting practices and bounty system left spaces for the predators to live and reproduce. In 1745 the fishing village joined Ipswich, Manchester, Beverly, and Wenham to offer a bounty for wolves destroyed "in the Woods between" the towns.[10]

Hunting wolves with guns was a skill at which few colonists excelled, but some did become accomplished wolf trappers. Towns tried to encourage these experts. Instead of offering a general bounty, some communities hired hunters and granted trapping monopolies. In 1644 Amesbury, Massachusetts, engaged Richard Goodale to hunt wild canids for the six weeks leading up to Michaelmas. For his work Goodale earned "a peck of Indian corne from each townsman," three pounds worth of wheat, and two shillings for every fox and two pounds for every wolf he destroyed. In 1645 Amesbury renewed its association with Goodale, this time hiring the hunter to stalk foxes and wolves one day every week, "wether there be any occasion or no," for a salary of thirteen pounds. The contract stipulated that Goodale "not hunt in any other towne." Amesbury's reluctance to share its hunter with others highlighted Goodale's value. He was a hot commodity, a skilled wolf killer amid a crowd of bird slayers. Yet he still pursued wild canines only one day a week.

Amesbury's leaders worried that another town might cut into the limited time Goodale, a busy farmer, was willing to commit to hunting.[11]

The experience of New Haven's Richard Beckley, another "skilled" wolf hunter, mirrored that of Goodale. In May 1651 the town tempted Beckley with an offer to top the colony's fifteen-shilling-per-wolf bounty by an undisclosed amount if he "would indeavor and use meanes to kill wolves." Beckley answered the town's nebulous proposal with an elusive promise. He pledged to "doe what he could." In September of the same year the town clarified its terms. The selectmen gave Richard Beckley and William Fowlers permission to set guns for wolves. These shotgun traps were horribly dangerous. In 1655 the town of Easthampton on Long Island barred "set guns" from within a half-mile radius of the town and required trappers to remove the guns at sunrise. The gun traps threatened both livestock and children. Easthampton passed the set gun regulations after a small boy tripped a wire and lost his life. New Haven tried to mitigate the collateral damage of these devices by limiting them to nighttime use and by giving Beckley and Fowlers immunity from prosecution if someone's heifer wandered into the line of fire. No other trappers had such "liberties."[12]

At least no one did until a town meeting a few months later. In October 1651 the New Haven selectmen revoked Beckley and Fowlers's monopoly on set guns and granted the liberty to all the men in town. New Haven's experiment in specialization had ended. Livestock protection became the responsibility of all the grown males in the community, as it was before the town had approached Beckley.

Both New Haven and Amesbury encouraged men who displayed a gift for wolf killing to devote more time to their talent, but neither Goodale nor Beckley seized with much relish the opportunity to hunt for bounties. And the reasons for their tepidness are not hard to find. Beckley and Goodale were farmers with crops to sow, animals to watch, and children to feed. An original settler of Amesbury, Goodale amassed an estate valued at eighty pounds including lands, cattle, swine, and an "8th part of a barke." He could afford a servant, Cornelius Conner, who inherited his master's clothes in 1666. In 1650 New Haven granted Beckley and three other farmers five thousand acres on a "necke of land by the seaside." The group agreed to pay a penny an acre, stay and improve the land for five years, and not sell any of it without the town's approval. Both Goodale and Beckley had plenty of work. Bounties no doubt fattened their purses, but wolf killing would always run a distant second to their main occupation: raising plants, animals, and children.[13]

Beckley and Goodale were examples of a peculiarly American invention: the yeoman hunter. In England kings, queens, and aristocrats protected wild creatures from the lower classes in order to kill the beasts themselves during elaborate hunts. The powerful chased, coursed, and gunned for sport, while the rest of society poached or resisted the temptation to attack the island's wildlife. Few aristocrats emigrated to North America. The English colonists, therefore, had little experience hunting. But it would be a mistake to over-state the long-term ramifications of this ignorance. The English colonists lacked woodcraft, but they were not bumbling fools. They could adapt. In New England, for example, most colonists were neophyte farmers as well as naive hunters. In time they learned to grow crops and kill game. Their hunting just looked different. Instead of running after charismatic fauna (deer and fox) with hounds on horseback, the colonists in New England trapped mammals and shotgunned waterfowl. They tried to kill as many animals as possible, quickly and easily. Unlike their upper-crust brethren, they had farms to work. The New World's yeoman hunters were predators shackled to plants.[14]

But New England did contain a group of men with no vegetable responsibilities: Algonquians. Like the English colonists, the Algonquians in southern New England depended on agriculture for most of their calories, but in their society women did the farming while the men hunted, warred, and conducted diplomacy. The patchwork landscape of strongholds and buffer zones looked different from the perspective of these native hunters. They frequented the spaces few colonists dared enter. They hunted and trapped in the woods and forests, and, like wolves, they used swamps as safe havens. Indian women and children hid in swamps during wars and plagues. This practice tantalized colonists. They imagined heathens gathering in "dark and dismal swamps" with their powwows to worship in "a horrid and devilish manner." Both Indians and wolves haunted wild places, and this spatial association fed the Europeans' habit of seeing Indians and wolves as metaphorically equivalent. But it also prompted the owners of domestic beasts to ask for help. Skilled woodland hunters, the Algonquians were potential allies in the colonists' efforts to make New England safe for livestock.[15]

The English colonists tried to recruit Indians to join them in a common front against a rival predator. The alliance should have worked. The Indians already killed wolves. The English needed only encourage them to destroy more. The colonists, however, fumbled their attempts at uniting humanity against wolves. In 1642 the leaders of Newport commissioned Roger Williams to ask Miantonomi, the Narragansett sachem, to send his warriors to kill all the wolves on the island of Aquidneck (renamed Rhode Island in 1644) in one grand hunt. Williams and Miantonomi were friendly, and the sachem agreed to the hunt. The Newport authorities rewarded Miantonomi's aid with a series of laws restricting the Narragansetts' access to Aquidneck's deer. They banned the Indians' snare traps; they forbade the Indians' burning of the island's undergrowth; they barred the Indians' wigwams; and, finally, they outlawed the Indians. A 1643 law instructed magistrates to arrest any Indian found "skulking about in any part of the Island." The Aquidneck episode demonstrated the problem with New England's humans killing wolves together out of friendship: the colonists returned favors with restrictions.[16]

But perhaps money could succeed where camaraderie failed. The English colonies enacted wolf bounties designed to encourage Indians to slaughter wolves. In 1651 Plymouth voted to give any Indian who turned in a wolf's head a "coat of trading cloth." Ten years later the colony increased the bounty to a coat plus a half a pound of powder and two pounds of shot. Connecticut and Massachusetts also passed wolf bounties aimed at Indians. Connecticut traded shillings for wolf heads, while Massachusetts tried money, corn, wine, and bullets. Measuring the effectiveness of these bounties is difficult. Town and colony governments kept track of the rewards they granted, but their records were neither systematic nor comprehensive. Still, Indians appeared in them. Plymouth paid "Kokawehewan an Indian" for killing a wolf in 1679. "Nimrod Indian" and "Sam the Indian" collected bounties from Providence in 1687. Kokawehewan, Nimrod, and Sam stand out because Indians are scarce in the bounty lists that have survived. The colonists tempted Algonquian hunters with cash and trade goods, but it appears only a few seized the bait.[17]

A closer look at the disbursal of wolf bounties explains why few Indians claimed them. To collect their reward, wolf hunters had to follow a series of bureaucratic procedures. After killing the wolf and detaching the head, the bounty seeker traveled to town and presented his trophy to a local official. The official then administered an oath. The hunter swore that he slaughtered said animal within the town's boundaries and that said animal was indeed a wolf. If convinced of the hunter's truthfulness, the local official accepted the head and either displayed it in a public place or buried the skull in an unmarked grave. At the next town meeting, the official would vouch for the hunter, and the town treasurer would pay the bounty.[18]

Collecting a wolf bounty in colonial New England was a nightmare for Algonquian hunters. They had to prove their honesty to a group of people who viewed them as inherently devious. The Indians who received bounties needed the help of reputable Englishmen. Nimrod Indian brought notes from Thomas Harris, John Steere, and Captain William Hopkins when he appeared before the Providence town meeting in 1687. The letters declared that Nimrod killed two wolves, one in June and another at "about michelmas time." The solid reputations of the letter writers secured Nimrod's bounties. Wolves' heads raised suspicions few Indians could assuage on their own.[19]

First the English enacted bounties to persuade Indians to kill more wolves; then they attached oaths, tests, and procedures to the rewards, making it nearly impossible for Indian hunters to collect them. The colonists were not imbeciles; why would they sabotage their own bounties? The reason was fraud. English wolf hunters frequently abused the bounty laws. In 1648 the Massachusetts Bay General Court ordered town magistrates to bury the wolf heads after hunters presented them to collect their bounties. The court wanted to stop wolf killers from taking the head of a single wolf on a multitown tour, collecting a bounty at each stop. In 1684 the court again outlawed the practice of transporting heads from one town to another. In 1650 Connecticut forbade "any person so ever, either Indians or English," from stealing "any Wolfe out of any pit made by any other man to catch wolfes in, whereby they would defraude the right of the owner of their due from the towne or country." The punishment for wolf theft was ten shillings or a whipping. Bounty seekers also tried to defraud towns by turning in a dog's puppies and claiming that they were a wolf's whelps. In 1740 the General Court of Rhode Island refused to pay Joseph Eady for several infant canines, "it being uncertain whether the young creatures were wolves or not." The suspicion that greeted Indian bounty seekers was hardly surprising given that the English colonists mistrusted each other with wolf heads.[20]

Instead of uniting New England's humans, predator eradication exposed the fault lines that separated them, and the region's wolves escaped a common front only to fall in the middle of the humans' squabbles. The animals' heads became symbols in the colonists' and Indians' struggle over land and political ascendancy. During the seventeenth and eighteenth centuries, New England Algonquians and English colonists fought several major wars and engaged in a series of raids and skirmishes. The violence sometimes plunged the bipeds into the basements of hell. During the Pequot War (1636–37), English militia burned a fortified Indian village along the Mystic River, slaughtering men, women, and children as they ran from the fires. In 1703 in the midst of Queen Anne's War, French, Abenaki, and Canadian Indian fighters raided the English town of Deerfield, killing fifty residents and carrying a hundred into captivity. Many of the instances of colonists labeling Algonquians animals came from these periods of intense conflict. John Underhill, an English captain who watched the bodies burn at Mystic, compared his Pequot enemies to "roaring lions." After King Philip's War, William Hubbard called Metacomet a den-dwelling "beast." A war hostage, Mary Rowlandson likened her Narragansett captors to "hell-hounds," "ravenous bears," and "wolves," while Rev. Solomon Stoddard wrote, a few weeks before the raid on Deerfield, that Indians "act like wolves and are to be dealt withal as wolves."[21]

Violence and heartbreak led English writers to question their Indian adversaries' humanity, but the actual lines of cultural division in wartime were never as clearly drawn as their animal metaphors implied. War generated cross-cultural alliances as well as inhuman violence. The English, for instance, fought the Pequots with the assistance of Narragansett warriors. Later, during King Philip's War, the colonists battled the Narragansetts with the aid of Mohegan fighters. Wolf symbols and metaphors signaled the cultural distance between warring peoples; they also helped bridge this gap through military alliances.

Severed wolf heads stood at the juncture of peace and war in colonial New England. Nailed to the side of a meetinghouse or set atop a post in a public space, the heads symbolized the colonists' desire to punish outlaw animals and bring order to a rambunctious natural environment. In England criminals and traitors received similar treatment. Displayed in public, the human skulls served as warnings to would-be thieves and rebels. Of course, no human signal however vivid could prompt a hungry wolf to mull the consequence of biting a lamb, and the predators' inability to read the messages disgruntled colonists were sending them makes the public display of wolf heads a puzzling activity. They were signs, but signs for whom?

In 1671 Metacomet, known to the English as King Philip, negotiated a treaty with the Plymouth Colony, and this document illustrated the multiple signals sent by lopped-off heads in colonial New England. The Wampanoag sachem agreed to abide by Plymouth's laws, to pay a fine of one hundred pounds for past "misdemeanors," to "not make war without approbation," to allow the court at Plymouth to settle future disputes, and to submit to a ban on selling Wampanoag land without the approval of the court. He also promised to send five wolves' heads to the governor every year as a "token of his fealty." Later that year Metacomet escorted Takamunna, sachem of the Saconet, to the Plymouth Court. Takamunna signed a similar treaty and pledged one wolf's head a year. The wolf-head tributes the Plymouth Colony extracted from Metacomet and Takamunna represented the colonists' attempt to fashion a symbol that communicated their right to control the demarcation, transference, and ownership of territory. Metacomet contested this right. Four years after signing the treaty, he led an uprising against the English. Many skulls rolled during King Philip's War, but only one ended up rotting on a pole in Plymouth town—Metacomet's.[22]

Propped up for display like a wolf's head, King Philip's skull was a symbol of English ascendancy. The colonists tried to use human skulls as tokens of power from the earliest years of settlement. In 1623 Miles Standish decapitated Wituwamat, a Massachusett Indian accused of conspiring to destroy the English settlements, and stuck his head on a pole outside of Plymouth's fort. The colonists received Wituwamat's head "with joy"; it signaled their ability to defend themselves and punish their enemies. This was an overestimation of prowess. In 1623 the Plymouth Colony could barely feed itself, much less fend off a coordinated Indian attack. Wituwamat's head symbolized the colonists' yearning for power, domination, and control, aspirations thwarted by the continued presence of human rivals who interpreted skulls differently. Standish seized physical command of an Indian body when he chopped off Wituwamat's head, but the English never acquired the cultural authority to determine the skull's meaning.[23]

During the Pequot War, the colonists' Narragansett and Mohegan allies offered Pequot heads as gifts. For the Indians the gifts reinforced their equal partnership with the English. The colonists, however, saw the skulls as tokens of not only the Pequots' subordination but the Mohegans' and Narragansetts' as well. The heads represented the Indians' "service" and "fidelity." In 1637 Roger Williams indulged in the ultimate power fantasy. In a letter to the governor of the Massachusetts Bay Colony, John Winthrop, he suggested that the conquered Pequots be dispersed throughout the colonies. They would live in small, isolated groups and send an annual tribute of wolves' heads to the governor: "As once Edgar the Peacable did with the Welsh in North Wales, a tribute of wolves heads be imposed on them . . . which I conceave an incomparable way to Save much Cattell alive in the land."[24]

Williams's plan linked the conquests of wolves and Indians through communication and territory. The vanquished Pequots would destroy wolves to communicate their fidelity to and compliance with English authority. In the process, they would make the wilderness safe for the colonists' meandering property. Williams imagined a line of communication that worked like a chain of command. Indians would subordinate wolves in order to collect the emblems of their own subordination. The plan, however, contained a glaring weakness. Controlling the symbolism of wolves' heads was beyond the colonists' power. The Algonquians exchanged both human and animal body parts for their own reasons. They traded black wolves' skins to heal alliances and restore reciprocity. It is hard to tell what wolves' heads meant to Indians, but the events leading up to King Philip's War hold a few clues. Metacomet's revolt in 1675 makes more sense if he understood the wolves' heads he committed to give in 1671 as symbols of restored equality instead of imposed fealty. The skulls may have hastened the war by convincing both the English and the Wampanoags that each had broken promises neither had made.

With each battle, raid, and treaty, English fantasies of power became more real. While wolves disappeared slowly and Indians never vanished from southern New England, both experienced a loss of territory and self-determination. Wolves needed space in which to linger, and, as the English population grew, the havens between towns shrank. Farmers drained swamps and cleared thickets. At some unrecorded and quiet moment in the eighteenth century, wolves succumbed to lost habitat and human predation. Dispersers may have traveled back through the region looking for territory and mates, but the population stopped reproducing itself. The Algonquians living along Massachusetts Bay, Cape Cod, Narragansett Bay, coastal Connecticut, and Long Island Sound followed a similar path, except, unlike wolves, they camped at oblivion's edge instead of falling in. Reduced to small enclaves, these southern Algonquians lived as subordinates in the colonists' world.

Rival predators need space, food, and clear lines of communication to live together in peace. In New England, wolves, colonists, and Native Americans never assembled the elements necessary to share an ecological niche. Colonists imported a food supply that invaded their neighboring predators' territories. Unable to impress upon their nichemates the importance of not eating property, the colonists offered rewards to one rival (Native Americans) to hunt the other (wolves). Wolf killing gave the human predators a set of symbols that helped mitigate the communication difficulties brought on by their flexible languages, but the bipeds' alliance shattered on the ground beneath their feet. Unlike wolves, the Algonquians inhabited landscapes—cleared fields and villages—colonists adored. The English bought, stole, and negotiated for Indian land, yet they struggled to convince the Algonquians to respect and adhere to their notions of property. The human predators fought over plots of land as well as the rules for creating, maintaining, and transferring territory. Each tried to invent symbols of power that signaled their control over cultural definitions as well as physical resources. Wolf heads represented one such token. The Algonquians and the English wrestled over the heads' interpretation, one predator insisting the craniums embodied fealty and submission, the other equality and reciprocity. In colonial New England language, land, and domestic beasts trapped three top predators in a pit of violence and misunderstanding, and only one escaped to continue its journey.

PART TWO THE NORTHEASTERN WOODLANDS

CHAPTER FOUR

Predator to Prey

WOLVES' JOURNEY THROUGH THE NORTHEASTERN

WOODLANDS

TWICE ALONG Maine's coast in the 1660s, John Josselyn and his hunting partners captured wolves alive and tortured them for fun. The men happened upon their first victim while gunning for waterfowl on the beach. Their dogs, led by a female mastiff, chased the wolf across the flats at low tide. After an "excellent course," the mastiff grabbed the wolf by the throat and pinned him in the surf. The hunters bound the animal's paws and carried him home swinging "like a Calf upon a staff between two men." That night, they unleashed the predator inside their living room. The beast sank to the floor. No biting, no snarling, he just slouched there, staring at the door. The men tried to rile him up with the dogs, but the pack was listless and uninterested, too worn out to care following that afternoon's long chase. Their evening's entertainment ruined, the hunters took the wolf outside and crushed his skull with a log.[1]

In 1664 Josselyn's mastiff caught another wolf under a tree in a swamp. Once again the giant canine pinned the wolf by the throat, and the hunters bound his paws and carried him home between them. They staked him out in the yard with a rope around his neck and baited him with small dogs. "We," wrote Josselyn, "had excellent sport." The only glitch in the fun was a broken hind leg that prevented the wolf from defending himself properly. After the animals tired and stopped fighting, the men "knockt out his brains."[2]

John Josselyn was an enlightened human who found pleasure in wolves'

69

pain. An educated member of the English gentry, he traveled to New England twice in the seventeenth century, describing his trips in two books published in England. He recounted the Maine wolf stories to tantalize his London audience. He assumed that his readers would enjoy the blood sport as much as he did, and these people were not low-class reprobates. Josselyn wrote to impress England's well-heeled amateur naturalists who gathered together in societies to mull over the reports of biological oddities coming from the New World. To please this crowd, Josselyn included observations about pedestrian flora and fauna (mushrooms and raccoons) as well as rumors about fantastic monsters (sea serpents and mermen). Wolves straddled the line between science and exotica, a line that was by no means fine in the seventeenth century. After the lurid brain bashings, Josselyn cataloged the scientific uses of wolves: wolf fangs hung around a child's neck kept them from "frighting"; the fangs also lessened teething pain when rubbed against a baby's gums; wolf gall prevented the "swelling of the sinews"; and wolf excrement mixed with white wine "helped with the *Collick*."[3]

In the seventeenth century humans swallowed wolf dung spritzers for their health and baited wolves with domestic animals for their entertainment. These were strange people with peculiar habits. They burned witches at the stake, disemboweled criminals, and tormented wolves for sport. As history progressed, as humans crawled from beneath the rock of superstition into the light of understanding, they stopped brutalizing defenseless creatures. Right?

They did not stop. John James Audubon enjoyed the spectacle of the Indiana farmer baiting wolves with hounds in 1824, and Americans continued to savage canine predators well into the twentieth century. In 1937 the federal government of the United States published an instruction manual for killing puppies in their den. The guide focused on coyote pups (few wolves remained in the United States in 1937), but the techniques of den hunting or "denning" were the same for both species. The pamphlet offered several methods of destruction. Hunters could snag the puppies' fur with wire twisted around a forked stick, fish them out, and smash them with a club. Or they could try to smoke the infants out, a technique that required "a shotgun loaded with BB shot." The weapon was essential for "hunting pups that have left the den but are still together." After scurrying from the hideout, groups of youngsters "may be found lying under the sagebrush or among the rocks and are more easily hit with a shotgun than with a rifle when they start to scatter."[4]

FIGURE 2   Hunter Bill Shaw with wolf puppy, a lure for adult
predators. Courtesy Denver Public Library Western History
Department.

Examples of ugliness toward wolves stained every period of American
history. It marked John Josselyn in the seventeenth century as well as the
sport hunters who shot wolves from Piper Cubs buzzing low over Alaskan
snowfields in the 1950s. Euro-Americans fractured wolf skulls and shotgunned wolf puppies. They set the animals on fire and dragged them to
pieces behind horses. They destroyed wolves for a host of pragmatic reasons:
to safeguard livestock, to knit local ecosystems into global capitalist markets,
to collect state-sponsored bounties, and to rid the world of beasts they considered evil, wild, corrupt, and duplicitous. Their motives appear as blunt as
a gunshot to the head, but wolves' deaths were neither that quick nor that
straightforward. They died with fractured spines and severed hamstrings,
gifts from a predator dissatisfied with mere annihilation. The brutality of

FIGURE 3 Poisoned gray wolf with pups. Courtesy Denver Public Library Western History Department.

wolf killing transformed bloody-but-understandable acts of agricultural pacification into deeds as inexplicable as they were horrendous. Why did Euro-Americans terrorize wolves? Why was death not enough?[5]

The European conquest of North America brought livestock owners and predators together in a series of time periods and landscapes. Following the French and Indian War, for example, New England colonists, who had for generations huddled in towns along seashores and in river valleys, fanned out north and west. By 1825 descendants of New England families planted crops, shepherded livestock, and hunted wolves in forests from Vermont's Lake Champlain to Ohio's Sandusky River. Territorial expansion rejuvenated wolf killing, as well as the legends and rituals associated with predator eradication. Through stories and hunting traditions colonists seized command of woodland environments that appeared unruly and frightening to them. They symbolically pacified northeastern forests as they struggled to make a living from these landscapes. Thus folklore and history sustained activities like wolf baiting and puppy shooting, giving agricultural expansionists the means to express their anger and frustration with their new homes.[6]

And biology? Here the life sciences throw folklore and history a curve. Biology offers a model of interspecific bloodshed—predation—that undercuts the central assumption of the humanist disciplines: the notion that people's

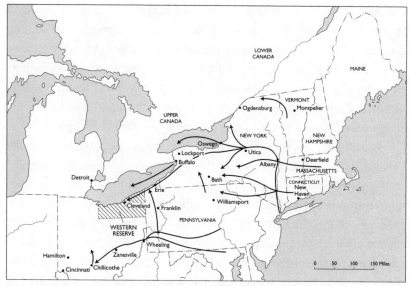

FIGURE 4 Immigration paths through the northeast woodlands.

actions, objectives, and belief systems mattered. Biologists view predation as a relationship, not a set of violent intentions. Wolves, for instance, have digestive yearnings for most herbivores they encounter, but herbivores survive by thwarting wolves' desires. Prey species have evolved an impressive array of defenses, and they routinely overmatch would-be devourers. The predators' violent intentions help shape their relationship with prey, but even the most ferocious carnivores resemble Wile E. Coyotes chasing after Road Runners rather than angels of doom swooping down on cringing bunnies.

Vulnerability—not hunger, not anger, and certainly not spite—is the key to predator-prey relationships. The skill and viciousness of the hunter matters less than the size, speed, strength, health, and ferocity of the hunted. Vulnerability explains why large predators tend to kill the old, young, and sick members of prey populations. Predators eat the mild and the weak because those are the animals they can catch and kill. A full-grown herbivore in good health has little to fear from predators under most circumstances. Of course, situations change. Prey vulnerability is contingent upon thousands of environmental factors. A sudden snowstorm can immobilize the sturdiest prey, turning a two-ton moose with antlers the size of car doors into someone's dinner. A drought may kill the grass in the hillside sanctuary of a herd of

Dall Sheep, forcing them to the valley floor in search of food. Invincible in the steeps, the climbers become juicy targets on level ground. The shifting dynamics of vulnerability make the predator-prey relationship a driving force in evolution. Prey species adapt to minimize their vulnerability, while predators try to stay ahead of their food supply's defenses. Prey sprout tusks, crowd together, and emit noxious chemicals; predators hunt in packs, squirt poison, and pounce from trees. Over time, this arms race alters both species.[7]

Euro-American cruelty looks different from the perspective of wildlife biology. Humans lose their place as the focal point of abusive episodes. The cringing wolf becomes the creature that must be understood, not the vicious hunter. In most predator-prey relationships, the prey species dominates. Predators follow the rhythm of their prey's population cycles; they fight against and many times fail to overcome their prey's defense adaptations; and they mold their behavior to suit their prey's migration patterns and seasonal calendars. Predation is an unequal partnership in which the food often controls the feeder. The first mystery that needs to be solved then is not why humans behaved so cruelly, but rather why wolves responded so ineffectively.

Magnificent killers, wolves struggled as Euro-Americans' prey. Unlike the herbivores they devoured, wolves' biological niche or ecological occupation (top predator: an animal that feasts on others and upon which no other animal feasts) offered neither the time nor the prior experience necessary for outrunning, outsmarting, or out-reproducing organisms intent on ending their lives. Wolves' predatory achievements laid the groundwork for their deficiencies as prey, and understanding their problems as quarry begins with their experiences as hunters.

But first a warning: there are no perfect models or steadfast rules for predation. Scientists have searched long and hard for the mathematical equation that would reveal and predict the interplay between predators and prey. So far, they have woven intricate and informative theories, but the laws of predation have proven elusive. Instead of rules, scientists have discovered contingencies. Weather, disease, and perhaps even sunspots affect the interaction. With the fundamental role of contingency in mind, let us look at how wolves make their living by causing the deaths of others.[8]

In 1818 Henry Hosmer witnessed an event few people have ever seen. He watched a wolf kill a deer. Euro-American colonists beheld evidence of many wolf kills. Livestock owners dreaded walking their pastures and finding pieces of their animal property spread across the clover. Yet while familiar with the aftermath of predation, colonists almost never spied the act. They filled the void created by their lack of firsthand knowledge with gory speculation. They imagined squadrons of wolves, coordinating their attacks with barks and howls, setting ambushes for prey. They imagined wolves slicing the hamstrings of their quarry, immobilizing the beasts in order to suck their blood. They imagined orgies of flying blood and snapping teeth as packs dismembered their victims with such enthusiasm that they began to injure and eat one another. Henry Hosmer stumbled across a spectacle that inspired outrageous fantasies.[9]

Hosmer was out hunting that spring morning. But he did not have a gun. He entered the woods surrounding his home in Guiliford, Ohio, armed only with "a very good dog." After tromping through the greenery for a while, he spotted a deer near a brush fence. He watched the deer halt, sniff the air, and run. In a moment, Hosmer spied the reason for the deer's flight: at "a little distance, a large wolf that was evidently waiting for its approach." He tried to sic his dog on the wolf, but the dog refused the order. Hosmer followed the wolf chasing the deer. "After having gone up the creek fifty yards," he wrote, "I found them a short distance from me, and saw that the wolf had caught the deer, killed it, and was sucking his blood." He scared the wolf away from the corpse and took the deer for himself.[10]

The most fanciful detail in Hosmer's account—the vampirelike blood drinking—is also the most revealing. Unbeknownst to him, Hosmer was seeing how wolves kill. He missed the initial takedown. The wolf and deer outran him and his dog, and he lost sight of them for several minutes. Wolves attack the hindquarters of prey first, biting into the animal's meaty rump or ham. They stay away from the tendons near the hooves. People hamstring wolves; wolves do not hamstring prey. Hard, sharp, and lethal, hooves are the last things wolves want near their heads. They aim for the flanks, grasping for a hold in the large muscles, hoping to bring the mammal down. A trip, a stumble, a fall, and the wolves go for the throat. The animals in the rear begin feasting as their partners crush and remove the herbivore's windpipe. Gallons of blood spill in this process, but none enters wolves' stomachs through calculated jugular sucking.[11]

Dumb luck brought Henry Hosmer and the Ohio wolf together, and luck would continue to act as the key enabler of humans' observations of wolf predation until wildlife biologists took to the air in the 1950s. In his landmark 1944 study of Alaskan wolf ecology, Adolph Murie revolutionized people's understanding of wolf predation. He based his cutting-edge interpretation, however, on no firsthand observations of wolves killing prey. Murie and his associates spent more than two years, April 1939 through August 1941, in Mount McKinley National Park (now Denali National Park and Preserve) studying wolves in the field. They collected wolf scats and Dall sheep skulls for analysis, they observed denning sites, and they examined kill sites. They possessed neither airplanes nor radio collars.

Catching wolves in the midst of taking prey in a study area as large and rugged as Mount McKinley on foot was highly unlikely. Murie described incidents of wolf predation, but he reconstructed these events from reading the tracks in the snow around a munched carcass. For example, in October 1939 Murie found a recently killed male lamb, and "the tracks in the snow plainly told this story . . ." A wolf had surprised a group of five or six sheep eating grass in a valley. Prey and predator rushed for higher ground. The stronger animals stayed above their pursuer, but the slower lamb lost the race for positioning. The wolf claimed the high ground and seized the youngster. Murie used the tracks in the snow to make two crucial arguments about wolves and Dall sheep. First, wolves tried to attack the sheep from above, and, second, they adopted this strategy because full-grown sheep were nearly impossible to catch from behind while running uphill. The incident helped explain why the Mount McKinley wolves tended to eat only the young, old, injured, and sick. Those were the animals they could grab.[12]

Murie had other evidence to back up his interpretation of predator and prey tracks. His examination of sheep skulls found at kill sites showed that "in a mountain habitat having considerable degree of ruggedness and extent, the wolf catches a few of the strong animals but preys mainly on the weak members of the population." The tracks at the kill site merely confirmed a tendency found in the skulls.[13]

Murie was a careful observer. Paw and hoof prints, however, led other, less rigorous, witnesses astray. Trappers and hunters interpreted the tracks surrounding kill sites and used their readings to confirm people's worst fears about wolves. They concocted the stories of wolf armies descending on prey with military discipline. They reported that female wolves often distracted targets with their feminine wiles as their male comrades detached the beasts' Achilles tendons. Finally, hunters and trappers looked at the bloody and trampled snow and imagined horrific scenes of slashing teeth and cannibalism. The tracks suggested many story lines, but some readers believed only the grimmest scenarios.[14]

In 1958 a group of scientists led by Durward Allan, a professor at Indiana's Purdue University, initiated a long-term wolf study at Isle Royale National Park, an island in Lake Superior walking distance from the north shore across the ice that forms in deep winter. These investigators used a plane to observe wolves in the act of killing. The airplane allowed a glimpse into the predator-prey relationship, but only a glimpse. The scientist witnessed a surprisingly low number of incidents in which a pack took a life. Rolf O. Peterson, a wildlife biologist who has studied Isle Royale for twenty-five years, estimated that out of "a couple hundred wolf-moose confrontations" he had seen "ten . . . that resulted in a kill." This paltry record of firsthand sightings of wolves in the act of killing was due to two reasons. First, the Isle Royale wolves, like all wolves, were most active at dusk and dawn. Most of their kills occurred in the dark. Second, the high ratio of confrontations to kills reflected a critical feature of the predator-prey relationship. The wolves challenged, prodded, and teased moose on a regular basis. They tested many more animals than they killed. Looking for signs of vulnerability, the wolves engaged their prey in a dialog or, in Peterson's words, a "dance of death."[15]

This dance had a series of steps. L. David Mech, another alumnus of the Isle Royale study, divided the hunt into five stages: locating prey, the stalk, the encounter, the rush, and the chase. Wolves locate prey through scent and sight as well as by chance. The predators may also consult a "mental map" of their territory, using previous sightings of animals to home in on a target's current location. Once the prey is found, wolves approach their quarry in a slow crouch. During this stalk, the predators sneak closer while gathering and interpreting signals from their prey. They may spot a limp or smell the rot of an abscessed tooth. The encounter begins the moment the prey detects the stalkers. Some animals stand their ground; others run, kicking off the final two stages of the hunt, the rush and the chase.[16]

The rush can lead to an abrupt kill or a chase that can last for days. Wolf packs, especially small ones, can be remarkably patient. On Isle Royale, Mech observed the caution and fortitude of both predator and prey. From an airplane he watched a pack stalk, encounter, rush, and chase a moose. The predators caught the animal within fifty yards. They attacked the flanks, legs, and back. The moose fell. A wolf bit into the animal's fleshy nose. The moose rose and carried the wolves, fastened to its body like leeches, into a stand of trees. Perhaps afraid that the herbivore would comb them off in the branches, the wolves released their grip. There the chase stalled. The moose, bleeding from the throat, stood in the trees. The wolves harassed the animal every so often, but they seemed content to let the animal bleed and weaken. Darkness forced Mech to land. The next morning, he found the moose still standing in the trees. The wolves had given up on the stubborn beast and killed another moose nearby.[17]

As they circled over Isle Royale, wolf biologists observed hundreds of encounters between moose and wolves. These sightings formed the basis for a striking interpretation of the wolf-prey relationship. The Isle Royale study demolished wolves' reputation as formidable killers. One hundred thirty-one times Mech observed individual wolves or packs detect a moose. One hundred twenty times the wolves sneaked up on their potential meal undetected. Ninety-six moose ran. Wolves caught up to fifty-three. Of these fifty-three, wolves attacked seven and killed six. The Isle Royale wolves tested more than a hundred moose in order to find six creatures they could eat safely. Instead of bloodthirsty aggression, wolves approached moose hunting with cautious restraint. Their prey did not have to deploy elaborate defense strategies to survive. A moose need only stand her ground and display some vigor to end an attack. "To my knowledge," writes Rolf Peterson, "no one has ever observed wolves killing a moose that did not run when first confronted by its predators." Wolves interpreted flight as a sign of vulnerability, and detecting weaknesses was the ultimate goal of their constant harassment of prey.[18]

Both the Mount McKinley and Isle Royale wolves subsisted on young, old, injured, and diseased animals. But how universal is this tendency? Murie's research is more than fifty years old, and Isle Royale has serious drawbacks as a case study. Islands distort and intensify population dynamics. At one time, Isle Royale supported an incredibly high density of wolves, much higher than any mainland population. Then in the early 1980s the population crashed. Wildlife biologists are still searching for the reasons behind the die-off. Furthermore, the wolves in the forests of the northeastern United States in the late eighteenth century and early nineteenth feasted mainly on white-tailed deer, not moose or Dall sheep. Does wolves' tendency to eat the weak apply to mainland deer as well?[19]

Deer pose less of a physical challenge to wolf hunters than moose, and they do not scale mountainsides for protection like Dall sheep. Yet wildlife biologists looking at the wolf-whitetail relationship in Canada's Algonquin Provincial Park and northern Minnesota discovered the same selection tendencies in deer as those found in sheep and moose. The wolves ate the vulnerable. In Algonquin Park deer remains appeared in 80 percent of the scats analyzed, and fawn hair made up 71 percent of the deer follicles found in wolf droppings. In the winter, the analysis of mandibles (jawbones) of deer killed by wolves showed "a strong selection for deer that were 5 years of age or older." In Minnesota wolves dined on fawns in the summer and older animals in the winter, like their colleagues to the north. These findings raise a quandary: if in general deer are easier to kill than moose or Dall sheep, why do wolves continue to select the vulnerable instead of feasting on the entire population?[20]

Mech has examined this question. In a 1981 study of wolves and deer in northeastern Minnesota, Mech and his associate Michael E. Nelson argued that migrations, social groupings, and spacing provided deer with critical defenses against wolves. In the summer the deer spread out through their home range. Males spent the summer alone, while does traveled with their fawns. This solitary behavior evened out grazing pressure across a habitat as well as forcing wolves to hunt one deer at a time. "The optimum strategy for summer is a wide dispersion of does," wrote Mech and Nelson. "Even if wolves do locate some vulnerable fawns, they would have to hunt far and wide to find others." In the fall this strategy changed. The deer gathered into herds. As temperatures dropped, as snow limited their mobility, and as the disappearance of browse robbed their strength, the whitetails "yarded."[21]

Spending the winter in a group held several advantages for the deer. The extra noses, eyes, and ears aided the detection of predators. The time individuals used to spend on lookout could be spent foraging for scarce food. When wolves harassed the group, vulnerable members—the young, sick, old, and injured—stuck out. Given a choice between attacking a robust buck or a wobbly old-timer, the wolves selected the old-timer. Finally, in a herd the ratio of wolves to deer would decrease, reducing the "relative predation level through sheer mathematical effect." For these reasons and more, wintering together helped deer thwart the ravenous desires of wolves. Mech noted one more spatial strategy employed by white-tailed deer in Minnesota that deserves special attention. The animals tended to collect in the buffer zones between pack territories. The deer exploited the social anxieties that kept wolf packs apart to carve out safe havens in the spaces wolves feared to tread.[22]

The seasonal migrations of the white-tailed deer exemplified the complexity and nuance of the predator-prey relationship. In Minnesota wolves and deer evolved offensive and defensive strategies that included spacing habits and social organization as well as fights and flights. It is important to remember that evolution created these behaviors, not animals huddled in strategy sessions. Over time, deer that hung out in the buffer zones between wolf territories, that gathered together in the winter, and that dispersed singly in the summer reproduced more successfully than deer that did not. Likewise, wolves that attacked the old, young, injured, and weak generated more offspring than those that wasted their energy running after the fleetest does or sacrificed their ribs to the kicks of the toughest bucks. Evolution transformed predators and prey, giving both frailties and strengths. Their relationship endured because neither predators nor prey could fulfill their desires. Prey species could never completely protect themselves; predators could never kill at will.

Yet before rejoicing in the balance of nature on display in the predator-prey relationship, we should revisit the wildlife biologists hunched over their deer mandibles and wolf droppings. Using airplanes, radio collars, and careful field observations, these scientists have dismantled the lies and superstitions that once veiled wolves' interactions with prey. They cannot, however, count the balance of nature among their numerous discoveries. Wolves tend to eat the vulnerable, but their predation ensures neither a well-regulated nor a healthy prey population. In many instances, disease and nutrition, not wolves, cause fluctuations in prey populations. Prey numbers can vacillate wildly, and wolves may have nothing to do with the changes. Conversely, wolves can cause swings in prey populations while still eating only vulnerable animals. Vulnerability is a shifting condition. A harsh winter can make the strongest herbivores targets for predation. Wolves thrive in miserable winters. They may even engage in "surplus killing," a form of exuberant bloodletting deeply disturbing to wolves' human admirers. Normally, wolves devour everything, hide, hair, and bone, leaving only a stain in the snow. But when bad weather makes entire prey populations vulnerable, scientists have come across multiple corpses at kill sites with only their choicest parts nibbled on. The triggers for this behavior remain a mystery, but it appears to be brought on by a sudden shift in the prey animals' ability to defend themselves. Surplus killing is an extreme case of the imbalance that can result even when wolves restrict their diet to the vulnerable.[23]

In February 1990 Rolf Peterson watched from a small airplane as a pack of wolves killed a moose on Isle Royale. The scene he witnessed encapsulated the dynamics of the wolf-prey relationship. Peterson's subjects ignored the buzz of the single prop; they had grown accustomed to the presence of strange machines shadowing their movements. The five-member pack—a mating pair and three pups—attacked the moose in a thicket of trees. The alpha male initiated the assault, rushing the moose and latching onto the animal's hind leg when the chase began. Jaws locked, the wolf held tight as the moose ran, tossing him "up and down through the air like a rag doll." In another thicket, the alpha female joined the attack while the frightened pups watched. She bit into the moose's other hind leg. The moose fell. The animal, bleeding heavily from holes torn in his rump, struggled to his feet and kicked furiously at the alpha male still attached to his leg. The female wolf danced in front of the moose, looking for an opening to the throat. The moose "whirled back and forth" and took off on another sprint. The female grabbed onto the moose's hindquarters, and the three beasts rocketed through the forest. The moose dragged the wolves over logs, bashed them against trees, and finally forced the predators to release their hold by sitting on them. The fight, however, was over. Weakened from exertion and blood loss, the moose succumbed, and the pack fed.[24]

The image of the Isle Royale wolves flying through the air, teeth buried in the hide of a creature with the power to crush their skulls, is a fitting metaphor for wolves' experiences as predators. Wolves often find themselves taken for a ride by their food supply. Weather, disease, and nutrition cause prey populations to rise and fall. Whether wolves effect these oscillations or not, the predators have little control over the abundance or scarcity of prey. Neither do wolves control their encounters with prey animals. The Isle Royale wolves killed the moose, but they accomplished the task by risking the survival of their pack. The moose could have easily killed both adults, leaving three pups, too young to hunt, to feed themselves. Wolves tend to eat vulnerable animals because hunting carries dangers as well as rewards. Predators approach their prey with caution and restraint, knowing well the consequences of biting into an animal with fully developed defenses. In the dance of death, smart hunters follow their quarry's lead.[25]

In the sixty-odd years since Adolph Murie's Mount McKinley study, scientists have collected volumes of data describing the behavior and ecology of wolves. Today, wildlife biologists track wolves on foot, in planes, and from space. Platform transmitter terminal (PTT) collars emit signals to orbiting satellites, pinpointing a wolf's location for up to 253 days. When the batteries run down, the scientist simply presses a button, and two small injector needles mounted in the collar anesthetize the animal. The humans swoop in, replace the old batteries with the three fully charged C-cells, and the wolf awakes groggy and clueless to his status as well-monitored subject. Whereas luck once brought humans and wolves together, now pricey gadgets allow people to spy on the elusive beasts. Humans know more about wolves today than at any time in the two species' eons-long association on this planet. Ironically, this knowledge has accumulated at a low point in this relationship. Human beings learned about wolves at the same time as they pushed the animals to the edge of extinction. Enlightenment and annihilation occurred in tandem.[26]

Wolves eat the vulnerable. They survive by exercising caution and restraint. While intelligent and tough, they are often at the mercy of their environment and their food supply. These constraints reflect the species' ecological occupation or niche. Over millennia wolves have secured a highly specialized job. They are group hunters that mostly eat large herbivores.[27] As such, wolves stand at the apex of a pyramid of calories, and an energy drain shapes their perch. Vegetables outnumber herbivores and herbivores outnumber carnivores because the residents at each tier of the pyramid (ecologists call these tiers trophic levels) consume more energy than they pass on. Organisms need calories to grow, move, and reproduce. Heat radiates from bodies, escapes from nostrils, and wafts from less-fragrant orifices. Only a share of calories of each pyramid level is available to the level above. Life sucks energy, and only a few animals can exist on the dribble of calories that reach the top trophic levels. This explains the relative scarcity of large carnivores; it also explains why no archpredators have evolved to consume the energy embedded in top-tier killers like bears, mountain lions, and wolves. There is not enough juice for another trophic level.[28]

As agriculturalists and livestock tenders, human beings are energy cheats. They gather calories from multiple trophic levels, allowing them to live like lions (no beast hunts them) but reproduce like rabbits. As the ecologist Paul Colinvaux explains: "People are animals that have learned to change their niches without changing their breeding strategy." If wolves wanted a population as large as the herds they eat, they would have to live like herbivores, devouring tons of vegetable matter to generate and support their large numbers. They would have to acquire a niche to match their breeding strategy. Through agriculture, human beings funnel herbivore levels of energy into their predacious offspring, making them especially dangerous to other top-tier animals that cannot reproduce beyond their niche. Wolves can replenish their populations quickly—in times of high mortality, for example, more than one female pack member can breed in a season—but they cannot pull off the human trick of finding new energy sources for growing masses.[29]

New Englanders and their offspring were niche hoppers, and the documents they left behind certified their talent for claiming and safeguarding calories from multiple energy sources. State wolf bounty records have survived from Vermont between 1777 and 1799. Housed in the state archives, this collection includes 492 slips of paper listing the name of the hunter, the date, the location, the number of wolves killed, a brief description of the wolf (Vermont paid bounties only for "grown" wolves), and the amount of the bounty. In that span 360 Vermont hunters destroyed 577 wolves. Bounty records also exist for two counties in Ohio's Western Reserve. One hundred eighty-four certificates have survived from Ashtabula County in the northeast corner of the state covering the years 1811–27. In Cuyahoga County 284 bounty records exist for the period 1810–21. The Ohio documents mirror their Vermont cousins. Each lists the name of the hunter, the date, the location, number of wolves killed, whether the wolf was "grown" or a whelp, and the price of the bounty. In Cuyahoga County 156 hunters killed 375 wolves, while 97 Ashtabula County hunters collected bounties for 213. As with most historical sources, the wolf bounty certificates raise more questions than they answer. They do, however, provide a view into how Euro-Americans combined hunting and agriculture to acquire and protect calories from several trophic levels, and how this combination of predation and plant tending endangered wolves.[30]

The bounty records from Vermont and the two Western Reserve counties reveal a pattern of peaks and valleys (see figures 6, 7, and 8). Did people cause these oscillations? Measuring the effect of human predation on wolf populations through wolf bounties is tricky. For example, the Cuyahoga records (figure 6) appear to tell a stark tale of extermination. Cuyahoga County measures 459 square miles. Biologists estimate that the average density of wolves in a forest environment is one wolf per ten square miles. Thus about forty-six wolves haunted Cleveland and its environs between 1811 and 1821. Given that human hunters collected bounties for sixty-six wolves in 1814

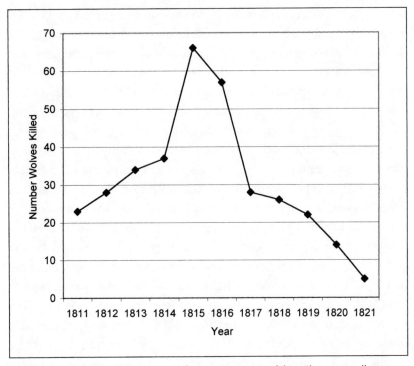

FIGURE 5 Cuyahoga wolf bounty certificates. Source: Handel M. Shumway, collector, wolf scalp certificates, 1810–21, Cuyahoga County, Ohio, Western Reserve Historical Society, Cleveland.

alone, it seems safe to assume that not only did they influence the wolf population, they demolished it.[31]

But the place names listed on the bounty certificates complicate this interpretation. Sixty-seven of the 284 certificates (114 of the 339 wolves killed) list "Huron" or "Huron Township" as the hunter's residence. The town of Huron sits dozens of miles outside the current boundaries of Cuyahoga County, where the west branch of the Huron River flows into Lake Erie. The hunting territory described by the bounty certificates was much larger than 459 square miles. It included Cuyahoga County and extended up the coast of Lake Erie to the watersheds of the East Black, Vermilion, and West Huron Rivers.

Too many variables affected wolf populations and informed the writing of wolf bounty certificates to make the records accurate gauges of the human predator–wolf prey relationship. Figures 6, 7, and 8 show a peak-and-valley pattern, but most wildlife populations, even those free from human

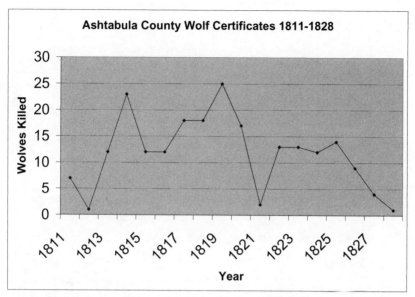

FIGURE 6 Ashtabula wolf bounty certificates. Source: "Wolf-Scalp Payment Certificates (1811–1828)," in Ashtabula County, Ohio, records, 1811–70, Western Reserve Historical Society, Cleveland.

predation, fluctuate in a cycle of boom and bust. Changes in the weather, shifts in the disease climate, and vacillations in the food supply could have caused wolf populations to rise and fall independent of human predation. Even if people influenced population swings, they may have contributed to wolf mortality through actions other than killing. By transforming habitats —clearing underbrush, damming rivers, hunting deer—humans can alter the carrying capacity of an ecosystem. (The carrying capacity is the sum of the resources—cover, water, food—that determine how many of one species can live in a habitat.) The bounty records do not account for the changes in carrying capacity that killed wolves.[32]

Finally, the bounty records are unreliable because early-nineteenth-century humans wrote them. Local officials filled out the certificates, and they differed on the type of information they included on the forms. For location, some recorded where the hunter resided, others where he killed the wolf, still others where he turned in the scalp for his reward. For the date, some officials wrote the day the hunter killed the wolf, while others noted the day he turned in the scalp. Wolf bounty certificates spread as much murk

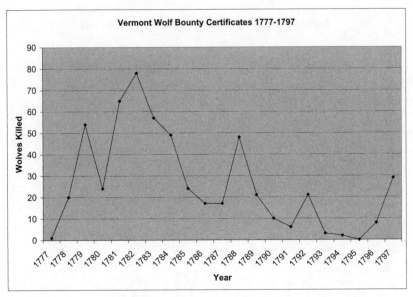

FIGURE 7   Vermont wolf bounty certificates. Source: *Vermont State Papers,* vol. 40, "Wolf Certificates," in the Archives of the Secretary of State, Montpelier, Vt.

as light onto the human-wolf relationship in the northeastern woodlands between 1780 and 1820.

Yet while the bounty records obscure rather than clarify the big picture of human predation, the documents can help illuminate wolf killing on a less grand scale. They can help us understand the wolf hunters as a social group. Who were these people? What was their place in their rural communities? Were they prominent and permanent, or transient predators chasing wildlife across the northeastern woodlands? Was wolf hunting a widespread activity or a job reserved for a few experts? This last question is critical. Unlike wolves, a species of multitaskers, humans divide their labors. All adult wolves, males and females, alphas and omegas, perform the work of the pack. They hunt, fight, howl, deposit scent marks, and socialize pups. By contrast, humans segregate jobs by gender, class, age, knowledge, and prestige. Human males monopolized wolf eradication. No women appear in the bounty records. In theory the bounty systems could have encouraged further specialization, creating a roaming class of archpredators who hunted wolves for a living. However, the records from Vermont and Ohio show only a modest level of specialization. Some men killed multiple wolves, but none of them took up predation as a full-time occupation. Despite the attempts of some colony and then state officials to create a class of highly skilled and devoted wolf hunters, predator control remained an amateur endeavor, a chore men performed in concert with the work of tending crops and livestock.

Wolf hunting in the northeastern woodlands was a task shaped by the demands and rhythms of agriculture. The bounty certificates from Vermont and Ohio support this notion. Hunters in Vermont and Ohio submitted bounties unevenly throughout the year. This is to be expected; agricultural work is famous for its seasonal bursts and lulls. Activities peak in the spring and the fall as farmers sow, tend, pick, mow, and pull their vegetation. Work calms after the harvest. Days grow short; plants die or lay dormant. Winter gave eighteenth- and nineteenth-century yeoman hunters the two things they needed most: time and cold. Freed from their plants, the men not only had time to kill, they could preserve their trophies in nature's icebox. This combination of freedom and frigidity helps explain why many communities in Ohio and Vermont organized grand circle hunts at Christmas time. At these gatherings, squadrons of men surrounded hundreds of wild mammals, slaughtered them, and then threw wild parties amidst the bodies. The depth of winter was the perfect time to kill multitudes of wild animals and drink copious amounts of alcohol. The venison steaks and bear shanks would keep, and no one had to plow in the morning.

While full of symbolic portent, these communal hunts actually destroyed few wolves. They rid patches of forests of livestock-devouring beasts, but the blanket extinction the agriculturalists sought required a sustained effort over a vast landscape. The bounty certificates document this effort, and they hold a surprise. Wolf hunters turned in scalps and filled out certificates in a seasonal pattern, but spring, not winter, marked the zenith of these activities (see figure 8). In both Ashtabula and Cuyahoga Counties, May was the busiest month, while in Vermont the records piled up in June. Remember, local officials dated certificates according to their own whims. Some recorded the date the hunter killed the wolf; others scribbled the date the hunter brought in the scalp. Given this confusion, what can we learn about the seasonality of wolf hunting from the records? A hunter could have killed a wolf in January and certified the animal's death in May.

While certainly a problem to keep in mind, the mixed-up dating criteria may not have spoiled the records as indicators of seasonal fluctuations. Wolf hunters had incentive to document their kills soon after they happened. It

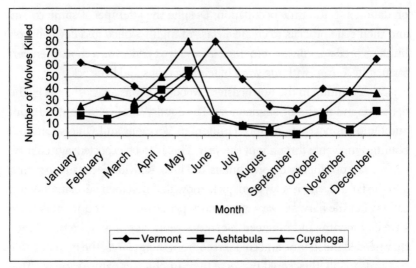

FIGURE 8 Wolf bounty certificates by month. Sources: Handel M. Shumway, collector, wolf scalp certificates, 1810–21, Cuyahoga County, Ohio, Western Reserve Historical Society, Cleveland; "Wolf-Scalp Payment Certificates (1811–1828)," in Ashtabula County, Ohio, records, 1811–70, Western Reserve Historical Society, Cleveland; *Vermont State Papers*, vol. 40, "Wolf Certificates," in the Archives of the Secretary of State, Montpelier, Vt.

took a long time for bounties to work their way through town, county, and state officials. The sooner the process started, the sooner the money would filter back to the hunter. Moreover, fraud was a constant worry. Hunters who turned in scalps quickly raised fewer suspicions than those who petitioned for a reward long after the event had faded from local memories. In general the dates on the bounty certificates recorded acts of predation that probably occurred a few weeks prior. Early spring, therefore, truly seems to have been the season for killing wolves in the northeast woodlands between 1780 and 1820.

This, of course, raises a question: what were these farmers doing hunting wolves when they should have been getting ready to plant their crops? The humans destroyed more wolves in the early spring because this was when the animals were most vulnerable. Wolves traveled all winter long; then, in spring, they denned. In winter their mobility protected them from human predators, whose favorite method of capture was immobile traps. Digging pits and trenches around a spring denning site offered yeoman hunters their best chance of slaying a bunch of wolves quickly and easily.[33]

The spring peak in bounty certificates reflects the compromise at the heart of Euro-American predation. To be successful the yeoman hunters had to exploit the wolves' springtime vulnerability, even if this violated the seasonal ebb and flow of agricultural labor. They slaughtered as many wolves as possible in the early spring and then turned their attention to their crops, explaining the sharp drop-off in the bounty records in June (Ohio) and July (Vermont). Stationed at their rendezvous sites, the wolves would remain vulnerable to human predation into August. The farmers, however, could not stretch their hunting—whether tracking beasts or tending traps—that far into the growing season. The agriculturalists displayed a predator's talent for striking when the killing was easiest, but they remained yoked to their plants.

The bounty certificates from Vermont and Ohio highlighted the agricultural context of wolf killing in other ways. They showed the brevity of most wolf hunters' careers. For the majority of bounty petitioners, bagging a wolf was a singular event (see figure 9). Of the 613 Vermonters and Ohioans who killed a wolf between 1777 and 1824, 409 (67 percent) killed only one. Eighty-nine percent destroyed three or fewer. For the overwhelming majority of hunters, therefore, wolf eradication was neither sustained nor widespread. They happened upon wolf scalps and the cash they represented like a person on the street stumbles across a fifty-dollar bill. The experience was pleasing and lucrative, but no one in his right mind based his livelihood on such windfalls. This included the hunters at the other end of the wolf-killing spectrum. Sixteen hunters collected bounties for eight or more wolves. This top tier represented less than 3 percent of the bounty petitioners, but they accounted for 15 percent of all the wolves taken. Four of the sixteen hunters reached these high numbers by killing whelps, a practice discouraged by lower bounties and rife with fraud (the skins of dog and wolf puppies being nearly indistinguishable).[34]

This left a group of twelve truly accomplished human predators. These were local nimrods, legendary men who excelled at all forms of hunting. (The nickname was a biblical reference: a mighty hunter, Nimrod was the son of Cush in the book of Genesis.) Yet even these experts stayed tied to agriculture. They may have possessed the skill to pull off sustained and widespread wolf-hunting careers, but none of them seemed to possess the urge to do so.

Nathaniel Whitney, a Vermont hunter who collected bounties for eight wolves between 1779 and 1783, exemplified the nimrods' double lives as

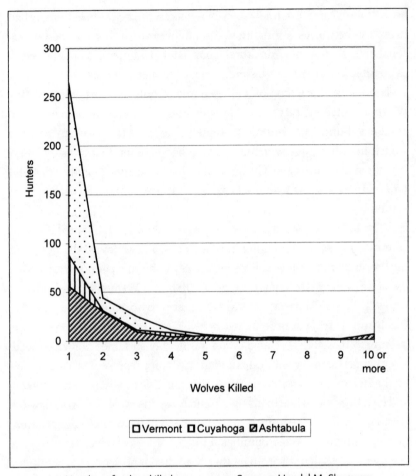

FIGURE 9   Number of wolves killed over a career. Sources: Handel M. Shumway, collector, wolf scalp certificates, 1810–21, Cuyahoga County, Ohio, Western Reserve Historical Society, Cleveland; "Wolf-Scalp Payment Certificates (1811–1828)," in Ashtabula County, Ohio, records, 1811–70, Western Reserve Historical Society, Cleveland; *Vermont State Papers,* vol. 40, "Wolf Certificates," in the Archives of the Secretary of State, Montpelier, Vt.

farmers and hunters. Born in Shrewsbury, Massachusetts, in 1749, Whitney emigrated to Marlboro, Vermont, in 1770. A militia captain, he fought in the Revolution. After the war, he became a farmer with a reputation for faunacide. No one excelled Captain Whitney as "a hunter and a trapper." Apparently, no one rivaled his talent for self-promotion either. Whitney loved describing "the exciting scenes of the hunter's life" to anyone who would listen. Marlboro boys remembered the white-haired captain recalling the time in 1773 when he shot a treed bear five times only to watch the "enormous creature" descend the branches and lay his brother's hound stiff with a swipe of a paw. Whitney eventually killed the bear, and the animal's ferocity added to his legend. Over an illustrious career, he destroyed "100 bears, 100 dear, one moose and 14 wolves, to say nothing of the multitude of lighter game." Yet even with all this success, Whitney remained an agriculturalist rooted in a community. Married with twelve children, he owned the "whole right" to section 23 of the land grid and was a member of the Congregational Church. Marlboro counted him an "influential citizen."[35]

The eleven hunters besides Whitney who killed eight or more grown wolves in Vermont and Ohio between 1777 and 1824 shared many of the captain's social credentials. Ten of the eleven were veterans of the Revolutionary War or the War of 1812. The predominance of veterans is not surprising. Military service was nearly universal at the time, and most bounty recipients, whether they killed one wolf or eighteen, spent time in uniform. Militia training and combat prepared and motivated men to destroy wolves. Militia companies often engaged in circle-and-drive hunts to hone their marksmanship and practice their formations. The military structure of the communal circle hunts and "grand drives" of the period reflected this training. Combat experiences could also enflame wolf hatred. Following the Battle of Hubbardton, Vermont, in 1777, for example, American soldiers watched in horror as "the wolves came down in numbers from the mountains to devour the dead and even some that were in a . . . manner buried, they tore out of the earth." Wolves had scavenged human battlefields for centuries. To them, the carnage was a smorgasbord. But for the soldiers, the sight of wild animals tearing into their comrades' flesh turned an already unpleasant scene into a vision of hell.[36]

Military service united the top tier of wolf hunters. In the case of John and George Brooks, it also revealed their social status. Cuyahoga County hunters, the Brooks brothers collected bounties for twenty-seven wolves between 1812 and 1815. John captained an Ohio militia company in the War of 1812. George served as his aide. American militias were democratic organizations; enlisted men chose their officers. Militia captains were usually prominent members of their communities whose qualifications for leadership ran the gamut from the depth of their military experience to the breadth of their land holdings. A reputation as a magnificent slayer of wild beasts could only have helped John Brooks secure his captaincy. During the War of 1812, the bogeymen that haunted the nightmares of the Americans living in Western Reserve were not British soldiers but their Native American allies. The colonists feared raids and ambushes, attacks made possible by the natives' superior wilderness skills. A local nimrod was the perfect antidote to the Indians' wood- and warcraft. John Brooks's leadership rested on his hunting prowess as well as his social prominence.[37]

The most dangerous humans, the men who killed eight or more wolves, resembled the hundreds of bounty recipients who slew three or fewer. Ten of the twelve top-tier wolf hunters appear in town histories, militia rolls, or tax records. Based on these documents, we can reconstruct the following social profile: they were farmers. They owned land, participated in militias, and went down in history as respectable citizens. The numbers of wild animals these men slaughtered over their lifetimes distinguished them from their neighbors. These killings, however, did not place the nimrods outside of their communities. In fact, the ability to rip the life from numerous furry creatures moved the men into leadership positions. Along with land ownership, military service, and church membership, hunting made these human predators substantial, influential, and memorable.

The bounty records from Vermont and Ohio underlined the agricultural context of wolf killing. The state bounties encouraged respectable farmers to eradicate vermin. Wolf hunting was an amateur pursuit; no one dropped his plow and took up stalking predators as his profession. Wolves may have been better off if they had. Farm work could threaten the animals as much as hunting. Predacious vegetable cultivators not only pursued wolves, they girdled trees, drained swamps, dammed rivers, and gunned down wild herbivores. They introduced diseases, imported weeds, and transplanted livestock. They erected fences and cut roads. They killed wolves with traps, and they killed wolves with altered habitats as they acquired calories from multiple energy sources.

Euro-American colonists dismantled forests as they moved north and east out of coastal New England in the eighteenth and nineteenth centuries to grow oats, hay, barley, rye, cows, pigs, sheep, and children. They rerouted the habitats' energy flows to fuel agricultural economies. Measuring the impact of this redirection on historic wolf populations is difficult. Ecological imperialism could reward native creatures as well as rob them. Euro-

Americans hunted deer to near extinction in sections of the northeastern woodlands, pilfering a critical wolf resource. The deer slayers, however, also herded alternative sources of calories into these habitats. They replaced venison steaks with pork chops, plugging new animals into old energy flows. Yet while the thermodynamics may have remained the same, the social context of these BTUs changed radically. Livestock muscle was private property. Utilizing this energy made wolves vermin.

Euro-American colonists lumped a number of species together under the vermin banner. Wolves shared the category with crows, bluebirds, "crow-billed black birds," robins, rattlesnakes, squirrels, rats, mice, mountain lions, bears, and foxes. All these animals, with the exception of rattlesnakes, ankle biters that achieved vermin status out of sheer meanness, were energy thieves. They raided the humans' biological larders, the domesticated plants and animals that warehoused calories. Euro-American agriculturalists altered their environments to siphon as much energy as possible into their bodies and pocketbooks. To prevent noxious beasts from swallowing illicit calories, governments paid cash rewards to encourage their removal. Bounty hunters turned in squirrel tails, snake rattles, bear paws, wolf scalps, and crow-billed blackbird heads. Wolf killing was part of a larger project to secure agricultural landscapes.[38]

American farmers' attempts to monopolize the calories moving through ecosystems made some species metabolic outlaws, and their place in the energy flows singled out large predators—wolves, mountain lions, and black bears—for special punishment. Thermodynamics made these animals especially vulnerable to Euro-American colonization. The energy drain between trophic levels kept the numbers of large predators small, and their scarcity prevented the animals from responding to aggressive plant tenders with the full arsenal of biological defenses. Sexual reproduction is the chief weapon of most prey species: they combat mortality with fecundity. Some prey "swamp" their devourers, hiking up their reproduction at unpredictable intervals to generate more offspring than predators can eat. Wolves, bears, and wildcats did not have the luxury of swamping. They inhabited a thermodynamic cul-de-sac, and this made them both ferocious and fragile. When a predator attacked them and their habitats, their defenses were meager compared with those wielded by a deer herd or a ground squirrel colony.

Top-tier beasts would never out-reproduce a predator that consumed energy from multiple trophic levels. Human predators possessed the biological

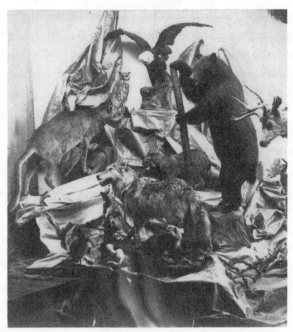

FIGURE 10 Top-tier predators in taxidermy pose. Courtesy
Denver Public Library Western History Department.

howitzer of reproduction, leaving wolves, bears, and panthers to fight for
survival with the popguns supplied by their niche: avoidance and sociality.
Black bears and catamounts ran and hid; they exploited their forest habitat,
climbing toward safety whenever possible. Wolves stayed grounded and tried
to signal their way out of trouble. The species' occupation—group hunters
of large herbivores—equipped them with impeccable social skills. Wolves
attempted to avoid conflicts through communication: howling, scent posts,
and postures of dominance and submission. They tried to incorporate human
predators into their social world by howling at a distance and cowering when
captured, a dreadful survival strategy given Euro-Americans' misinterpretation
of these behaviors.

Euro-American hunters recorded the defense tactics of top-tier predators
in local histories and pioneer reminiscences. These are extremely problematic
sources; no mere cultural assumptions or unspoken ideologies tinged the
hunters' observations. The men described animal behavior in stories that
celebrated their skills, secured their reputations, and buttressed their mascu-

linity. The temptation to lie pulled hard. The size of the bear, the fierceness of the panther, and the cunning of the wolf reflected back on the storyteller. Legendary animals made legendary hunters, and beasts could gain weight, grow meaner, and gather intelligence as stories passed through time and space.

But surprisingly few terrible beasts (excluding humans) roared and rampaged in the hunting anecdotes from the northeastern woodlands. Instead of creating legendary animals, Euro-American hunters filled their stories with timid creatures. Wolves, bears, and mountain lions scrambled up trees, hid in logs, and submitted to captivity. Far from outlandish, these behaviors seem reasonable avoidance tactics and defense strategies. The agricultural context of wolf killing explained the stories' realism. Unlike sport hunters, the farmers who stalked the carnivores at the top trophic level had little interest in mythologizing their prey. While stronger in tooth and nail than rodents or birds, the predators were still contemptible thieves. They were vermin. Neither empathy nor objectivity underwrote the yeomen hunters' honesty; they portrayed the animals in a realistic fashion because these depictions made the predators look cowardly. The agriculturalists would rather confirm the duplicitous nature of top-tier beasts—the animals savaged innocent livestock but trembled before humans—than enhance their own reputations as sportsmen.

The agricultural context of hunting encouraged hunters/observers to emphasize their quarries' fear, avoidance, and passivity rather than exaggerate the beasts' ferocity. The writings of William Cogswell, a skilled hunter from Ohio's Western Reserve, illustrated this tendency. In 1815 the teenaged Cogswell and three comrades were "cooning" in the forest near Granger, Ohio, when they heard a riot of barks and howls from their dogs in the distance. Sprinting to the ruckus, the young men found the canines hopping around the hollow of a massive fallen tree. The dogs snarled and bellowed at the opening. Growls and yelps answered from inside. Cogswell grasped the situation immediately. He dropped his ax and crawled into the hollow. He snatched a hound and extracted the dog. He squirmed back in and grasped another leg, but this one would not pull free. He yanked harder, and the dog inched back. Cogswell reached daylight and as the dog emerged Isaac Sippey, Cogswell's brother-in-law, jumped on the tree with his ax. When he spotted the reason for the dog's slow exit—a four hundred–pound bear had the canine by the throat—Sippey swung and carved off the bear's snout. The bear roared and withdrew into the hollow. The hunters waited quietly until "the bear poked out his mutilated head," at which time Sippey "buried the ax" in the animal's skull.[39]

In 1818 Cogswell and Sippey wandered into another "hazardous adventure" with a carnivore at the top trophic level. Hired to cut a road from Cuyahoga to Granger, the young men spent their summer in the woods felling trees and assaulting wildlife. One morning, the pair walked through the forest in search of a calf that had escaped the night before. They sent their dogs ahead, and soon an older hound was baying at something. Running to the spot, Cogswell and Sippey discovered a catamount perched in the high branches of a large tree. Neither had a gun, so Cogswell grabbed a stick and climbed toward the "critter":

> The green, glaring eyes made me feel uncomfortable, but my po-
> sition required that I should be courageous. With my left hand,
> I took firm hold of a limb, and with my right I wielded my blud-
> geon. As I stood watching, the wild-cat made first a few quick
> shakes with her tail, and instantly bounded for my face. Instantly
> I parried off its descent with the club, and sent the animal to the
> ground. The dog was on hand, and made "jaw love" to "pussy."
> A hard fight of scratching and biting ensued, until Sippey, with
> a blow of a club, ended the cat's life.

The most striking feature of these anecdotes was the animals' passivity in contrast to the humans' ferocity. Cogswell described the attacks as "hazardous adventures," but the bear and the wildcat remained peaceful long into the encounters. They hid and lashed out only after being prodded with sticks or harassed with hounds. The animals' mildness fuels our repulsion. Removing the snout of a creature that obviously wants to be left alone seems cruel and unsporting. Cogswell and Sippey, however, brutalized animals without shame, and their lack of embarrassment signaled the cultural context of their behavior. Cogswell felt no compulsion to tone down the violence in his stories or cloak his actions in the language of fair play. He slaughtered as many animals as possible quickly and easily. In his agricultural society, human predators savaged prey with a clear conscience.[40]

William Cogswell recorded the defense strategies of bears and panthers. The hounds initiated the chase, and the bear and panther sought refuge to avoid tangling with the canines. In a forest environment, trees served as the first line of defense for many prey species. This explains the ubiquity of axes in the hunting narratives. Human predators felled trees to counteract the avoidance tactics of climbers like raccoons, bears, and wildcats. By cutting off escape routes and invading safe havens, the humans and their canine allies goaded prey animals into violence. Cornered bears and panthers bit and slashed at their attackers. Aggression, however, only inspired more hostility. Humans were not cautious predators. They risked their lives for sport and entertainment as well as nourishment and livestock protection. In the end, nothing the bears and panthers tried worked. They fell victim to an animal whose behavior mocked the rules of predation. Human hunters not only attacked without restraint, they often expended more calories killing beasts than they gained digesting them. Cogswell and his colleagues leveled trees to catch wildlife. A giant bear rewarded this expenditure of energy, but the Ohio youths chopped as hard for raccoons. Euro-Americans' willingness to take injuries and waste calories made them truly dangerous predators.

Backed into a corner, bears and panthers used violence to fend off human attackers. The third resident of the highest trophic level tried a different tactic. In the hunting stories, wolves remained docile under some of the most provocative circumstances. In 1814 Joshua Redfield, a sixteen-year-old nimrod, caught a wolf by the toes in an iron trap outside of Harrisville, Ohio. Afraid that the animal would escape the metal jaws' tenuous hold, Redfield pounced on the wolf. He cuffed the predator's ears "and put the foot into the trap, carrying it in this way into the settlement." The animal was "completely cowed." Redfield played with his captive. Even when he twisted the wolf's nose, "it offered no resistance." We have already encountered similar instances of passivity. The wolf that John Josselyn captured in the Maine surf in the 1660s refused to fight, as did several of the Indiana wolves Audubon saw captured in the pit trap in 1824. The wolves attacked dogs, but they melted before people. The farmer leapt into a pit with three of them, sliced their Achilles tendons, and emerged without a scratch. Thomas Morton commented on wolves' skittishness in 1637, and in 1820 a Catham, Ohio, boy met a pack of wolves in the forest a mile from his home, "but it seems the beasts were as much taken with fear as the pioneer lad, for they disappeared quickly at the sight of him." Flight and submission, hardly the defensive tactics one would expect from robust predators—yet wolves fled and trembled throughout American history.[41]

As with panthers and bears, avoidance represented wolves' first line of defense against human predation. The animals ran and hid. If these tactics failed, wolves tried to signal their rivals with howls. Discerning wolf intentions from historical accounts is a knotty exercise at best. Wolf howls provoked the colonists' anxieties and anthropocentrism. In 1818, for example, a group of Ohio settlers who huddled together in a two-room cabin on a winter night "were serenaded by a pack of hungry wolves." The experience so badly frightened an elderly woman "as to cause a hemorage of the nose, which nearly cost her life, and from effects of which she never fully recovered." The incident revealed the fear howls evoked as well as the self-absorption of the human listeners; Euro-Americans invariably believed that wolves howled for them. But why would a species that hoped to avoid encounters with a terrifying predator declare "here I am" with a song? When threatened, most prey species freeze in silence. Wolves, however, were not a prey species. They indulged in the luxury of the strong, big, and elusive: noisemaking. A top predator, the wolf felt free to be loud. Large packs regularly advertised their strength and position to rival groups, seeking to avoid violence by communicating their dominance. Howling was predatory behavior that exposed wolves' shortcomings as prey.[42]

An 1814 howling incident in Wadsworth, Ohio, illustrated the dangers wolves courted when they treated a group of humans like a rival pack. A member of a surveying crew, Benjamin Dean, recorded the interspecific conversation. "The wolves," he wrote, "howled about us nearly all night, but did not come within sight." When the animals stopped, the surveyors would "make a little noise or increase our fire a little" and the howls would return. Some evenings, the men elicited howls by rapping on dry trees. They discovered that the wolves passed by their campsite "every alternate night" on a "line of travel from Wolf Creek to Chippewa," and the animals continued this pattern as the Wadsworth settlement grew. They followed "the road, until the settlement became so large that they went around it. But they always, in passing, saluted us with a specimen of their music."[43]

Benjamin Dean uncovered the travel itinerary of a wolf pack through an exchange of tree raps and songs. Wildlife biologists believe that packs howl to one another to convey precisely this kind of information. Wolves vocalize to advertise territories, warning rivals to "stay away from us" by announcing the location and strength of a pack. The surveyors learned that the wolves passed by their campsite on alternate days and that they loped the same course from Wolf Creek to Chippewa. Packs broadcast these details to keep rivals at a distance and prevent chance encounters along travel corridors.

(The Wadsworth colonists built their road along the wolves' "line." Both wolves and Euro-American road builders followed paths of least resistance. The choppers probably expanded a trail used by multiple species. This also explained why path hackers met up with so many bears. They were on the animals' highway.) The Wadsworth episode was extraordinary for two reasons. First, it showed humans and wolves communicating, and, second, even after the humans learned the wolves' route, they continued to hear howls along the road for a number of years. The wolves should not have lasted this long. By revealing their travel habits, the howlers notified wolf killers where to place their traps. An able trapper could have silenced the pack in a matter of days.[44]

The Ohio wolves seemed to howl to keep their rivals at a distance. Yet while some yowls frightened American colonists into bloody noses, notifying human trappers of your location could be an awfully bad idea. Instead of inspiring the anxieties that created space, warning yowls often collapsed buffer zones, encouraging hunters to pursue the noisemakers. Howls aroused anger and curiosity as well as the agriculturalists' desire to safeguard energy caches, and these sentiments prompted the strenuous pursuit of wolves. Humans sounded alarms, encircled woods, and dug traps. They passed bounties, hired hunters, and purchased hounds. Through their eradication efforts, hunters came face-to-face with wolves, and these encounters could be cozy to the point of horror. Pit traps, the favorite method of destruction in the northeast woodlands, created moments of brutal intimacy. Trappers handled wolves. They touched the animals' fur, smelled their panting breaths, and peered into their eyes. Wolves' reactions to these examinations defied their vicious reputations. The beasts that provoked such violent human emotions often met their end with a cringe and a whimper.

That wolves would try to signal their human executioners is not surprising. Their willingness to accept people as pack leaders has made wolves prime targets for domestication. Wolves and humans inhabit compatible social worlds. They can establish hierarchical relationships using the signs of dominance and submission. The Euro-American colonists who captured live wolves and tortured them for fun ignored the animals' pleas for clemency. Instead, they interpreted submissive postures as evidence of cowardice and duplicity.

The colonists lived with animal allies that could have helped them read wolf behavior. Euro-Americans witnessed submissive canine displays on a regular basis. Their dogs winced, trembled, and tucked their tails; far from denouncing these postures, the humans welcomed them. Submissive postures signaled the animals' friendliness and loyalty. Wolves' gestures, however, brought no sympathy. In fact, the colonists tried to force wolves to abandon their acquiescence and fight by siccing their distant genetic relatives on them. They baited their captives with dogs, exploiting one species' compliance to break through the other's passivity. Both John Josselyn and the Indiana farmer succeeded in instigating fights with dogs. Their captors may have wanted snarls and bites, but most wolves only volunteered their throats.

Fathoming a group of people so cruel that they ignored a frightened creature's obvious pleas for mercy brings us back to the agricultural context of wolf killing. Classified as vermin, living wolves had no redeeming attributes, and the hunters who disposed of the animals felt no compulsion to introduce redeeming attributes at the scene of the villains' deaths. Even though a valiant yet doomed foe may well have boosted their reputations, the hunters refused to romanticize the destruction of wolves.

The agricultural context of wolf killing shaped the actions and the stories of Euro-American colonists. Both their behavior and their narratives were often atrocious. Many rural Americans considered brutalizing wild creatures amusing. They recounted instances of stabbing, hacking, and pitchforking animals with fondness. They baited captive wolves with dogs, twisted their noses, and sliced their hamstrings. Today these activities seem cruel and un-usual, but wild animal abuse neither embarrassed nor sickened Euro-American storytellers. As a result, their narratives not only raise a historical and ethical conundrum—how could people be so mean?—but they also documented the defense strategies and tactics of large woodland carnivores and omnivores. Their extreme bias enhanced the hunting anecdotes' value as a historical and a biological source.

Euro-Americans told gruesome stories that betrayed their cultural as-sumptions and their conquest ideologies, as well as their deepest fears. Yet, however ugly, human attitudes did not eradicate all of the top-tier beasts that roamed the northeastern woodlands. Predation is a relationship. Human ideas figured into their relationship with prey, but prey vulnerability was equally critical. Perched atop the food pyramid, wolves, panthers, and bears had little experience as prey. They ran, hid, and lashed out when cornered. Wolves howled, and advertised their subordination. Humans accosted both timid and ferocious animals. Indeed, they seemed to relish chasing the fierce beasts no other creatures hunted. Bears, wolves, and mountain lions needed time to adapt; they needed the accumulated experiences of generations of offspring to invent behaviors to counter such quirky and aggressive killers. The short supply of energy at the top of the food pyramid denied them this time. Euro-American colonists attacked animals in a vulnerable niche, creatures stuck with few options in a thermodynamic dead end.

CHAPTER FIVE

Surrounded

FEAR AND RETRIBUTION IN THE NORTHEASTERN

FORESTS

FEW CHILDHOOD memories conjure up warmer emotions than a bed-time story told by a doting grandparent. But in Brecksville, Ohio, there once lived a grandfather who tucked his loved ones in with wolf stories, and his tales inspired dreams more sour than sweet. Imagine yourself cozy under the covers when a blood relation walks in and assaults you with this legend:

"It was a terrible night that night we left Batavia, New York, on our way west to our new home in the Western Reserve of Ohio. There were Father and Mother and us eight children all in a great big sled. By the time we had passed the last little log hut on the outskirts of the town the snow was coming fast and was soon near a foot deep."

The father in Grandpa's story urged the oxen forward as the drifts reached the animals' knees and buried the sled's runners. Next to him, the mother turned and hushed the children nestled in skins and quilts. As darkness fell, they heard the first howls. The father grumbled, the mother prayed, and the children cried. The wolves closed in. Near a creek, one lunged at the off-ox, missing his skull by inches.

"There's no other way out," said the father. "We must protect the oxen; they are our only salvation."

"What do you mean?" the mother asked, the panic rising in her voice. "Oh, I can see it in your eyes. You are going to sacrifice one of the children."

"It can't be helped," the father replied. "It can't be helped."

The couple began feeding their brood to the wolves one by one. They pitched three toddlers and had nearly tossed a fourth when the leader of the wolf pack signaled his companions to halt the attack. The family settled in Brecksville, and the children who escaped the wolves told the story of the winter journey to their grandchildren at bedtime.[1]

Babies devoured by wolves—no scenario could possibly misconstrue the actual vulnerability of predator and prey in the northeastern woodlands more. In these forests Euro-American travelers and their livestock were the marauding packs, wolves the besieged quarry. Grandparental flights of fancy aside, no wolf ever tasted the flesh of a living human child (or adult, for that matter) in the recorded history of North America. People frightened wolves; a creaky sled filled with howling children would tempt them to flee, not rouse their appetites. Why did the colonists tell such outrageous lies about the danger wolves posed to them? Even more, why did they perpetrate these falsehoods on their sleepy grandchildren?[2]

Fantastic legends littered the paths of New Englanders as they moved north and west into Maine, Vermont, New Hampshire, and Ohio's Western Reserve in the late eighteenth and early nineteenth centuries. These tales survived in documents published generations after their initial telling. They are curiosities from an oral culture, mementos of a wild past reprinted to enliven a tame present. As historical sources these stories bedevil, and the legend of the Ohio immigrants tossing their children to the wolves typified their fiendishness.[3]

Thomas A. Knight, the field secretary for the Western Reserve Historical Society and executive secretary of the Early Settlers Association, collected the tale from Emma Parsons, a local clerical worker, in 1945. Parsons heard the story from a descendant of the immigrant family still living in Brecksville. The woman swore her grandfather put her to bed with the tale. An anonymous grandfather recounted a family legend to an unnamed granddaughter who told it to Emma Parsons who passed it on to Knight. The legend's provenance grows murkier near its source. We know more about the Cleveland typist than about the grandfather, and he was the critical figure in the legend's diffusion. He invented it, most likely with considerable help from a Victorian poet and a western novelist.[4]

Robert Browning depicted babies flying into the mouths of wolves in his 1879 poem "Ivan Ivanovich." On a frigid Russian night, a pack of wolves follows a young woman and her children. To save herself, the mother feeds her

FIGURE 11   "Deadly Attack of a Wolf Upon Man, and Heroic
Conduct of the Man's Wife." Illustration in *Frank Leslie's Boy's
and Girl's Weekly*, 1867. Library of Congress.

children to her pursuers. She arrives alive and childless in a village where
Ivanovich, a family friend, beheads her with a carpenter's ax for her maternal
lapse. Willa Cather included a similar winter chase scene in *My Antonia* (1918).[5]

The genesis of the Ohio family legend appears straightforward: the
grandfather cobbled together a macabre tale with scenes stolen from books
he read. The narrative, however, was not complete faux-lore. The baby flinging
came from books, but the rest of the Ohio legend fit into a larger tradition
of wolf folklore that stretched back to New England, the region of origin for
most Western Reserve immigrants. These stories featured defenseless trav-

elers. Alone in the woods, the travelers hear howls. Soon a pack of wolves surround them. The animals frighten the humans, but they never attack. A hair's breadth escape is a crucial element in the tale type. By eschewing the happy ending, the grandfather added a sick twist to an old story.[6]

The Ohio grandfather concocted a wildly inappropriate bedtime story from a string of legends with similar motifs, settings, protagonists, and villains. Storytellers from Maine to Brecksville recycled the "wolves surround defenseless travelers" plot. Like the Ohio grandfather, these storytellers tailored the legends to suit their objectives. The wolf stories traveled through a process that combined innovation and repetition. Repetition carried stories and rituals across territories and generations, but folklore's value as a tool of conquest lay in its ability to combine both tradition and innovation. Individuals adapted folklore to novel situations through their performance. Storytellers added details, changed settings, and altered endings. Groups imbued rituals with new meanings. Persistence through adaptation: Euro-Americans preserved their culture by adjusting their legends and customs to fit new environments.

Reconstructing the meaning of the wolf legends Euro-Americans spread during their conquest of the northeastern woodlands is difficult because the historical contexts of the stories' performances are missing. The storytellers' gender and community standing; dramatic flourishes, facial expressions, and hand gestures; moments of silence and exaltation, laughter and applause —all this critical information has vanished. Local historians like Thomas Knight collected wolf legends in town annals and family reminiscences, but they rescued the stories for their own purposes. In their hands, the legends became markers of progress. The tales of ravenous beasts attacking vulnerable travelers measured the distance communities had traveled from their wild beginnings. Local historians retold the legends to titillate an audience nestled in the safety of a wolfless world. Without the events, behavior, and assumptions that surrounded their telling, the wolf stories remain intriguing fragments taken from one context to serve another.

By themselves the legends say little about the people who destroyed and brutalized wolves. When placed alongside communal wolf hunting rituals and inside the historical context of colonization, however, the legends provide a glimpse into the role of folklore in the eradication of a species. The wolf legends and hunting rituals depict two mirror-imaged worlds. In the legends wolves prey on humans, while in the hunts humans prey on wolves. In the legends wolves surround humans in the woods, inducing panic with their hideous howls. In the hunts humans surround wolves in the woods, inducing panic with drums, horns, and conch shells. Working in tandem the community hunts and the wolf legends spread the methods and the meanings of wolf eradication.

Colonization entangled wolves in human beings' attempts to reproduce their culture as well as their property. Through these stories, an aggressive group of animals intent on expanding their territory, transplanting their culture, and growing their wealth expressed their frustration and protested their vulnerability. In the legends, the planet's top predator imagined life (and death) as prey. Human beings experienced the raw panic of being another organism's dinner. The communal hunts returned this upside-down world to its upright position. The legends and rituals created the illusion of regeneration through violence. Richard Slotkin has chronicled the astonishing resilience of this idea in American culture. Regeneration through violence, he argues, was the guiding myth of the conquest of North America. In cultural forms as diverse as sermons and motion pictures, Euro-Americans fantasized that planting a civil society in a wilderness required acts of extreme brutality. To overpower savagery one must lash out savagely. In their stories, Euro-American colonists invented and broadcast a vision of wolves as threats to human safety. They then modeled their behavior on the ferocity they perceived in wolves. Thus folklore explains not only why humans destroyed wolves but why they did so with such cruel enthusiasm.[7]

On a winter night in 1742, the farmers of Pomfret, Connecticut, had their "common enemy" trapped in a cave. A brilliant sheep killer, the wolf had been tormenting the humans for years. She avoided their snares, dodged their bullets, and outran their hounds. When pressed, she vanished into the western forests, only to return the next year with a new litter of whelps. In 1742 the slaughter reached epic proportions. Israel Putnam, the largest landowner in the county, lost seventy sheep and goats in a single night. Putnam and his neighbors vowed to hunt the wolf day and night until they killed her. Working in pairs, the men tracked the animal west as far as the Connecticut River. From there, the wolf circled back toward Pomfret. Her trail halted in a den three miles from Putnam's farmhouse. The den's mouth was "two feet square"—just wide enough for a hero to enter.[8]

Falling back into colonial New England after visiting snowy nineteenth-century Ohio may seem jarring, but wolf legends skipped across regions and decades, and following them will require some spatial and temporal gymnastics. It is worth the risk of chronological whiplash to consider Israel Putnam's famous encounter with the she-wolf. The story demonstrates how folklore and history inspired human cruelty.

The news of the wolf's entrapment drew a crowd. Townspeople arrived with muskets, sulfur, torches, straw, and hounds. The dogs went in first. They came out "badly wounded" and would not reenter. Next, the men set the straw and sulfur on fire and threw it into the cave. Smoke roiled from the den, but the wolf did not appear. Finally, Israel Putnam "proposed to his Negro man to go down into the cavern and shoot the wolf." After watching the beast overpower dogs and defy brimstone, the servant declined. Angered by this display of "cowardice," Putnam "resolved to destroy the ferocious beast" himself. The twenty-four-year-old farmer crawled into the hole armed only with a torch.[9]

In the farthest reaches of the cavern, Putnam met the "glaring eye-balls of the wolf." She growled. He yelped. The men outside panicked. They heaved (with "great celerity") on the safety line fastened around Putnam's waste. The vigorous tug knocked the crouching Putnam to his stomach. His "shirt was stripped over his head and his skin severely lacerated" on the way out of the cave. Bloodied but undaunted, he entered the den again, this time with a musket loaded with "nine buckshot." He found the wolf in the same spot. As he moved closer, the animal assumed a "fierce and terrible appearance." She howled, rolled her eyes, and snapped her teeth. Putnam leveled his musket and fired. Again, the commotion prompted the men to drag him from the den. After waiting for the gun smoke to clear, he crawled into the cave a third time. The wolf lay dead. Grasping the animal by the ears, he kicked the rope, and the cheering farmers pulled him and the she-wolf from the "mansion of death."[10]

Colonel David Humphreys first popularized the story of Israel Putnam and the she-wolf in 1788 during a Fourth of July address to the Connecticut State Society of the Cincinnati, a fraternal organization for the veterans of the American Revolution. Having served as Putnam's aide-de-camp during the war, Humphreys decided to present the major general's biography in order to "preserve [his] actions in the archives of our State Society." Humphreys considered Putnam a model patriot, and he hoped "Old Put's" life story would inspire others to imitate the general's "native courage" and "unshaken integrity." The she-wolf episode was an early indicator of Putnam's heroism, foreshadowing his bravery and leadership in the French and Indian War and the Revolution. The youthful destroyer of wolves would blossom into a killer of savages, papists, and tyrants. Famous for ordering his men not to "fire until you see the whites of their eyes" at the Battle of Bunker Hill, Putnam first met and extinguished the gaze of hostile eyeballs in a she-wolf's den.[11]

Humphreys incorporated elements of folklore into the tale of the she-wolf's demise. For instance, he structured the story around threes. The hunters tried three methods of extraction: hounds, fire, and then Putnam. The young farmer entered the den three times, and the crowd dragged him out three times. The repetition of threes gave the story the rhythm of a waltz, and this cadence made the tale communicable.

David Humphreys constructed a legend that would outlive him, Putnam, the wolf, and the historical circumstances that prompted its creation. He recounted the she-wolf episode to comment on the relationship between personal character and social status, an excellent theme for a Fourth of July lecture sponsored by a group of Revolutionary War veterans. These men wanted to believe that character, not wealth or inherited titles, prepared individuals for social leadership. The best men, those with courage, honor, and virtue, should rise in society and rule the new nation. Through a wolf story that transformed a young farmer notable for the size of his sheep herds into an American hero famous for his strong character, Humphreys reaffirmed the republican values of his audience.

And he did something else: he traced the development of civic character to violence. Putnam discovered his intestinal fortitude in the commission of a murder, and he verified his bravery throughout his life by engaging in war. This martial vision of public virtue contrasted with the elitist (and equally republican) notion that only disinterested gentlemen, persons with the means to establish their economic and political independence, met the criteria for leadership in a commonwealth. Humphreys laid down an alternative route to power, a path every combat veteran could follow. By showing courage under fire, the Connecticut soldiers had displayed their "unshaken integrity." Military service, not the leisured pursuit of enlightened disinterest, qualified them to wield authority in the republic. While gentlemen cultivated virtue in the privacy of their well-appointed libraries, hunters and soldiers visited a second birthplace of republican character—the mansions of death that housed the nation's fiercest enemies.[12]

Humphreys used a wolf legend and hunting ritual to celebrate the political righteousness of the veterans in the Society of Cincinnati. Swept along
with the immigration of southern New England livestock owners to Vermont, New Hampshire, and Maine, and later to the forests of northern Ohio,
these legends and rituals depicted two inverted worlds. In the legends wolves
surrounded humans in the woods, while in the hunts people encircled wolves.
In the legends, luck, courage, and providence rescued defenseless travelers
from cruel and painful deaths. In the hunts, nothing protected the animals
from human retaliation. Working in tandem the community hunts and the
wolf legends spread the methods and the meanings of wolf eradication. Folklore's motifs, types, and rituals eased the reproduction of wolf animosity and
human cruelty.

David Humphreys aided the maintenance and transmittal of wolf hatred, but harming wildlife was not his goal. He wanted to make Israel Putnam a national hero and secure veterans' claims to leadership in the young
republic. Folklore helped him accomplish these ends. Humphreys used the
traditions of wolf killing to lionize a man and renovate a political ideology,
and in the process, he broadcast legends and rituals that endangered wolves.
The tale of Putnam and the she-wolf dispersed wolf lore like a bear spreading seeds in a forest. Bears gather all sorts of nettles, buds, and pods in their
tangled coats as they rummage through brambles and grasslands in search
of calories. When the animals scratch, roll, or shed, they deposit these hitch-
hikers in new habitats. Bears are magnificent seed spreaders, but the furry
transports assist the diffusion of plant communities accidentally while pursuing their own omnivorous goals.

The history of wolf folklore is replete with examples of customs and stories that behaved like ambling bears with hides full of cockleburs. Wolf legends and hunting traditions reminded humans how to kill wolves and how
to feel about the animals' destruction. But like the seeds in a bear's coat,
these spores of wolf lore clung to stories and customs with their own objectives. People told wolf stories and participated in wolf hunts to create national heroes, to protest social and property relations, to mark their passage
into adulthood, and to overcome their feelings of powerlessness in an unfamiliar environment. The wolf legends and hunting rituals aided the transmittal of ideas, identities, and relationships across generations and regions.
At the same time, the stories and customs stoked the animosity that hastened wolf eradication.

*   *   *

The legend of Israel Putnam and the she-wolf is extraordinary because the historical context of its telling survived in print. Most wolf tales in early America originated as oral presentations, and when they resurfaced decades later in local histories, almanacs, gazetteers, and family reminiscences, the circumstances of their creation and repetition had disappeared. David Humphreys presented the Putnam wolf legend to a crowd of Connecticut Revolutionary War veterans on the Fourth of July. These basic facts—when, where, and to whom—provide springboards into the text, platforms for investigators to leap in and recover the legend's meaning. The mundane details of authorship and audience distinguished the Putnam legend from the bits and pieces of wolf lore and ritual that Euro-Americans spread across the northeastern woodlands in the eighteenth and nineteenth centuries, and these fragments resist methods of analysis that utilize the facts surrounding stories and rituals to make sense of them.

The following stories answer some questions collectively that no one tale could answer alone. Stripped of the contexts of their performance, they lack the depth of the Putnam legend, but grouped together these bits of lore reveal the themes of social inversion and violent restoration that gave wolf stories and rituals their transcendence.

One afternoon, John Marsh shouldered his gun and headed for town. The sun set as he strolled through the forest between his home and his destination, Harrisville, Ohio. As woods grew dark, the farmer became disoriented, but he did not panic until he heard "the howls of wolves echoing in his ears." Stumbling through the brush, Marsh discovered a tree bent close the ground and climbed up for safety. From his perch, he fired at the "row of shining eyes" beneath him. A yelp followed one shot, but the varmints refused to leave. Marsh began shouting for help. After an hour, a line of torches inched toward him, and the wolves slunk away as "the light of the torches was shed upon them."[13]

In Geauga County, Ohio, Theodocia Patterson got lost in the woods riding to her cousins' house. She had been following notches cut into the trees that marked the path through the forest when a bout of daydreaming led her astray. She searched for notches until nightfall. Taking refuge in the branches of a fallen tree, she heard howls. Twigs broke near her hiding place. She heard panting and growling. Theodocia folded her hands and promised to "always trust and serve God" in exchange for surviving the night. After an eternity, the animals left. The next morning, Theodocia discovered a wagon road and followed the tracks home. She remained a staunch Christian the rest of her life.[14]

Farther south, in the woods outside Henderson, Kentucky, a pack of wolves surrounded an African-American fiddler named Old Dick on his way to a wedding dance at an outlying plantation. The animals "yelled," "bellowed," and "clamored," driving the fiddler into an abandoned cabin. He slammed the door and leapt onto the roof through a hole in the shingles. Just as "a great gaunt head, lit by two eyes like globes of green fire," thrust itself through the hole, Dick broke into a song. He played "Yankee Doodle" with such "desperate energy" that the pack quit howling and settled on their haunches. The music turned the berserk squadron into an "attentive audience." Time passed and as Dick played encore after encore, the wedding crowd grew worried. They outfitted a posse with lanterns and barrel staves and sent them into the forest to locate the wayward musician. The lanterns scattered the wolves, concluding Dick's recital.[15]

The stories of Theodocia Peterson, John Marsh, and Old Dick exemplify the tradition of "wolves surround defenseless travelers" legends. These were stories about wanderers that wandered themselves, following the immigration paths of American families as they moved west across the Appalachian Mountains. All the tales shared similar plots, themes, and characters. A woodcutter, a preacher, or perhaps a couple of newlyweds set off on a trip at dusk. To reach their destination, the travelers must pass through a forest. As the darkness grows, they hear howls off in the distance. Soon the wolves surround them. The woodcutter fends off the animals with his ax; the preacher scrambles up a tree; the newlyweds fling the remnants of their picnic lunch to the ravenous pack. They all escape, barely. The next morning, the hero of the folktale appears. Alarmed by the howls in the night, the farmers living near the woods have assembled a hunting party. Armed with muskets, pitchforks, and clubs and led by a grizzled hunter or a militia captain, the farmers surround the wolves and destroy them.

The legends depicted a frightening natural order in which wolves hunted humans. When the travelers entered the forest, they passed from a world controlled by people to one ruled by animals. This passage was marked by a series of oppositions: day and night, clearing and forest, community and individual, hunter and hunted. Alone at night in the woods, the travelers' world—that of the day, the clearing, and the community—turned upside down. The hunters became the quarry. To live, some fought and others fled. But the predominant method of survival in the wolf legends was some sort of sacrifice. In a version of the legend from Maine, a woman carrying a baby and a string of fish met a pack of wolves on the forest path between Harpswell and Brunswick. She escaped, the story goes, by throwing her fish to the wolves. In Starksboro, Vermont, Sam Hill encountered wolves on his way home from a neighbor's house with the dressed carcass of a lamb. To escape, he fed pieces of the sheep to his pursuers. Wolves ambushed Samuel Stanwood of Topsham, Maine, as he was walking home from a day's work at his sawmill. The miller staved off his attackers by feeding them portions of his unfinished lunch. The tossing of babies to pursuing wolves was an especially grim version of a well-worn theme in the wolf legends. The sacrifice of food epitomized the legends' inversion of the natural order. Humans were not supposed to feed nature; it fed them.[16]

The wolf legends resembled another tale type collected by local historians: lost-in-the-woods stories. Not all Euro-Americans marched purposefully into the forest to conquer the wilderness; many roamed aimlessly in the trees for days after losing their way. In 1633 a "maid servant" of a Mr. Shelton lost her way traveling from Salem to Sagus. She wandered in the Massachusetts woods for seven days with no food in the depth of winter. "She was so frozen into the snow some mornings," wrote John Winthrop, "as she was an hour before she could get up." The next fall, a fifty-year-old alderman from Bear Cove roamed through the woods and swamps between Dorchester and Wessaguscus for three days and two nights. With his legs battered and his hope nearly gone, "God brought him to Scituate." In 1643 two men from Ipswich got lost in the forest near their home. They stumbled around for six days, eating nothing, until an Indian found the pair "almost senseless for want of rest, etc." In seventeenth-century New England, the woods subdued the colonists as many times as they subdued it.[17]

Lost-in-the-woods stories followed Euro-Americans as they spread through the northeastern forests. In the fall of 1800, eight-year-old Milo Hudson strayed into the woods. His family, rushing to complete a cabin before the Ohio winter set in, did not notice his absence until sunset. They combed the area, but the boy had vanished. The temperature dropped, and the only noises that interrupted the cold night were "the crackling of the timber frost, the tremendous howling of wolves, and the hollow reverberating sound of the horns" calling for the lost child. The next morning, Hudson limped home with frostbitten toes. He had survived the night huddled under a pile of leaves next to a hollow log.[18]

In April 1824 Abel Beach's daughter, a twenty-six-year-old woman who could neither hear nor speak, got lost in the woods during a spring snowstorm. After scouring the forest all night, a search party discovered footprints in the morning. They followed the trail until the rising sun melted the snow. The woman was never found. Samuel Cross lost his way and his life in the winter of 1813. Traveling home to Harrisville, Ohio, after delivering a load of oats to Wooster, Cross, his son, and eighteen head of cattle froze to death in the wilderness along the Little Killbuck River. Missing all winter, the travelers' remains were discovered by a farmer in the spring. He found an ox yoke, an overcoat, and a human skull bone. Wolves had eaten the rest.[19]

The colonists' misadventures in the forests provided a basis for the wolf legends. Sunset plays a featured role in both narratives. In the lost-in-the-woods stories, the wanderers realized their predicament at dusk. The defenseless travelers in the wolf legends heard the first howls at nightfall as well. The yowls panicked the already nervous humans. The differing biological clocks of wolves and humans could explain the timing of these meltdowns. Humans are daytime animals, their sense organs work poorly in the dark, and they look for safe places to curl up as the sun drops. Wolves, however, go to work at dusk. Bimodal, their activity levels peak at sunrise and sunset. The most likely time for wanderers to hear howls was also the moment their bodies urged them to find a safe place to rest. Frightened, they ran or hid only to hear another pack answer the first howl. Given humans' tendency to see themselves as the pivots around which all creatures' lives spun, the bewildered travelers assumed the wolves were talking to them. They felt surrounded—hunted—and when they found their way home, they described their experience as narrow escape from eminent digestion.[20]

The wolves would offer a far different interpretation of the same events. A wolf howl can travel dozens of miles in the shifting acoustics of a forest. A pack trading "stay away from us" warnings with another pack may not know and does not care that a human is listening in on the conversation. Wolves howl to communicate with other wolves, not to scare people. They neither coordinate their attacks nor drive their prey with howls. They sing to maintain territories and to keep rivals away from kills. The wolf legends may describe actual encounters between humans and wolves, but instead of people escaping the jaws of ravenous beasts, these episodes involved a jittery animal, terrified of the dark, eavesdropping on another species' banter.[21]

The wolf legends were lost-in-the-woods stories with a howling villain. The tale types contained similar settings and emotions. Darkness triggered the events in both stories, and vulnerability was the emotional theme of both. The prime difference between the tales was the solutions they offered. The colonists could not punish the woods for being confusing. They could widen paths into roads and open clearings for farms, but this conquest was slow and passionless compared with the slaughtering of wolves. The wolf legends demanded immediate revenge. Groups of colonists entered the forest, killed the predators, and restored their mastery over nature in a day. Both the wolf legends and the lost-in-the-woods stories highlighted the colonists' vulnerability, but the legends offered a quick solution: regeneration through violence.

Communal wolf hunts turned the upside-down world of both the wolf legends and the lost-in-the-woods stories right side up. The hunts reordered biotic communities. They demolished the top tier of the food chain, the beasts that ate other beasts, and established humans as the forest's top predators. The humans' behavior mimicked the behavior of the wolves in the legends. Like wolves, humans surrounded their prey in the forest, pushing them forward with hideous noises. Both humans and wolves committed savage acts. Yet whereas the wolves' cruelty threatened the natural order, the hunters' brutality restored it. The humans' behavior was not beyond the pale of civilized society; rather, their savagery was a crucial element in its foundation.

Communal wolf hunts were common in New England. The first took place in 1642 when Rhode Island colonists organized a "grand hunt" to drive the wolves from the island of Aquidneck. Numerous examples of "circle" or "drive" hunts appear in the histories of frontier towns in Massachusetts, Maine, New Hampshire, and Vermont. In 1753 the citizens of Lynn, Salem, and Reading, Massachusetts, assembled to rid the forest between the towns of wolves. In 1797 the towns of Rockingham, Springfield, Charlestown, and Walpole, Vermont, contributed hunters to track down a single wolf. "A sagacious old wolf" with a talent for maiming sheep, the animal led the men all the way into Connecticut before Colonel Samuel Hunt, a "most noted wolf hunter," shot the predator. In 1805 a posse from Amherst, Massachusetts, surrounded and killed two wolves that had "ranged for some time" in the neighborhood and "killed many sheep." In 1810 a large group of men, women, and children encircled Spruce Peak near Chittenden, Vermont. The circle hunters captured six wolves. In 1831 the New Port *Spectator* ran an announcement for a drive hunt on Croydon Mountain near Goshen, New Hampshire. "It is earnestly hoped," the editor wrote, "that the people will turn out, as the wolves have made great destruction among the sheep in the vicinity of the mountain within the last few weeks—Captain Comings has had 48 killed and about the same wounded."[22] These New England hunts established the model for future wolf drives and circle hunts throughout the northeastern woodlands. Described at length in a gazetteer published seventy-nine years after its performance, an 1803 Vermont wolf hunt lays out the key features of the ritual.[23]

The story of the Great Wolf Hunt on Irish Hill begins with a boy lost in the woods. In February 1803 Daniel Baldwin walked toward the home of his brother-in-law, Israel Dewey. Like so many victimized travelers before him, Baldwin started his trek at dusk. He anticipated an easy trip. The trail was familiar, his destination only four miles off. Near Northfield Falls, he passed the Johnsons' cabin on the edge of the trees. The Johnsons stopped the boy and warned him to stay out of the forest. "The varmints," Mrs. Johnson said, "have been prowling in the woods every night for a week." Mr. Johnson concurred: "Daniel, you must not try to go through the long woods to your sister's tonight, for [they] will catch you." Varmints, however, did not scare Baldwin. He refused to stop. The couple gave the boy a torch and watched him walk into the woods.

The rest of the story follows the worn grooves of the tale type. Darkness closes in; Baldwin hears a howl in the distance. He quickens his pace. The wolves yowl again, closer this time. Daniel runs swinging his firebrand before him. Beasts growl and bark all around him. He feels their breath on the back of his neck. The moment before the varmints snatch him, the boy sees the light in the window of his brother-in-law's cabin. Pale and exhausted, he tells the tale of his narrow escape to his horrified relatives.

Daniel Baldwin's near gobbling inspired the farmers living around the long woods, known locally as Irish Hill, to organize a community hunt. Abel Knapp, Esq., the town clerk of Berlin Center, the closest settlement, served as ringleader. He sent out an invitation to the men living in a twenty-mile radius of Irish Hill to gather at Berlin's meetinghouse on Saturday morning. Between four hundred and five hundred hunters showed up. The men created a giant circle and advanced to the center under the direction of local militia officers. When the hunters could hear the shouts of their cohorts across the circle, their commanders ordered a halt. Thomas Davis, the best marksman among them, entered the ring and killed the wolves and foxes trapped there. The farmers scalped the wolves and marched to the town clerk's office to collect the bounty. With the proceeds, they purchased a keg of rum. The group then retired to Esquire Knapp's haymow and got snockered: "It was said that Knapp's haymow that night lodged a larger number of disabled men than were ever before or since collected in Washington County."[24]

The circle hunt was a ritual that traveled through space and time by word of mouth and physical example. No instruction manual existed for organizing and executing a drive hunt. Older, experienced humans taught younger ones how to surround wild animals and kill them en masse. The circle hunt belonged to a set of communal rituals that traveled with Euro-Americans. Wherever they moved, colonists gathered together for cabin raisings, maple sugar frolics, and road-chopping bees. In 1817, for example, the men of Medina County, Ohio, assembled at Rufus Ferris's farm to build a barn. Work began at the crack of dawn, but the carpenters managed only a half-day's labor before they had to stop. "Fond of fun," Ferris plied his workers with "large pales of milk punch, sweet but strong with whiskey," and before noon "six or eight of those who drank most freely were on their backs feeling upward for terra firma." The barn rose the next day after everyone sobered up. The circle hunt followed the steps of the community ritual: first, a group came together to accomplish a task no one individual could tackle alone, and second, work quickly turned to play as the participants become inebriated. The party was as important as the barn, or the dead predators.[25]

Euro-Americans often chuckled as they slew their ecological rivals. Fear—a solitary traveler lost and besieged in the howling wilderness—justified the grand wolf hunts, but these rituals, begun in terror, ended in fun as groups of besotted men toasted their victory over nature. This provocative blend of mirth and bloodshed illustrates the allure and the frustration of folkloric evidence. The stories of lost travelers, drive hunts, and wild celebrations raise beguiling questions: Why did Euro-American colonists consider wolf killing a pleasure as well as a necessity? How could people be so callous? But to these queries, the surviving remnants of wolf lore offer only the sketchiest of answers. Gathered together, the snippets of narrative display linked patterns and shared themes. Alone, they are out-of-context fragments that survived in local histories for their strange antiquity rather than their historical import. Skimming their surfaces for commonalities works. Delving into them for a historical understanding does not.

Wolves, however, were not the only prey species that suffered Euro-Americans' wrath and laughter. Bear stories dotted town histories and local reminiscences from New England and Ohio's Western Reserve. Applying the skimming technique to these narratives generates clues to the relationship between animal slaughter and communal celebrations in early America. Bears, it seems, were funnier than wolves, and an examination of the bear lore New Englanders and their descendants broadcast over northeastern woodlands demonstrates how animal comedy often masked human pain.

Euro-American colonists fantasized about packs of wolves hunting them down, but bears posed an actual risk. No credible record exists of a healthy (nonrabid) wolf killing a human being in North America from the onset of European colonization to the present day. Bears, however, have been known on occasion to flay humans, and the Euro-American colonists understood that, unlike wolves, bears would attack them, given the right motivation. A story from seventeenth-century Chelmsford, Massachusetts, illustrated the colonists' bear savvy. While searching for kindling in the woods, a mother and her two young daughters stumbled across two "balls of fur." They were cubs, and the mother understood that in the pantheon of bad ideas, wandering between a bear and her offspring ranked near the top. She grabbed her daughters, ran home, barred the door, and refused to come out until hunters killed the she-bear.[26]

Euro-Americans knew that bears were dangerous, and they knew how best to avoid bear trouble. New England bears, reported William Wood in 1643, were "most fierce at strawberry time," when their cubs were young. Yet despite their bear knowledge, few colonists acted wisely in the animals' presence. Indeed, most dropped any pretense to intelligent thought when they encountered a bruin.[27]

The history of bear hunting in the northeastern woodlands is a festival of strange, atrocious, and idiotic behavior. Abial Bugbee met a group of excited men by the side of the road on his way to Woodstock, Vermont. The men pointed at the bushes: a bear was in there. "Why don't you kill him?" asked Bugbee. "We have no powder." Appalled, Bugbee grabbed a pine knot and ran into the brush. He stunned the bear with a smack on the head and yelled for the men to throw him an ax. They did, and Bugbee decapitated the animal. Peter Abbott and a man named Durfee spotted a bear while working in a cornfield near Pomfret, Vermont. They attacked the animal with a hoe and a handspike. The skirmish ended when the bear bit Abbott's thigh and escaped. In Francestown, New Hampshire, a bear sneaked into Robert Butterfield's barnyard, seized a calf, and headed toward the woods. Butterfield followed with an ax, and recovered his property after some carving. In Carlisle, Massachusetts, a woman, an infant in her arms, listened in the doorway to a riot of yells and barks in the distant woods. Her husband and some neighbors were out hunting "a savage and destructive bear" with hounds. The noises grew louder and louder; the chase was headed her way. She left the infant, boarded up the house, and ran into the forest to meet the bear with a musket. The men found her standing over the carcass. In Charlestown, New Hampshire, a bear stepped out of the bushes on the edge of a meadow being mowed by Stephen and Samuel Farnsworth. Samuel jumped the bear and stabbed him with a jackknife until the blade broke. Stung and angry, the bear rushed the farm boy. "Not knowing what else to do," Samuel "thrust his hand deep into the creatures throat, calling to his brother 'Run Stephen, for the bear has got me!'" But Stephen stayed and killed the bear with a pitchfork.[28]

Euro-Americans possessed better, safer, and less gruesome means of bear destruction, but some colonists could not wait for pits to be dug, iron traps to be set, or muskets to be loaded. Why did bear killers act like lunatics when saner methods were available? Spontaneous bear hunts encouraged accidents, miscalculations, and technological breakdowns. These mishaps flipped the human-animal relationship. For a brief moment, people appeared wild, violent, and irrational. Storytellers exploited the comedic potential of these antics, creating a tale type—the wacky bear hunt. Oral culture preserved and transmitted the funniest incidents, and local historians printed versions of the narratives in almanacs and gazetteers. In most cases, bear killing in the northeastern woodlands was neither bizarre nor humorous. But when guns misfired, handspikes hit belly fat instead of arteries, and bears appeared unexpectedly at community gatherings, the animals' deaths entered history as folk legends. Like wolf tales and hunting rituals, the bear narratives depicted an inverted natural order, but in these worlds-turned-upside-down humans and bears competed for laughs as well as survival.

Violence against bears entertained crowds and induced guffaws in the northeastern woodlands in the late eighteenth and early nineteenth centuries. Dead bears appeared at social gatherings. A bear corpse, for instance, brightened a 1781 corn husking in Dublin, New Hampshire. Aaron Marshall, the bee's host, had set gun traps in his cornfields to punish ursine cob robbers. On the night of the event, the guns went off. The shuckers ran to the field and discovered a bear well ventilated with lead shot. They carried the animal to Marshall's house and laid him on the floor. The merrymakers woke up Marshall's son, Benjamin, "then a small boy," and placed him on the bear's back. Locating the fun in this scene is a challenge. Did the look (terror? excitement?) on the child's face when he spotted the monster in his living room inspire chuckles? Perhaps the symbolic contrast between sleeping-babe tranquility and wild-animal ferocity amused the huskers. Whatever the source of their pleasure, the incident demonstrated how a bear carcass could spice up a party in 1781 Vermont.[29]

Dead bears also served as comic relief at chopping frolics. In 1829 a group from Medina County, Ohio, gathered to cut a road through the forest that stood between them and Cleveland. Chopping wagon routes was hard labor, and the men lightened the task by hewing bears as well as maples: "This work was enlivened by quite a number of adventures with bears, a large one being killed with an ax, by some of the Wadsworth company, on the present site of the residence of George A. Shook."[30] The Ohio road choppers transformed a community ritual into a bear hunt; other groups turned bear hunts into community rituals. In Francestown, New Hampshire, the local newspaper recounted an 1836 communal hunt. "The citizens of Francestown," the reporter wrote, "had quite a treat last week in the shape of a bear hunt." Hunters "mustered" to destroy a bruin that "had been doing much mischief among the flocks in the vicinity." In a short time the men treed the animal "and killed his sable majesty." The animal weighed 171 pounds.[31]

In community jokes the carnage of bear hunting often served as a backdrop to other forms of humor. For instance, a hunting tale from Cornish, New Hampshire, concerned marital infighting as much as bears. One day, Ezra Stowell spotted a bear in his cornfield. Afraid the animal would hurt him, Ezra's wife asked him to let the scavenger be. Ezra ignored the advice and ran after the bear with a musket. He shot once. The bullet, however, bypassed every vital organ and enraged the bear. The animal turned and charged him. Hastening to reload, Ezra discovered that he had forgotten his bag of shot at home. He could have turned and run, but flight would only prove his wife right: he should leave large, wild creatures alone. To save his pride, Ezra risked his life. He loaded the musket with powder and fired the ramrod at the bear. The iron bar pierced the animal's skull, and the body crumpled at Ezra's feet. The humor in this anecdote arose from the strange way the bear died and from the absurd lengths to which Ezra Stowell went to avoid confirming his wife's low opinion of his hunting skill. He would rather be torn apart by wild animals than hear her say: "I told you so."[32]

The Stowell anecdote used the violence of bear hunting to make fun of married humans. Other stories went a step further and mined the pain humans inflicted on each other while pursuing bears for laughter. A trap anecdote from the same neighborhood as Ezra Stowell's ramrod incident shows colonists turning the dark humor of bear hunting on themselves. Colonel Jonathan Chase owned an iron bear trap that he often lent to his neighbors. As payment, he asked for the hide of any bear captured in its jaws. One day Chase lent the massive contraption to Benjamin Dorr. With the help of a neighbor, Dorr set the trap on a partially cleared hillside bordering his farm. The next day, he returned to check for captives. But in the confusion of stumps, trunks, and fallen limbs, he forgot the trap's exact location. Thinking the device lay further up the hill, he jumped down from a log and discovered that the device did not lie further up the hill. It took two men to free his mangled leg, and from that day forth the community retold this story as a joke with this punch line: "And that's how Benjamin Dorr came to owe his hide to Colonel Chase."[33]

Part of the fun of bear hunting resided in the ample opportunities the activity offered for humans to look foolish. They hopped into monster traps and fired ramrods. They ran after the beasts with broomsticks, levers, hoes, and pocket knives. In Pomfret, Vermont, during the 1830s, a posse of farmers cornered a bear a half-mile from the post office. Armed with muskets "old enough to be from Queen Anne's War," the defenders of the community counted to three and squeezed the triggers in unison. The guns emitted a chorus of clicks; not one worked. The bear stories transformed acts of butchery into burlesques. In these routines, the bears played the straight men while the people cracked up. Many bears died in the production of folklore, but Euro-Americans targeted their laughter at their human colleagues. People were the butts of bear jokes.[34]

Like the lost-travelers legends and communal wolf hunts, bear anecdotes featured the disruption of agricultural life. Bears interrupt the Farnsworths' hay mowing, waylay Abiel Bugbee on his journey to town, escalate the joviality at the Dubliners' husking bee, and break up the Ohio woodchoppers' frolics. The destruction of a bear was an extraordinary event made more so by the inversion of normal relationships. Spontaneous hunts turned everyday farm tools into bludgeons, spears, and swords. Women dropped their infants and grabbed their muskets to search for destructive bears, taking the place of male hunters; firearms malfunctioned and men forgot their shot bags at home, flipping the power dynamics of predator and prey as the bulletless hunters found themselves at the mercy of their aroused targets; and trappers stepped into forgotten snares, transposing the human and animal relationship completely.

Bear anecdotes often switched the roles of people and beasts. Humans abandoned their high-powered brains. Gut instincts overwhelmed intellects, culminating in foolhardy procedures like defensive tonsil grabs and hoe battles. The stories turned strong into weak, high into low, dignified into silly. The legends' humor arose from the depiction of human predators as goofy instead of dangerous. With their misfiring guns dangling in their hands, the men exuded impotence. Yet aside from Benjamin Dorr with his mangled leg, the bulk of farmers escaped their bear encounters with their major appendages in working order. In the end, the anecdotes restored the humans' deadliness. After their pratfalls, the madcap pacifiers of agricultural landscapes killed their straight men. The violence in the bear stories worked like the violence in the communal wolf hunts: it returned an agricultural society disrupted by a ferocious animal to its proper order. Like the wolf legends and hunting rituals, the bear tales offered male colonists regeneration through violence.

Still, while they were kindred folk traditions, the bear stories differed from the wolf legends and hunting rituals in one respect: before the kill, there was nothing funny about wolf hunting. The participants in communal wolf hunts drank, guffawed, and lounged in the glow of masculine camaraderie only after they shot the wolves. They completed the inversion ritual before tapping the whiskey barrels. In the bear legends, comedy erupted at the moment of inversion. Laughter transformed industrious farmers into hapless buffoons. The stories' lighthearted tone camouflaged the real emotions of bear encounters. In contrast to wolves, bears mauled and ate people. The farmers knew that a chance meeting with a burly omnivore could end their lives. Bears, therefore, posed a serious challenge to their supremacy over wild animals, and they countered the gravity of this threat with satire. They turned bear encounters into jokes to deny the horrible prospect that, instead of their ruling the northeastern woodlands, the forest might swallow them.

Euro-American colonists told stories that cast humans as lost, defenseless, and comically inept; then they participated in communal hunts that restored their species' dominance through ritualized violence. Placed together, the shards of folklore reveal the pattern of cultural inversion. The stories and hunts circled back to the notion that violence could remedy chaos like a pack of wolves revisiting a favorite scent post. When wolves hunted humans in the lost-travelers stories, they violated the natural order so egregiously that only the harshest retaliation could repair the breach. Why did the colonists lie about the danger wolves posed to them? They lied to regain a sense of power lost during their conquests. Their legends expressed their vulnerability, while the hunts exterminated any notion of weakness. Which raises another quandary: why did Euro-American colonists, the most dangerous animals in the northeastern forest, feel so vulnerable?

Two epic and well-documented wolf hunts from 1818 Ohio and 1844 Illinois can help answer this question.

CHAPTER SIX

Metaphors of Slaughter

TWO WOLF HUNTS

ON CHRISTMAS EVE 1818 a small army of Ohio farmers fought a war of extermination in the dense forest of Hinckley Township. Armed with muskets, clubs, axes, pikes, pitchforks, and butcher knives, the "able-bodied men and large boys" encircled their enemy at sunrise. An officer ordered "All Ready," and the combatants advanced, blowing conch shells and tooting horns. The ruckus drove the enemy deep into the woods, and the men followed, walking within arm's length of one another to ensure that nothing escaped alive. Upon reaching a frozen stream, the ones with muskets climbed into the trees to avoid shooting their colleagues wielding clubs and knives. With a shout, they stabbed, smashed, and shot the foe trapped in the creek bed. The farmers emerged victorious, killing three hundred deer, twenty-one bears, and seventeen wolves, as well as an assortment of raccoons, turkeys, and foxes.[1]

The Great Hinckley Hunt, as the 1818 battle between the species in the Ohio woods came to be known, is at once understandable and mystifying. The able-bodied males from the farms and villages surrounding the Hinckley forest set out on that Christmas Eve morning to solve a common problem in the northeastern woodlands. They surrounded the woods in order to eradicate the wolves that had been feasting on their property. But their desire for safe pastures only begins to explain the hunters' behavior on that Christmas Eve.

After the massacre, the men scalped the wolves, and several men rode to the nearest town to collect the four-dollar reward the state of Ohio offered.

With the bounty money, they purchased whiskey for four hundred hunters. Returning with the liquor at dusk, they built a fire to barbecue a massive bear. One of them, "frisky perhaps by the cheering supplies just partaken of," cut a piece of fat from the roasting bear and mashed it into his neighbor's beard. This triggered a fat-smearing frenzy that soon had "every face glisten[ing] in the glare of the fires." The hunters frolicked through the night. The next morning their wives and children joined them and everyone enjoyed a "jolly Christmas" in the shadow of the carcass pile.[2]

The Ohio farmers killed wolves to safeguard animal property: the sheep, cows, goats, oxen, chickens, horses, and pigs that provided them with food, clothing, labor, mobility, and wealth. Domestic beasts were crucial partners in their agricultural society. Yet why did they wage their war of extermination against all the wild animals in the Hinckley forest, not just the predators? Even more, how does one account for four hundred drunken men smearing bear grease on one another deep in the woods on Christmas Eve? The eradication of predators made sense to the agriculturalists; so did the yuletide bacchanal. To understand why humans persecuted wolves with such ferocity and, in the case of the Great Hinckley Hunt, with such glee, we must place both the carnage and the carnival in their historical contexts. Luckily, unlike most early American wolf hunts, the Hinckley episode left an extensive record. The corpse pile and glistening beards caught people's attention, and reports of the event appeared in local newspapers, pioneer reminiscences, amateur poems, and, later, in national sporting magazines. Although farmers organized several drive hunts in the woods of northeastern Ohio in the winter of 1818, the lethal exuberance of the Hinckley hunt inspired documentation.

A "Wolf Hunt" planned and nearly executed in 1844 in Nauvoo, Illinois, also grabbed notice. The governor of Illinois and several Nauvoo residents described the incident, and since a group of Latter-day Saints stood at the center of the event, the Mormon Church kept records as well. These documents help establish the historical context for another performance of wolf lore, and it is impossible to overstate the value of the dates, names, and observations contained in the archived pages. Tracing motifs, themes, types, and patterns across centuries and regions through fragments of wolf lore yields valuable insights, but wolf stories and hunting rituals spread because people embedded in particular times and places found the lore attractive and useful.

Euro-Americans integrated wolf stories and hunting rituals into conflicts peculiar to the northeastern section of Ohio in the years following the War of 1812 and to Nauvoo, Illinois, in the months following the assassination of Joseph Smith, the Mormon prophet. In both cases, the hunts restored a world turned upside down to its upright position. Yet while the participants wielded familiar wolf-killing themes and symbols, they performed their rituals of renewal in social and ideological settings that altered the ceremonies' meaning. In the Hinckley woods, frustrated agriculturalists attacked wildlife to protest their economic and social isolation, while in Nauvoo vigilantes organized a "wolf hunt" to rid their territory of a religious sect whose beliefs repelled and angered them. Wolf symbols and metaphors played central roles in both Hinckley and Nauvoo, but at heart neither hunt really concerned wolves. These were human conflicts over land and religion enacted through the narratives and rituals of wolf killing.

Back to the pile: any examination of the Great Hinckley Hunt must reckon with the hillock of animal bodies. In one day, a group of colonists transformed a working food pyramid—a small number of meat eaters subsisting on a large number of herbivores—into a pyramid of food. The Great Hinckley Hunt resembled a thousand frolics, bees, barn raisings, and communal labors organized by rural males in nineteenth-century America with one glaring exception: the prodigious kill. Pragmatic on their surface, the community rituals may have been excuses for men to gather together and drink liquor, but the inebriants still had to tap the maples and blaze the trails in order to maintain the rituals' façades of practicality. The stated purpose of the Great Hinckley Hunt was the killing of predators, but as the destruction spread to other species, the hunt's rationale lost focus. The Hinckley Hunt was like a group of men assembling to build a cabin and raising a castle instead, and the social context of the hunt helps explain the overkill.

The Hinckley forest was not a howling wilderness, but rather a howling real estate investment owned by the Honorable Judge Samuel Hinckley, a land speculator living in Northampton, Massachusetts. On Christmas Eve, four hundred armed men marched onto Judge Hinckley's land, emptied the property of both nefarious and edible beasts, and threw a wild party. The presence of wolves in the forest justified these activities, and the hunters drew upon folklore to legitimate their mob action. During the hunt the Ohio colonists attacked the wild animals living in the woods and the property relations that protected the beasts. They restored a world gone awry—a natural and social order that fed predators and distant landowners instead of them—to its rightful order.[3]

Society and nature conspired in northeastern Ohio to create a patchwork landscape of small farms and speculator woods. For both the farmers and speculators, this was a landscape of anger and frustration. To comprehend these ill feelings, it helps to know the history of the region called the Western Reserve. Like most colonial ventures, the Western Reserve began with an act of geographic hubris. In 1632 the English crown granted a charter to a group of Puritan colonists in the Connecticut River Valley. As it did with all the seaboard colonies, the crown left Connecticut's western boundary open. In theory, Connecticut stretched like a ribbon across the continent to "the western ocean to the South Seas." For more than a century, Connecticut's vast but slender Western Empire remained theoretical. But in the 1750s land-hungry farmers and profit-hungry speculators moved to claim the land. The only problem was that New York and Pennsylvania now blocked Connecticut's path to the South Sea. Undaunted, Connecticut colonized Pennsylvania. A group of settlers established a taxpaying Connecticut County in William Penn's domain. This adventure in intramural colonization ended during the Revolutionary War when British troops and the Iroquois allies demolished "New Connecticut."[4]

During the 1780s the seaboard colonies ceded their western lands to the new federal government. Connecticut gave up its empire in 1786, with one reservation. It held on to a 120-mile stretch of land along the southern shore of Lake Erie. This "Western Reserve" not only compensated the colony for the loss of its charter lands, it also rewarded the suffering of Connecticut's Pennsylvania settlers during the war. Connecticut finally possessed a colony, but the state had no intention of holding on to it. In 1795 Connecticut sold the Western Reserve for $1.2 million to a group of New England investors called the Connecticut Land Company. In a perfect world, settlers with cash would rush to the area, and both farmers and speculators would prosper. The Reserve, however, was far from a perfect world.[5]

The list of the region's woes was long.[6] To start, the rivers ran in the wrong direction. The Reserve's waterways emptied into Lake Erie rather than the Ohio River. The Ohio, with its links to the Mississippi and New Orleans, was the economic lifeblood of the Northwest Territory. To reach the Ohio, the farmers in the Reserve had to haul their goods overland. The region's roads, however, were monstrous. A running joke in the Reserve explained why few settlers gave up and returned to New England. They stuck, the joke went, not because "the country was so good, but because the journey [home] was so bad." Poor roads and the lack of water routes locked the Reserve's farmers in economic purgatory. The dearth of cash in the Reserve reduced the standard of living for most New England immigrants. When the shoes, pots, blankets, plows, teapots, harnesses, and spoons the immigrants brought with them broke or wore out, they struggled to replace them.[7]

The Reserve's poor economy also afflicted the speculators who had invested in the Connecticut Land Company. In 1809 the company dissolved after defaulting on its debt payments to the state, and the Western Reserve lands were dispersed to its former members. The individual investors, now in direct competition with one another, scrambled to recoup their losses. Many began selling land on credit to settlers, a disastrous strategy considering that the farmers had no cash for shoes, let alone land payments. When the farmers missed the installment payments on their land, many simply left, but the speculators felt tremendous pressure to keep the farmers on the land. In order to sell their holdings at the highest prices, they depended on the improvements the farmers made. By clearing away the forests, building roads, and establishing villages, farmers increased the value of the surrounding unsold land. That is, if they could keep their hands off the unexploited resources in the speculators' woods. Many investors watched their unsold lands decrease in value as neighboring farmers cut the best trees, exhausted the salt licks, tapped the sugar maples, and poached the wild game.[8]

The Western Reserve's patchwork landscape embodied the uneasy social and property relations that bound farmers and speculators. Neither side dominated. Both suffered from the Reserve's economic isolation. Speculators went broke while farmers went barefoot. Both competed for the scarce resources of a hardscrabble economy, and fought for these resources with the powers at their disposal. The speculators possessed the rule of law. Titles and contracts codified their relationship to the land and to the farmers. The farmers, on the other hand, held the power of custom. The communal wolf hunts epitomized the customary rights and obligations that defined the farmers' relationship to the land and the speculators. By allowing varmints to congregate on their unsold lands, the speculators broke no laws, but they did open their property up to invasion.

Wolves exposed the complexity of land rights in the Western Reserve.

The law may have given Judge Hinckley clear title to a patch of Ohio forest, but the customs of land use muddled his ownership. The Reserve's isolation stalled emigration and development, and the region teemed with owned but untouched property. The speculators who controlled these "wild lands" hoped to sell them to young families—couples with strapping children and cash for land payments. Families truly improved the landscapes they inhabited. They cleared forests, raised crops, and elevated the moral tenor of entire settlements. They were righteous neighbors, and immigrants would pay money to live next to them.[9]

Alas, few Reserve farmers reached the heights of wealth and decorum that impressed newcomers. Most were poor. They needed credit to buy their farms, and land payments devoured whatever money they could scrounge. (The most endangered species in the Reserve was specie.) Many families lived in squalor, and even prosperous farmers struggled to look respectable. Zerah Hawley, a Connecticut physician who traveled to Ohio in 1820 and described his trip in a published diary, recounted a meal he shared with a well-to-do family in Ashtabula, a Reserve town near the New York state border. The family's dinner plates indicated their affluence—every member had one. The silverware, however, undercut the dishes' effect. There were enough forks to go around, but the six eaters had to share one "decent knife," a "shoe-knife," and "a raiser" among them. This family, Hawley exclaimed, had been living in the Reserve for sixteen years. More than a decade and a half of labor and they still sliced their beef with shoe blades and shaving implements.[10]

Hawley disliked speculators, and he published his memoir to dissuade Connecticut farmers from believing the land sellers' propaganda. He depicted life in the Reserve as a moral freefall. Immigrant parents grew coarse in the backcountry, but their children "degenerated still more, so much so, that politeness, ease of manners, and every kind of grace, is almost entirely lost and obliterated." Colonization turned the gentle sons and daughters of New England into bumpkins. Of course, vulgarity was in the eye of the observer, and Hawley exaggerated the crudeness of life in the Western Reserve to drive home his point: speculators lured farmers west with lies. Ohio was not a pastoral utopia; it was a sinkhole.[11]

Hawley's aversion to real estate developers hopelessly warped his account. Yet while untrustworthy, the memoir does contain a redeeming surprise. While he loathed speculators, Hawley often sounded like them. The absentee landlords echoed the Yankee doctor's reservations about the moral fiber of

Reserve farmers. They bemoaned the agriculturalists' work habits and directed their agents to extend credit only to "industrious" settlers. According to the speculators, the Reserve's settlers fell into two camps. They were either "honest" or "unruly," and the appearance of a farmer's homestead reflected the category to which he belonged. Brush-covered fields and dilapidated shelters signaled the proprietor's laziness and potential criminality. Wild lands revealed their owner's character flaws.[12]

Whereas Zerah Hawley and absentee landlords disparaged the Reserve's farmers in books, letters, and court papers, the targets of all this documentation said very little in print. Did the farmers resent being slandered as untidy horticulturists when some of the roughest, most unkempt property in the Western Reserve belonged to upper-class speculators like Judge Hinckley? If they did, they kept these feelings to themselves. None of the sources from the time period include rebuttals from downtrodden farmers. The immigrants, it seems, never hoisted a pen in their defense. Fortunately, they did pick up their guns and pitchforks. The communal wolf hunts offer some hints to the farmers' understanding of property relations.

The wolf hunts did not attack the speculators' power head on. No one expected Judge Hinckley to improve all his holdings himself. His responsibilities differed from those of a farmer. Wild land indicated less the quality of his character than it did the absence of his person, and unoccupied lands were free in ways tended properties were not. Poor settlers sometimes helped themselves to the animals, apples, maple sap, lumber, and salt deposits located on wild property. They countered the land-equals-character hypothesis with their own wild-equals-free proposition.

Communal wolf hunts brought the notions of moral character and free property together. Wolves underscored the wickedness of disorderly land. Their presence demanded action, and communities had a right to enter private property to destroy the animals. And killing wolves improved the speculators' property. The hunters could argue that they were doing the landowner a favor, and they exacted a payment for their labor. The destruction of game animals transformed a landscape that filled wolves' stomachs and speculators' pocketbooks into a landscape that nourished the hunters and their families. With bear grease dripping from their beards, the farmers celebrated a restored natural and social order that engorged them, not their creditors. The discarded bodies of wolves ensured that these festivities stayed within the boundaries of acceptable behavior.

In the Reserve the communal wolf hunt became a cautious form of so-cial protest, and in the winter of 1818–19 these protests flourished. Following the Great Hinckley Hunt in December, communal wolf hunts took place in Chagrin, Newburgh, and Ashtabula. Between December 24 and January 16, nearly two thousand farmers participated in drive hunts. The *Cleveland Register* followed the action. On January 12, the newspaper reported, "the inhabitants of the towns of Newburgh, Warrensville, and adjoining towns convened to the number of 3 or 400, and after surrounding a part of the town of Newburgh and part of the town of Warrensville, . . . advanc[ed] in the usual manner to the center." Four days later, three hundred men assembled at Chagrin. The *Register* tallied the game at "23 bears, 17 wolves, and 10 turkeys." On the same day in Ashtabula, six hundred hunters convened and surrounded the town-ship. Upon reaching the center, they encamped for the night. The size of these gatherings of "well-armed" men was startling; so was the abruptness of the circle hunts' cessation. After the Ashtabula hunt, the drives stopped.[13]

They halted for a lack of wolves. The casualty list for the Newburgh hunt, according to the *Cleveland Register,* included twenty-four dead deer and two wounded men. The Ashtabula hunters were even more pathetic: "The next morning the game was all taken to the camp and divided, when it was ascer-tained that an owl was all that had been killed, but it was reported that one porcupine had been killed, and one badly wounded." Wolves were the pre-text for the farmers' invasion of the speculators' property. When gangs of armed men shot prickly rodents and one another instead of wolves, they di-minished the legitimacy of their mob action. And this legitimacy was crucial. Agrarian protest was a dangerous activity in the United States in the decades following the Revolution. The government dealt harshly with farmers who challenged property relations. Shays's Rebellion and the Whiskey Rebellion inspired but two examples of state crackdowns on rural unrest. The Ohio farmers killed predators to overturn an illegitimate natural order that fed animals and impoverished humans. In the process, they assaulted the social and property relations that protected the varmints. When the circle hunts injured porcupines, not wolves, the hunters became rebels, and that was a transformation the Ohio farmers were unwilling to make.[14]

Seventeen corpses lying frozen and skinless in a forest clearing: this was the physical aftermath of the Great Hinckley Hunt for Medina County's wolves. The Hinckley episode was a minor catastrophe for the beasts. The hunters destroyed seventeen individuals and killed hundreds of deer, robbing the surviving animals of their primary food supply. Wolves, however, are resilient. They can recover from population losses. While brutal, the Great Hinckley Hunt was not an extinction-level event. Exterminating species required a sustained campaign of violence. The humans not only had to kill wolves in bunches, they had to keep slaughtering them in sufficient numbers every year to prevent the animals from recovering through reproduction. Uneven thinning could actually increase the wolf population by encouraging neighboring packs to fill the voids created by sporadic repression. Given the opportunity, the wolves would repopulate Hinckley's forest.

The true danger of the Great Hinckley Hunt for the wolves could not be measured in bodies. The Ohio humans destroyed the animals during a performance of folklore. These were ritualized killings, as significant for the meanings they created and expressed as for the lives they ended. The social context of the Hinckley hunt provided one meaning, and there were others. A landless teenager in 1818, William Cogswell cared little about property relations or absentee landlords. Hunting was his passion. For him the Hinckley drive was a personal milestone as much as a social protest. It was a rite of passage. He stepped from adolescence into adulthood on that Christmas Eve. Cogswell's description of the Great Hinckley Hunt brought together the personal and the social, and the episode showed how communal violence could bring about multiple renewals, transformations, and initiations in rural nineteenth-century America.[15]

An excellent marksman, Cogswell answered the call sent out by the organizers of the Hinckley Hunt. On December 23 he left his home near Cleveland with his Uncle Gates. On their way south, the pair split up to hunt in the forests along the Cuyahoga River. Cogswell nearly killed himself trying to extricate a raccoon from an oak tree. Normally, he would have felled the tree and sicced his dogs on the disoriented animal, but the oak was too big. He knew that "if there was an Indian there he would contrive some way to the game without the trouble of cutting the tree." Not to be outdone by the native who haunted his imagination, the young hunter chopped down a smaller hickory next to the massive oak. The hickory fell against the limb where the raccoon clung, making a bridge for Cogswell to climb. Near the top, the slender tree began to bend and wobble. Cogswell jumped to the oak the moment before his bridge crashed to the ground. He grabbed the raccoon and threw the animal down to his hounds. When he reached the ground, Uncle Gates sauntered up. After hearing of his nephew's adventure, the older man declared that he would not have "undertaken it for all the land on the Cuyahoga River, from Old Portage to Cleveland."[16]

Hunting set William Cogswell apart from other humans. Snatching the coon from the oak demonstrated the lengths the teen would go to secure his reputation as a woodsman. He risked his life to prove that he could match wits with an Indian, and the Great Hinckley Hunt offered him further opportunities to outsmart and outgun his rivals. On Christmas Eve morning, Cogswell and Uncle Gates took their places in the ring of humanity encircling the Hinckley forest. They marched forward. Anxious that wildlife might escape through gaps in the circle, a captain asked Cogswell to choose a partner, enter the ring, and shoot as many furry creatures as possible. With his uncle, Cogswell walked toward the center. He had killed several wolves and a couple pair of bears when he spotted the largest bruin he had ever seen. He pursued the animal. On the bank of a stream he discovered a spot from which he could fire down on the bear from a distance of twenty-five feet. He leveled his rifle and sighted in the beast's massive head, but before he could squeeze the trigger, scores of bullets ripped through the forest. He had wandered too close to the south line of the circle. Seeing the bear (but not the boy), the men let loose with a volley. Cogswell described the scene: "Probably one hundred guns fired within a very short space of time, and the bullets sounded to me very much like a hail storm." Miraculously, the young hunter and the bear weathered the storm of bullets without a scratch. Cogswell leapt to his feet, leveled his gun again, and fired. The bear fell, and later that night his fat dripped from the whiskers of hundreds of drunken men.[17]

Cogswell devoted only one sentence to the Christmas Eve celebration in his account of the Great Hinckley Hunt. "That night," he wrote, "was spent merrily in singing songs, roasting meat, &c." This was a pregnant et cetera. By slaying the party's centerpiece, Cogswell attained an exalted position among the men. He had succeeded where dozens of hunters failed. Killing the "monster bear" signaled Cogswell's rise to prominence within the rural community, and, while he refused to recount the details of that night in his memoir, events he did describe provide a clue to his new stature. Christmas dawned with the Ohio hunters hungover and bickering. They could not agree on the fair distribution of the previous day's kill. Cogswell participated in the discussion, and he found the solution. Major Henry Coyt arrived in the morning from his home in Liverpool, Ohio. Cogswell asked the militia officer to referee the dispute. He did, the spoils were divided, and everyone traveled home happy. That Cogswell, a teenager, both joined and ended the argument over the division of meat showed his leadership. The Great Hinckley Hunt transformed him from a farm boy into a woodsman. By slaughtering animals with flair and courage, he became a man other men followed.[18]

William Cogswell ascended the dominance hierarchy of his pack during the Hinckley Hunt. By entering the circle and killing the "monster bear," he answered the Indian rival in his head. The native symbolized Cogswell's insecurities. A master hunter, the Indian was at home in the woods, a place that rattled many colonists' nerves. For Cogswell, hunting like an Indian meant overcoming a forest environment that exposed the vulnerabilities of many of his countrymen. Through the destruction of animals, the teenager abandoned several weaknesses: his youth, his anonymity, and his fear of the wilderness. Through violence, Cogswell remade himself into a woodland creature that induced anxieties instead of feeling them.

Euro-American colonists retold wolf legends and reenacted circle-hunt-binge-drinking rituals in many locales and time periods. William Cogswell's remembrance of the Great Hinckley Hunt showed how the meanings of these narratives and hunts changed according to the context of their performance. Wolf lore resembled a wrestling move that could flip a number of opponents. The immigrants repeated the move—stories that expressed vulnerability followed by rituals that restored dominance—but the targets they upended shifted over time and space. In 1780s Connecticut, for instance, Revolutionary War veterans asserted their Republican values through the memory of Israel Putnam's destruction of a she-wolf (another tale of individual distinction arising from a communal animal hunt). In 1818 Ohio farmers protested their geographic isolation and economic stagnation with a Christmas Eve circle drive and drinking spree. At the same event, William Cogswell overcame his boyhood vulnerabilities by outhunting an imaginary Indian rival. These episodes demonstrated the first law of wolf lore transmittal: wolf stories and rituals had to address the concerns and anxieties of particular historical circumstances to move beyond those same circumstances.

A circle drive and drinking party conducted in the social milieu of Medina County, Ohio, in 1818 could lead to a collective act of violence so impressive that people remembered and recorded the details. Observers celebrated the Great Hinckley Hunt, documenting the scene in diaries, newspaper articles, and poems. The pile of animals, often represented as a tally sheet of deer, fox, bears, turkeys, wolves, and raccoons killed, secured the hunt's fame. Yet for all the bloodshed and boozing, the Hinckley hunt remained a conservative event in its historical context. The hunters killed to restore order, not overturn it. They created a civic ritual—one that combined the definitions of wild lands as free and immoral—to express their anger and frustration through violence without appearing revolutionary. They invaded Judge Hinckley's land and drew blood, but they never openly criticized him or the power relations he symbolized. Other frontier communities pushed the wolf hunts to more radical conclusions: warring sects used wolf metaphors and rituals to attack one another directly.

In the late summer of 1834 Wilford Woodruff traveled south with two companions to evangelize in Arkansas and Tennessee. The missionaries had set out from the Mormon settlement of Independence, in Jackson County, Missouri, four months earlier, and they departed reluctantly. Mobs of armed frontiersmen suspicious of the beliefs and practices of the Prophet Joseph Smith and his Church of Latter-day Saints assaulted the community. Woodruff and his friends wanted to stay and protect the settlement, but the Prophet disagreed. Missionary work was as important as town building, and he sent the young men into the wilderness to win converts.

One morning, as the company approached the woods on the edge of an expanse of prairie grasslands, "a large black bear" ambled toward them. The men stood their ground: "for we were on the Lord's business." The bear rose up on his haunches, stared at the humans for a moment, and wandered away. That night the travelers encountered woodland creatures less respectful of their God. Walking along a dirt road in the forest's gloom, the men heard a howl. They quickened their pace. A chorus of howls surrounded them, and "soon a large drove of wolves gathered around and followed us." The predators "came very close, and at times seemed as though they would eat us up." To save their lives, the missionaries built a fire. The blaze chased the wolves away, and the humans slept.[19]

Until a bark woke them. It was still dark and the fire had died. Alarmed that the wolves had returned, the men scrambled to relight it. The sound of a cowbell calmed them. The bark belonged to a dog; they must be close to civilization. Armed with firebrands, they followed the bell's clanks to a shack with "an old blanket" for a door. Inside they discovered a man nestled in a pile of children and hounds. He startled awake and greeted the wanderers coldly. He was a hunter named Williams and a member of the mob that had assaulted the Mormons in Jackson County. "After the Saints were driven out," Woodruff explained, "he, with many others, went south." Williams let the travelers sleep in the cabin until morning, but he refused to feed them breakfast. The missionaries thanked their surly host and left, walking twelve miles in a downpour to a second shack. This one belonged to a hunter named Beamon, and, like Williams, he had been a Jackson County mobster. Beamon fed the men and harangued them with anti-Mormon slurs and curses. Starving after their long night, the missionaries withstood the insults and devoured the food. Recalled Woodruff: "The harder he swore, the harder we ate."[20]

Woodruff's story was a travelers-surrounded-by-wolves tale with an ending redrawn by religious conflict. The story proceeds along the familiar path of the tale type—evening falls; howls enfold; travelers panic—until the moment of deliverance. The hunter in the cabin should embody civilization. In the morning he should rally the community and lead them into the woods to destroy the wolves. But for Woodruff and his companions there would be no salvation. Their lives depended on the hunter staying at home and not rousing his community—the mob. Williams and Beamon were as dangerous as the wolves and the black bear. If the wilderness was a place where humans experienced fear, vulnerability, and powerlessness, then the Mormons' wilderness extended beyond the woods into the cabins of their fellow colonists.

Inspired by a series of divine encounters in upstate New York during the 1820s, in which angels revealed new sections of Scripture to a young, barely employed farm laborer named Joseph Smith Jr., the members of Church of Latter-day Saints had traveled west in search of a safe gathering spot. They stopped for a while in Kirtland, Ohio, a small village on the outskirts of Cleveland in the Western Reserve. There they converted a part of the congregation of Sidney Rigdon, a prominent evangelist, but following a bank scandal and mounting opposition from non-Mormon Kirtlanders, the Latter-day Saints relocated to northeastern Missouri, an even more hostile setting. Vigilante mobs attacked the immigrants, damaging property, burning haystacks and barns, and tarring and feathering church leaders. In October 1838 at Haun's Mill, a small settlement in western Missouri, 240 members of the local militia surrounded thirty Mormon families. The militia fired into the crowd and laid siege to a group of men hiding in a rickety blacksmith shop. The mob killed seventeen, injured twelve. Anti-Mormon violence drove the Saints farther west. In a swamp on the Illinois side of the Mississippi

River, they raised Nauvoo, a town that for a brief time rivaled Chicago for regional supremacy. By 1844 this newest Zion had a population of ten thousand, an enormous, half-built temple, and a thriving agricultural economy. The community also had enemies. After being arrested in his Nauvoo home, Joseph Smith was murdered in a neighboring town's jail by a crowd of nonbelievers. Following Smith's death, the Latter-day Saints again moved west, to Utah's Great Basin, this time without their Prophet.

The history of the Mormons could serve as a primer on human beings' talent for and insistence on transmitting their values, beliefs, institutions, possessions, and genes across miles and generations. In this the Latter-day Saints resembled their fellow Euro-American travelers. Indeed, while their doctrines marked them as distinctive, the Mormons extended rather than disrupted the patterns, attitudes, and folk practices found along the immigration path New Englanders and their descendants cut through the northeastern woodlands. Their migration passed through the familiar woods of northern New England, upstate New York, and Ohio's Western Reserve. The Mormons killed wolves, bears, and catamounts; they told travelers' stories about being surrounded by wolf packs along forest trails; and they organized community hunts. Armed with rifles and strychnine, the Mormons exterminated Utah's varmints at a pace that would have made a backwoods Missouri ruffian blush.[21]

Yet while the Saints ripped into wildlife with an enthusiasm reminiscent of earlier Euro-American colonists from Boston to Cleveland, their experiences with wolves and wolf lore also ran counter to familiar patterns. The Church of Latter-day Saints disturbed many nineteenth-century Americans. The Mormons, as the Latter-day Saints were derisively called, roused similar passions to those inspired by wolves. People disbelieved Joseph Smith and doubted his motives. They portrayed him as a confidence man who victimized converts with his animal magnetism. The Saints' critics disliked their secular cohesiveness: the way church members lived, worked, and voted as well as prayed together. This pack behavior struck many Gentiles (the Saints' term for nonbelievers) as a betrayal of American individuality and liberty. To mark their difference, nonbelievers applied a series of animal descriptors to the Latter-day Saints. Mormon immigrants resembled droves, their towns nests, and their leaders vermin. The Saints killed wolves, told wolf stories, and performed wolf hunts. They also struggled with other Euro-American colonists over the meaning and applications of wolf lore. Both Mormons and Gentiles fought for the right to call each other wolves.[22]

Joseph Smith's death unleashed a plague of malevolent canines. The Prophet's mother, Lucy, communicated with a howling reference the horror of the night an anti-Mormon posse arrested Joseph. Awakened by yells in the distance, Lucy Smith stood in the doorway of her Nauvoo home with her husband, Joseph Sr., and listened. Five or six gunshots split the dark. Convinced his son had died, Joseph Sr. crumpled in "unutterable" agony. Lucy wrestled her distraught husband to bed. More shrieks and yelps followed the couple to their sleeping quarters: "No heart can imagine the sensations of our breasts, as we listened to those awful screams. Had the army been composed of so many bloodhounds, wolves, and panthers, they could not have made a sound more terrible." The mob did not kill Joseph Smith Jr. that evening. Instead, they dragged him to a Carthage, Illinois, jail to await trial for banning a Nauvoo newspaper hostile to the Saints. The Carthage Greys, the local militia, protected the jail. On the second night of his captivity, an angry crowd walked through the Greys' "guard" (the sentinels fired blanks) and killed Smith, his brother, Hyrum, and several Mormon apostles.[23]

To Lucy Smith the mob's howls betrayed the wickedness in their hearts. The beast in their voices cut through the trappings of legal warrants and judge's orders that cloaked the posse's actions in legitimacy. When she heard their yawps, she knew wolves had her son. The Carthage mob was the first predator that attacked the Nauvoo Mormons in 1844. There soon were others. Since the movement's founding in 1830, groups of converts had broken with the church, and false prophets had challenged Joseph Smith's spiritual authority. Apostasy and schism uncovered numerous wolves within the flock. Following the death of Joseph Smith Jr., the wolf-in-sheep's-clothing accusations sprung from the lips of Mormon leaders like wasps from the mouth of a nest hit with a stick.

The murder of Joseph Smith Jr. plunged the Church of Latter-day Saints into a leadership morass. God had clearly marked Smith for command by revealing the Book of Mormon to him. No one else had such unquestionable authority. Left without a president, the church's high council, the Quorum of Twelve Apostles, governed in the interim. Brigham Young, a forty-three-year-old preacher and carpenter from western New York, headed the Quorum. A forceful leader, he organized the church's successful missions to Great Britain, converting thousands. He also oversaw the Saints' retreat from Jackson County, Missouri, in the face of mob violence. In New England when Smith died, Young returned to find a rival shepherd ministering to the Nauvoo flock. His name was Sidney Rigdon, and he was the second wolf that descended on the Saints following Joseph's death.

A fiery revivalist, Rigdon converted to Mormonism in 1830 along with a portion of his Kirtland, Ohio, congregation. He was a close adviser to Joseph Smith Jr., and with Joseph and Hyrum Smith he joined the First Presidency, a divinely ordained leadership committee of three, in 1832. As the surviving member of the original troika, Rigdon had a genuine claim to power. Joseph Smith, however, was an energetic prophet, and his pipeline to the supernatural hummed with instructions. Over the years he blessed numerous successors, including the Quorum of Twelve Apostles. The dueling revelations set the stage for a showdown. On August 8, 1844, the Nauvoo Saints gathered to choose their leaders. They voted Brigham Young and the Quorum of Twelve Apostles Joseph's heir. But the dispute did not end there. Rigdon fled to Pittsburgh and continued his challenge. He published his own revelations, denouncing the Twelve as usurpers of his God-given authority. In November 1844 Amasa Lyman, speaking on behalf of the Twelve, published a reply in Nauvoo's newspaper, *The Times and Seasons*.

Lyman countered Rigdon's prophesies with a quotation from the Bible. He flung Acts 20:29 at the pretender: "For I know this, that after my departing, shall grievous wolves enter among you not sparing the flock." Rigdon, Lyman proclaimed, was the worst kind of predator. Not a wolf in sheep's clothing but rather a thieving animal dressed in shepherd's robes. He had blown into town after Joseph's murder, held secret meetings, and plotted the armed overthrow of the church's leadership. Moreover, he had run away when Brigham Young confronted him. Rigdon portrayed himself as the protector of the LDS flock against the rapacious Quorum of Twelve Apostles, but unlike "the true shepherd" he had "let those pesky wolves, the Twelve, drive him off." Thus, Lyman concluded, Rigdon proved himself a "black-hearted cowardly wretch" who "would not come himself to see the black catalogue of his deeds held up to the gaze of thousands, but like the wolf, sought to be secluded."[24]

The Twelve pounced on Rigdon with a ferociousness all out of proportion to his threat to their authority. Stationed in Pittsburgh, Rigdon snarled at the Nauvoo leaders through the press, but Young and the Quorum had more immediate problems. Fearing the return of the anti-Mormon mobs, many people wanted to leave Nauvoo. Young fought all summer against "the disposition in the sheep to scatter," and he did so by rhetorically biting all aspiring herders. The vigorous attack on Rigdon served notice to all Saints: follow the Twelve to salvation; follow others to ruin.[25]

By transforming Sidney Rigdon into a wolf, the Twelve announced their intention to oppose all men who "will not stop striving to be great and exalted, and lead away parties from us, thereby weakening our hands." In August, Young publicly warned Lyman Wight and George Miller to halt their plans to lead groups away from Nauvoo: "I tell you in the name of Jesus Christ that if [they] take a course contrary to [the Twelve's] counsel, they will be damned and go to destruction." Young continued: "You get a party to run here and another there, and our enemies will flock around us and destroy us." The church's survival depended on the bonds of faith, family, and community that held the Saints in one place. If the people scattered, these ties would break and Mormonism would become one of the many colorful experiments in religion, spawned by the awakenings of the early nineteenth century, that ultimately fizzled. The image of the wolf in shepherd's clothing was a tactic employed by a weak interim government to keep a Prophet-less movement together.[26]

In the fall of 1844 Nauvoo, Illinois, was ripe for a wolf hunt. A group of colonists felt besieged by howling mobs and wolfish usurpers. To recover their mastery over their environment, they could encircle a patch of forest and return order to their existence by killing wild animals. The Nauvoo Saints had all the ingredients for a "great" hunt: guns, a sense of vulnerability, and, most important, wolves. In the early 1840s the *Times and Seasons* published announcements asking the citizens of Nauvoo to present their receipts to the tax collector. The fees could be paid in "State auditor's warrants, wolf scalp Certificates, or Cash." With real wolves around, the colonists could ravage the woods with impunity. And an invitation for a communal wolf hunt did indeed circulate in the final weeks of September 1844. The notice bid men and strapping boys to assemble at Nauvoo on Friday, September 27, with their weapons ready to eradicate vermin. This "great wolf hunt," however, threatened to agitate the Mormons' vulnerable feelings instead of purging them. For the Saints did not organize the hunt; their enemies did. The call went out to the militias in the counties surrounding Nauvoo to encircle the city on the twenty-seventh. The mob would be the hunter, the Mormons the wolves.[27]

The "wolf hunt" never happened. The governor of Illinois, Thomas Ford, arrived in Nauvoo at noon on the twenty-seventh with his own troops to halt the event. He commissioned Brigham Young a lieutenant general, thereby sanctioning the Saints' militia, the Nauvoo Legion, as a lawful army. He also proclaimed his willingness to use force "to help maintain the supremacy of the laws in Hancock [County] and bring [Joseph Smith's] murderers to justice." Confronted with the governor's army of 470 men as well as an incensed Nauvoo Legion, the anti-Mormon forces backed down. The governor's intercession narrowly avoided the spectacle of two groups of Euro-American colonists trading bullets, each side viewing the other as wolves.[28]

It is little wonder that both the Saints and their opponents utilized wolf metaphors. Wolves' pack behavior made the animals the perfect symbols for representing human social groups. When one collection of humans wanted to comment on the inappropriateness of another group's social ties, it could use the image of wolf packs to communicate its displeasure. Saints and Gentiles each accused the other group of improper bonds. The Mormons, their enemies asserted, cooperated far too much. They corrupted state politics by voting in a block; they engaged in economic collusion; and they physically segregated themselves, gathering in isolated communities hostile to nonbelievers. The Saints, on the other hand, lumped their enemies into a faceless mob. The mob destroyed individual thought and responsibility; it was social bonding run amuck. When Lucy Smith likened the mob's shouts to animal howls, she transformed a posse of human beings into a single irrational beast. The Mormons and anti-Mormons feared and despised each other's communities.[29]

The participants' shared love of animal metaphors and verbal warfare makes evaluating the true danger of the 1844 wolf hunt difficult. The Latter-day Saints and their foes exchanged insults through newspapers, pamphlets, and exposés. Both sides lied and exaggerated, and each dehumanized its opponents, calling them mobs, hordes, beasts, and vermin. Yet the 1844 wolf hunt analogy stuck out amongst the din of incendiary rhetoric for one reason. It brought a response from Governor Ford, a man not easily moved.[30]

A Democrat, Ford wobbled under the political burden of Mormon support. Nauvoo had backed him unanimously in the last election, and Illinois's Whigs pummeled Ford with this fact at every opportunity. The murder of Joseph Smith placed him in a tough position. He needed to uphold the law and prosecute the vigilantes (to protect his own power as much as LDS lives), but if he acted, the Democrats would label him a Mormon puppet. Ford spent the summer trying to devise a plan that would transfer his problem to someone else. First, he turned the job of securing arrest warrants over to Brigham Young. He advised Young to go to a non-Mormon justice of the peace in an outside county and convince him to file the complaint. "I will help," Ford implied, "but only if I can pretend I am not helping *you*." Second, he sent a request to Colonel Stephen Kearny in St. Louis to dispatch federal troops to Hancock County to maintain order. Kearny refused, leaving Ford to confront an escalating situation with state militiamen, most of whom despised the Latter-day Saints.[31]

Ford's appearance in Nauvoo on September 27 was truly remarkable. The wolf hunt flushed him from his political cover. He took risks that day that he had been avoiding for months. The question is why? Why did the threat of a faux hunt goad a reluctant governor to act on behalf of a group of religious deviants?

In 1844 Illinois the Mormons and the anti-Mormons stepped to the brink of genocide. While Governor Ford's actions prevented them from plunging into bloodshed, the symbolism of the folk ritual helped him stop the slaughter. The preservation of order redeemed the bloodshed of the circle hunts. Men butchered wildlife to return the inverted world of the forest, a world where animals hunted people, to its upright position. They invaded the woods to restore a natural hierarchy. Militiamen rampaging through a frontier town—shooting people, hacking limbs, stabbing children, getting drunk among the corpses—hardly qualified as orderly behavior. The analogy faltered because it promised degeneration into chaos, not regeneration through violence.

Religious strife revealed the dark side of the social rituals that summoned frontier communities to action. The same communal impulse that brought people together to shuck corn, chop roads, and raise barns prompted crowds to attack those with whom they disagreed. Anti-Mormon mobs were quilting bees gone horribly awry. Travelers' tales, the wolf legends that often preceded and justified circle hunts, illustrated the dangers of collective action in colonial Missouri and Illinois. When wolves surrounded hapless travelers in the woods of Vermont or Ohio's Western Reserve, the community was the protagonist that encircled and killed the predators the next day. In 1844 Nauvoo a group of colonists assembled to rid their environs of a nightmarish pest, but the heroism of their collective action was no longer an assumption shared by all. Calling one another wolves, Mormons and Gentiles attacked the legitimacy of each other's communities. The social bonds celebrated in bees, frolics, and raisings turned into corrupt ties that melded individuals into dangerous mobs and swarms. Along the banks of the Mississippi River in the months following Joseph Smith's assassination, wolf lore darkened the bonds of human society instead of refurbishing them.

The Great Hinckley Hunt and the aborted Mormon "wolf hunt" offer two examples of folklore in history. In each episode human beings adapted tales and rituals to the unique circumstances of their lives. This duet of improvisation and pattern explains the longevity and intensity of Euro-Americans' hatred of wolves. Wolf lore's transcendence, its ability to slip historical contexts, equipped Euro-American colonists with a set of legends and rituals that addressed the frustrations and disappointments of territorial expansion. Western Reserve colonists relocated to find profitable farmlands for themselves and their children, while the Latter-day Saints moved west searching for a gathering spot to preserve and grow their infant church. Colonization let both groups down: instead of improving economic conditions and allowing for religious freedom, it endangered the very things the wandering humans hoped to conserve and pass down.

Wolf legends and hunting rituals countered the radical tendencies of territorial conquest—the maddening habit of geographic movement to dash hopes and upset plans. The colonists' wolf lore was conservative. The legends and rituals brought out-of-control situations back to order. The Great Hinckley Hunt and the Nauvoo "wolf hunt" demonstrated the array of social, economic, political, and religious disorders wolf stories and rituals could remedy, as well as the pitched battles colonists waged over the lore's application. In some historical circumstances, wolf killing inched toward human murder. Animal symbols legitimated mob violence, indicating how quickly conservative folklore could mutate into radical behavior.

In the end, the notion that wolf killing healed natural and social orders by restoring dominion to the proper authorities prevented Euro-American colonists from exterminating one another like vermin. Taking this last step, killing people labeled wolves, would have destroyed wolf lore's righteousness, and this sense of moral superiority was critical to the job of colonization. The hunters who butchered wolves—chopped their hamstrings, mashed their skulls, wired their muzzles shut—performed their acts of cruelty over an ethical safety net spun by folklore. Their violence repaired a malfunctioning world, bringing harmony to nature and society. If wolf killing became associated with radicalism—instigating chaos instead of order—the brutal treatment of wolves looked fiendish rather than heroic. The perpetrators of cruelty would stand outside of society and their deeds would harm worlds, not heal them. Taken too far, wolf lore could force conquerors to examine the moral implications of their conquests, and this is why Euro-Americans were careful not to take their animal metaphors too far.

PART THREE THE AMERICAN WEST

A Wealth of Canines

MORMON AMERICANS ON THE GREAT PLAINS

ON A SUNDAY afternoon in April 1847 a large wolf interrupted a trailside prayer service near the Loup Fork of the Platte River. The canine's appearance was a small miracle: one of the meeting's leaders, the Mormon apostle George A. Smith, had just launched into a sermon about showing kindness toward animals. The wolf trotted out of a nearby patch of woods at the moment Smith exhorted the crowd to follow the Prophet Joseph Smith's instructions "not to kill any animals or birds, or any thing created by Almighty God that had life, for the sake of destroying it." The wolf's cool demeanor seemed a taunt, as if "to say the Devil & I are determined to prove whether you will practice what is now taught." The Mormon immigrants adhered to the spirit of Joseph's words that Sunday, and the wolf loped off unmolested, but once the praying stopped and their wagons rolled forth, the Saints' benevolence shriveled on the plains.[1]

Mormon travelers on the overland trail killed adult wolves that threatened their livestock, and they slaughtered whelps that threatened no one. Thomas Bullock, Brigham Young's clerk and personal secretary, noted many wolf deaths in his trail diary. In May 1847 hunters killed "2 Wolves & 2 Antelopes" one afternoon and "4 Antelopes & [a] wolf" the next. In October, Simeon Howd collected "1 Hare, 1 Badger 1 White Wolf & 3 Sage Hens" during an eight-day hunt. On May 11, 1847, the men in charge of herding the cattle in Young's wagon train stumbled upon a den filled with wolf pups:

"There were 4 fine cubs in it which were brought out alive, but afterwards killed, to make caps." Later that spring, Brigham Young and Heber Kimball rode ahead of the wagons to scout for a campsite. They "saw five cub Wolves, succeeded in killing two, while three escaped to their den." In Missouri in 1834, Joseph Smith instructed his followers "to become harmless before brute creation." He preached reconciliation with the worst beasts, even snakes, the archvillains of Genesis. When humans "lose their vicious dispositions and cease to destroy the animal race, the lion and the lamb can dwell together, and the sucking child can play with the serpent in safety." A scant twenty-three years later, the leaders of Joseph's church were dragging puppies from their dens to make hats from their pelts. What ruined Smith's interspecific détente?[2]

A plague of real and symbolic wolves attacked the LDS flock between Joseph Smith's ban on indiscriminate animal destruction and Brigham Young's whelp killings. Smith had been taken and murdered by a howling mob; anti-Mormon militias had organized and nearly pulled off the 1844 "wolf hunt"; and Sidney Rigdon and the Quorum of Twelve had traded wolf accusations in the papers. Then, to heighten animosities further, biological wolves on the Great Plains ate the Mormons' livestock and desecrated the graves of the relatives they buried along the trail. Joseph Smith may have anticipated a peaceable kingdom in 1834, but the church's subsequent experiences with real and symbolic wolves permanently revoked that species' membership among the animal races deserving of human kindness.

A conflagration of history, folklore, and biology inspired and sustained the Latter-day Saints' animosity toward wolves. Mormonism breathed new life into biblical wolf and sheep metaphors. The LDS movement saw itself as restoring the true Christian church. As they trekked through the northeastern woodlands to the Mississippi Valley and onto the Great Plains, the Mormons relived Christianity's founding with all the attendant persecution, betrayal, and bloodshed. For them, the Bible described their turbulent present, not some distant Mediterranean past. The document's ravening wolves, false shepherds, and innocent herds were real and immediate, not mere allegories.[3]

Recapitulation—the belief that Joseph Smith's visions had ripped the fabric of time, opening a pathway for the repetition of a sacred history— guided the Saints' responses to the predators they met. Chosen by God to restore Christianity, the Latter-day Saints were distanced by their religious

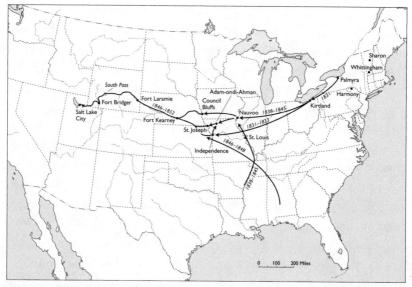

FIGURE 12 Mormon immigration paths.

beliefs from their fellow American colonists. Indeed, the reason the Saints colonized Nauvoo and then the Great Basin was to put space between their church and its enemies. Yet it is important to remember that both the Mormons and their tormenters shared a commitment to agrarian conquest. They both grew plants and tended livestock, and their success depended on channeling the energy flows of novel habitats into the seeds and kernels of the vegetables they liked and the flesh of the animals they owned. From a wolf's point of view, the line separating Mormon from non-Mormon was razor thin. The brutality of the Latter-day Saints' treatment of canine predators can be traced to their divergence from and adherence to a history of Euro-American colonization ushering from New England and the northeastern woodlands. They killed wolves to protect livestock like other American conquerors, but this violence grew in ferocity as Mormon colonists incorporated real and imagined wolves into their sense of difference and destiny.

But this path, strewn with anger and bones, was not the only one the Saints could have traveled. Joseph Smith's prohibition against animal cruelty marked one alternative route, and biology offers more. Historians are not accustomed to thinking of biology as revealing possible pasts or historical contingency. When they consider biology at all, it is usually in conjunction with the notion of determinism. For good reasons, humanities scholars cringe when topics like evolution and genes enter a discussion of human societies and their pasts. For more than a century, a collection of supremacists have abused evolutionary biology to justify systems of racial, class, and gender apartheid, cloaking social, political, and economic oppression in the language of scientific necessity. Recently, sociobiologists, philosophers, and evolutionary theorists have tried to rescue biology from eugenicists and their ilk, using the natural sciences to explain "human nature" with varying degrees of success. Most humanities scholars continue to reject these efforts: boiling down complex, contingent phenomena like aggression, language, and colonization to a few biological root causes, they argue, generates more delusion than insight.[4]

Yet what if instead of narrowing history down to a single cause, biology helped open the past up, exposing sightlines ignored by the humanities? Applying evolutionary and ecological ideas to the story of Mormons and wolves on the Great Plains in the nineteenth century expands history's vision, revealing trails American colonists chose not to travel. Whelp encounters, for example, offered a range of possibilities. Evolution equipped both the Mormons and the puppies with compatible social systems. Instead of skinning the youngsters, the humans could have adopted them. Wolves form packs to hunt large herbivores, and this sociability makes wolf puppies amenable to bonding with humans. Far from natural enemies, whelps will accept people as social intimates.

Humans can fall for whelps as well. Over thousands of years of evolution, human beings have developed a fondness for creatures with large heads, big, round eyes, and small bodies—creatures that resemble Homo sapiens babies. Walt Disney and the manufacturers of Kewpie dolls have earned billions of dollars exploiting the biological tug of balloon-skulled characters with small torsos and saucer eyes. Wolf whelps can also benefit from this phenomenon. Unlike snakes or insects, wolf puppies fit a definition of cute and cuddly based on the appearance of human infants. They have the right head-to-eye-to-body proportions. Humans have even tried to prolong this cuteness through breeding. Compared with wild canids, many domesticated dogs retain their juvenile characteristics into adulthood. Toys stay small, basset hounds keep the round, expressive eyes of an infant, and many breeds maintain a puppy's openness to forming emotional bonds into maturity. Human beings have manipulated natural selection to create friendly, attractive companions that behave and look like whelps. Evolution has hardwired wolves and humans with relationship options ranging from tooth-and-bullet antagonism to social intimacy. Nature both pulls the species together and pushes them apart; it is up to wolf and human representatives living in historical time to work out the meaning of their genetic legacies.[5]

Cultural beliefs, biological predispositions, and historical patterns offered an array of choices for the humans and animals that met on the Great Plains during the second half of the nineteenth century. Neither history nor evolution nor culture predetermined the course of their interactions. Americans, Indians, wolves, and bison traveled down one of the bloodiest and most tragic paths imaginable: by the end of the nineteenth century, Americans had imprisoned their human rivals on reservations and reduced the bison and wolf societies to heaps of skinless corpses. But the kill-off was not the only route the mammals could have followed.

What is the difference between a lawyer and a wolf? One is a ravenous predator who hunts down innocent creatures with his partners; the other is a canine. This joke is funny (or, at least, mildly amusing) because it mocks the notion that human beings, with their large brains, vibrant cultures, complex societies, and vaunted ethics, have little in common with animals. The joke exploits the unsavory reputations of lawyers and wolves to drag people down to the level of brutes. It does so playfully. Only members of a single profession get dehumanized. But replace "lawyer" with "hunter-gatherer," "pig farmer," or "cowboy," and the jest's edge, blunted by the attorney-as-villain cliché, regains its sharpness.

What is the difference between a human and an animal? The lawyer joke addresses this enormous question and then retreats to the safety of humor. However, to understand the history of humans and wolves on the Great Plains in the second half of the nineteenth century, we need to confront the query with a straight face. Differences between humans and wolves abound, but the animals exhibit surprising commonalities as well. Both species, for example, respond to environmental change through behavioral as well as genetic adaptations. Wolves can learn and pass along their knowledge to their offspring. In the spectrum of living beings, wolves rank among the fastest adaptors. While not as quick as humans, wolf populations colonized the northern half of the world through nimble adjustments. And the story of the Great Plains wolves should give all swift animals pause. Speed may ease the conquest of space, helping fast-adapting species infiltrate and flourish in a variety of landscapes. But as any highway patrolman knows, speed also kills.

Cultural quickness teamed with social affection opened an interspecific common ground, and humans and wolves defined their relationship by embracing or rejecting their similarities. Both species invest considerable time and energy in their young. To build quick-reacting minds, humans and wolves start life out slow. Juveniles need years of care and instruction before they can function alone. The responsibility of parenting large-brained, fast responders is so onerous that both species enlist the assistance of other adults. Social groups raise children and whelps, and, to facilitate this education, youngsters of both species develop strong emotional ties to grandparents, aunts, uncles, babysitters, and tutors. Affective bonds cement social alliances, and these relationships help communicate environmental information across lifetimes. Both humans and wolves can change their behaviors rapidly, and one of the consequences of this mutability is the emergence of intense and widespread emotional attachments. Humans and wolves are poly-amorous; they can bond with a range of "packmates," including each other.

Given Euro-Americans' history of wolf animosity, interspecific affection marked the extreme fringe of possibilities in the nineteenth-century trans-Mississippi West. Yet tenderness was an option, if a slim one. Americans could have bonded with wolves instead of dismembering them. Evolution gave the species choices, and a crash course in the biology of culture and love can help uncover the possibilities as well as the limits of the wolf-human relationship.

What separates humans from their animal relatives? The answer has to include Homo sapiens' fabulous brains. People have large brains for their body size. This fact explains the feats of intelligence that differentiate the species from other animals. Humans possess culture, language, art, religion, and technology. They have overspread the world, built civilizations, and shot themselves into outer space. Their fertile imaginations raise them above beasts, literally. Humans are the only creatures on the planet with the neural capacity and the gall to imagine themselves superior to other organisms.

Yet while a wolf may never file an amicus brief, it is easy to overestimate the degree of difference between humans and animals. People's high-powered intellects overwhelm the slow, rigid, and narrow thought processes of most creatures, but humans and animals use their divergent brains to solve similar problems. Take human culture as an example. Culture—the collection of myths, rituals, metaphors, ideologies, beliefs, symbols, and signs that create and express the collective mentality of a people—represented a giant leap in human evolution. Through culture, evolutionary biologists argue, humans greatly enhanced their fitness as a species. All organisms have to deal with the problem of environmental change. Certain frogs thrive in ponds but die in savannahs. Shifts in temperature, humidity, rainfall, sun, and shade can turn a pond into a savannah. Species modify their behavior, their form, even their anatomy to survive in environments undergoing constant alteration. This is the meaning of survival of the fittest. Those organisms best suited to a particular environment flourish, and, when changes occur, those quickest to adapt to them live on to reproduce.[6]

Culture sped up humans' adjustment time. People can reinvent their cultures with incredible swiftness. This seems obvious in an age when rapid communication allows fashions and fads to remake culture daily, but human beings were quick before they acquired high-speed modems. Compared with the glacial pace with which most living organisms react to environmental change, a medieval peasant was an adaptive Ferrari. Most creatures are limited to a single response when confronted with alterations in their environment: they die. Animals with minimal nerve systems like sponges and flatworms cannot invent new behaviors to match novel situations. They can adapt, but only through natural selection. Over generations, the lives and deaths of countless individuals slowly select organisms that can survive in the altered environment. Of course, the world may have shifted again by the time evolution reworks a species. To counteract the dangerous lethargy of genetic adaptation, organisms with large enough brains respond to environmental change nongenetically as well. They learn ways to survive in chaotic environments and pass this knowledge on to their children and neighbors. Through culture, human beings preserve and transmit information crucial to their survival, but Homo sapiens is not the only species that uses its big brain to respond to ecological change.[7]

Both humans and wolves belong to the club of neuron-endowed species that practice behavioral heritability. Wolf pups enter the world with stereotyped responses to environmental stimuli—instincts—encoded in their DNA. All young canids, for example, display a "chase-response." In one behavioral study, the ethologist M. W. Fox tempted wolves, domestic dogs, gray foxes, red foxes, arctic foxes, and coyotes with live rats. The first reaction of all the month-old pups and kits was to run after the rodents. Even when they caught and killed their bewhiskered stimuli, the young canids pawed at the corpses in the hopes of resurrecting the chase. The urge to pursue moving objects is a stereotyped reaction that serves predators well. By itself, however, the chase response does not ensure a harvest of calories. Just ask the canines stalking tennis balls and Frisbees in the park. Wolf pups may have an instinct for running after things, but their litter- and packmates teach them how to turn this gut reaction into a belly full of meat.[8]

Wolf puppies are roly-poly fuzz balls that frolic for a living. They devote their waking hours to pouncing, wrestling, tugging, and nipping. From a human perspective, romping wolf pups are devastatingly cute. But play is a serious part of a wolf's education. Old wolves socialize young ones. They introduce pups to the imperatives and mysteries of life as a top predator that hunts in a pack. Adults model social behavior and demonstrate hunting skills. They sniff, whine, defecate, and howl, unveiling the signs and scents of wolf communication. Wolf pups learn from their littermates as well. Through play, infants and juveniles practice communication, they exercise hunting and fighting skills, and, most important, they establish dominance. Around the age of two to three weeks, puppies cross the line separating friendly skirmishes from nasty fights. Milk teeth draw blood, and the combatants form an enduring relationship. The pack's dominance hierarchy grows to include a new generation as vanquished pups submit to stronger siblings. Young wolves jostle for social position at the same time that they develop the physical capacity to slaughter large mammals, and pack relations are as essential to survival as strong muscles. Wolves are social killers, and adults sacrifice to give pups the time and calories to build lethal bodies and relationships.[9]

Wolf packs typically raise only one litter a year. This means that most pack members have little biological incentive to help safeguard another couple's genetic legacy. Yet the reproductive strategy of wolves depends on the group's sharing the responsibility for pups. This strategy carries risks for the group. Packs limit their mobility to raise their young. Mothers give birth in a den, and when the pups can walk, the entire pack moves to a rendezvous site. Thus for much of the spring and summer, wolf packs are place-bound. Individuals and small groups leave for days to hunt, but they return to the rendezvous site to share their kills. During the pup-rearing season, wolves' hunting effectiveness declines and their ability to protect their territories drops. Packs try to compensate for their immobility by howling more. They voice their intention to defend their space despite the constraints of pupcare. Rival packs rarely test these bluffs. In the spring and summer, they have their own fuzz balls to worry about.[10]

Wolves' reproductive strategy also carries risks for nonmating individuals. They help shoulder the costs of mammalian reproduction (focusing scarce resources on a limited number of offspring) without receiving any of the benefits: the transmittal of DNA to a new generation. These wolves not only forgo their yearly opportunity to reproduce, they give to others the care and calories that could have gone to their own offspring. Wolves do not repress their libidos voluntarily. The pack's dominance hierarchy influences reproduction. During the breeding season, dominant animals harass, intimidate, and attack their subordinates. The alpha male and female do not always mate, but they help determine who will. Subordinate wolves face a dilemma. The social arrangement that provides them with food, defense, and companionship also prevents them from swapping genetic material as often as they might like.[11]

Dominance hierarchies, however, are mutable. A well-aimed moose kick can rearrange the social order and give sexually frustrated subordinates the opportunity to breed. Through endurance and sublimation, lowly pack members can ascend to dominance and extend their genetic legacy with the full assistance of the group. Subordinate wolves can also disperse. A recent study of the genetic relatedness among wolf packs in Alaska's Denali National Park found a surprisingly high level of interrelatedness across packs, as well as a correspondingly low level of genetic similarity within them. Scientists had always assumed that packs consisted of a dominant male and female living with their offspring from various litters. Family ties reinforced pack cohesion; incest was a common occurrence. The Denali study challenges this cozy picture. The mitochondrial DNA evidence indicates that wolf social relations are far less insular and far more dynamic than previously thought. Packs split, bud, colonize, and collapse. They adopt new members and raise multiple litters. All these activities foster genetic novelty, lessening the deleterious effects of inbreeding. In Alaska, subordinate wolves left packs fairly often to find mating opportunities, and they did so in the face of extraordinary intraspecific strife. The same scientists who discovered wolves mingling across pack lines watched half of their thirty-one radio-collared subjects die from attacks by neighboring packs. Dispersers risked their lives to smuggle genes across territorial boundaries.[12]

In wolf packs, as in human societies, power and sex are intertwined. Dominant wolves try to direct group reproduction, but the high level of genetic diversity within packs suggests the frequent loss of control. This should not be surprising. Being a top predator does not excuse wolves from environmental uncertainty. Chipmunks and wolves inhabit opposite ends of the food chain, yet both experience the same ecological whiplash when microorganisms, weather, and food shortages infest, freeze, and starve species along the chain. Wolves are especially vulnerable to population swings in their prey. After a series of mild winters, a prey population may blossom, encouraging wolves to increase their numbers as well. More wolves means more intraspecific conflicts as packs crowd into each other's territories. Abundance causes injuries, but scarcity can hit a wolf population like a wrecking ball. A harsh winter with heavy snowfalls can make the killing too easy. Large prey animals struggle through drifts while lighter wolves pursue on frozen crusts. Deer and elk "yard up," gather together for protection, and wolves feast on the old and weak as the snowed-in herds exhaust their food supply. The devoured, however, get their revenge. One winter's feast is another winter's famine, and the wolves will confront their own season of hunger when they try to support their growing numbers on a declining prey population.[13]

The life of a top predator is no easier than the life of the animals they consume. Wolves have little control over their environment. They can catch and digest a moose; they can boss and bully one another; but they cannot alter the weather, douse a forest fire, or rid their intestines of tapeworms. Wolves scramble to survive in an unpredictable environment, and knowledge is a key asset in this struggle. Like humans, wolves display a talent for gathering and transmitting information. They learn from their surroundings and adapt to environmental change. By sharing the responsibility for feeding, socializing, and protecting their young, wolf packs buy time for the pups to acquire the information that will help them survive in a volatile world.

Wolves' livelihood demands cooperation: they are top predators that eat large mammals by ganging up on them. Wolves band together to retrieve stores of calories inaccessible to them as individuals. Their sociality creates their niche, and this highlights the species' eccentricity. Most animals, the zoologist Charles Elton pointed out in 1927, eat prey that fit in their mouths. The size of organisms tends to rise along the slope of the food pyramid. The rare animals on the top levels need to be big enough to kill prey without injuring themselves. Wolves belong to the club of beasts that violate the size gradient of Elton's "pyramid of numbers." Baleen whales and elephants also fit into this group. They devour animals smaller than themselves, but the amount of bone, muscle, and blubber they devote to mauling leaves and krill seems excessive. Whales and elephants have evolved to finesse the pyramid. They bypass the intermediate trophic levels to scoop, shovel, and gulp the tiny but abundant organisms residing at the bottom, and they use these calories to build bodies no single predator can wrap its mouth around. North American wolves have evolved the capability to eat versions of these trophic-hopping behemoths (moose, elk, dairy cows). They have carved out a niche as a midsized predator that specializes in devouring huge vegetarians through teamwork.[14]

Their social groups are so central to wolves' existence that behaviors that increase pack solidarity appear easily understandable. Wolves bond, share food, raise pups cooperatively, and join forces to defend one another because these activities hold packs together, and wolves need their packs in order to feast on large prey.[15] Yet the clarity of purpose behind wolves' altruistic behavior is a mirage. It looks refreshingly simple, but biologists have wandered in the dry landscape of evolutionary theory for years searching for an explanation for altruism. Many organisms perform feats that, in the language of socio-biology, "increase the fitness of another at the expense of [their] own fitness." Soldier ants sacrifice their bodies for queen and colony; gibbons protect companions' food caches; and red deer "bark" to alert herdmates to nearby predators, a risky behavior that could draw the attention of the killer. Biologists observe plenty of nice behavior, but they struggle to comprehend why any creature would behave nicely.[16]

Altruism must aid the transmittal of DNA from one generation to the next. Yet if a red deer's bark draws a wolf, her days of gene swapping end with a bite while her colleagues live to fornicate another day. Given their reproductive advantage, dastardly deer that nonchalantly slip to the center of the herd after spotting a predator, leaving the oblivious browsers on the outskirts to suffer the attack, should have replaced upright barkers long ago. Signaling deer exist, however, and biologists have crafted ingenious theories to account for the continued presence of self-sacrifice, kindness, and cooperation in animal populations:

Theory One: Kinship. Animals behave altruistically to protect the DNA housed in their children. A mother wolf attacks a trespassing bear to defend a litter of pups. This dangerous act is sensible Darwinism. The wolf balances her life (and the chances for reproduction this life represents) against the potential for genetic longevity embodied in her offspring. Her choice could be expressed algebraically, and evolutionary biologists have indeed turned motherly love into a cost-benefit equation. They have created mathematical models to explain altruistic behavior among cousins, nieces, nephews, aunts, and uncles as well. An uncle, for example, may help feed and safeguard his brother's children, but doing likewise for the offspring of his nieces and nephews would be counterproductive, turning smart altruism into daft generosity. Calculating the costs and benefits, animals should heap the most care and attention on the closest relatives, thereby preserving the highest number and fullest copies of their genetic code.[17]

Theory Two: Reciprocal Altruism. Kinship, however, cannot explain altruism among nonrelated individuals. The red deer notifies despised rivals as well as beloved mates. Why hazard a wolf bite to extend a competitor's genetic reach? The deer accepts the risk, some biologists argue, in order to receive a warning bark in the future. Sacrificing one's food, labor, or health for unrelated associates makes sense only if the associates return the favor. But why should an organism blessed with an altruistic gift ever reciprocate? A selfish strategy seems best. Accept the gift, and when the time for payback arrives, stay mum and eliminate the competition. Time, however, militates against the double-cross. A herd of red deer confronts perilous situations often. A sleaze who betrays the group once will be punished at the next opportunity. Creatures share, cooperate, and alert one another to danger because in lifetimes filled with sacrificial moments the best strategy is reciprocal altruism.[18]

Theory Three: Affection. No theorist believes this one. Animals do not behave altruistically in the sense humans understand the term. Altruism is an imperfect metaphor scientists use to describe kindly actions that appear maladaptive: behaviors that seem to cripple one organism's chances to reproduce while improving the chances of another. The challenge facing evolutionary theorists is to unmask these behaviors, to reveal the functionality beneath their façade of benevolence. They argue that deep-down altruism conforms to Darwinism. Kindness, friendliness, solidarity, and self-sacrifice aid the transmittal of DNA from one generation to another. Motivation—the critical element in human altruism—has no place in this equation. People behave altruistically only if their actions come from unselfish motives. Pull a schoolgirl from the path of a speeding bus in order to steal her lunch money and you are a bully, not a saint. Altruistic acts require the proper inspiration. Evolutionary biologists not only reject affection as a reason for altruistic behavior among animals, they reject all motivations. No thought, feeling, or decision propels evolution. Evolution drives itself.[19]

And, of course, they are right. Even if an individual based every life choice upon a strategy calculated to maximize the dispersal of his genes, the effort would be wasted. The interaction of heredity, fitness, and environment determines the scattering of DNA. Organisms well suited to a particular environment produce more offspring than organisms poorly adapted to that environment. As environments change and natural selection alters species over generations, levels of fitness shift as well. All these transformations occur beyond the reach of individual organisms. Evolutionary biologists study altruistic behaviors to discover why natural selection seems to favor some organisms over others. They are intrigued by the choices evolution makes, not the decisions of individuals.

Thus biology turns love into a glum helpmate of evolution. Roses are red; violets are blue. Love has no meaning, except perhaps to aid the dispersal of genetic copies of me and you. Yet does functionality inevitably destroy love's subtle tenderness? Wolves are wildly affectionate animals, and their social bonds serve an obvious function. Emotional attachments hold packs together, and wolves secure their ecological niche—gang-hunting predators —through their sociality. While the purpose of wolves' social ties is clear, however, those ties are neither simple nor easily fathomable. Just ask the people who have bonded with the beasts. Humans have observed (and felt) wolf social attachments intimately, and the two animals have formed interspecific packs that restore the mystery to wolves' social bonds.

Lois Crisler first joined a wolf pack in the early 1950s. She and her wildlife photographer husband, Herb, purchased two wolf pups from Eskimo bounty hunters. They bought the animals to film. The Walt Disney Corporation had sent Herb to Alaska to make a movie starring the region's caribou. The picture would need kill-scenes with drama-enhancing close-ups, and the wolf captives ensured that Herb would get them. The Crislers acquired four more pups a year later when Herb robbed a den in the Brooks Range. Theft and cinematic exploitation may seem rickety foundations for an enduring interspecific relationship, but the Crislers turned out to be devoted wolf friends.

They justified stealing the puppies on the reasonable assumption that bounty hunters would soon destroy them, and the couple took their responsibility for their canine charges to extraordinary lengths. When the Alaska filming ended, they transported the four pups (the first two wolves had died on the tundra) to their home in the Tarryall Mountains of Colorado. For the next decade, they sacrificed their time, money, labor, love, and, eventually, their marriage to the canines.

Lois described their experience in two popular memoirs. The theme of social bonding runs through both books. Far from bloodthirsty, the tundra wolves impressed her as aggressively communicative. They smiled, wagged, talked, romped, howled, and kissed. They playfully stole her mittens and groomed her eyelids with delicate nibbles. The wolves' faces were a carnival of signs. Mouths, eyes, and ears flashed information. The Crislers even learned to read pupil dilatations for hints to the animals' moods and intentions.[20]

The couple mimicked the wolves instead of teaching them human commands. They never scolded, threatened, or punished their charges. The wolves greeted the humans with bows and hugs, and the Crislers reciprocated. The wolves howled and the Crislers joined in. The wolves turned serious or possessive and the Crislers left them alone. With patience and kindness, they assembled a collection of signals that integrated them into the wolves' pack. Yet for every communication breakthrough, there were tragic breakdowns. Neither animal fully deciphered the other's social cues.[21]

Captivity presented insurmountable communication problems. The wolves could not understand the terms of their imprisonment. Their urge to roam and hunt crashed against the high fences of the pens the Crislers built to protect them. Ranches surrounded the property. Instead of loping free, pen-breakers ran a gauntlet of rifles and shotguns. The Alaskan wolves escaped their first spring in Colorado. All four headed east to the plains. Only one, a female named Alatna, returned, and she narrowly survived a gunshot to the shoulder. Following the deaths of the three wolves, the Crislers reassembled the pack around Alatna, using dogs, wolf-dog hybrids, and themselves. Lois, especially, bonded with the female. She considered the wolf a friend. The wolf's opinion of the woman was harder to discern. Alatna "loved" Crisler, greeted her enthusiastically, played, smiled, and licked her. She also protected the woman from her aggressive wolf-dog offspring. In order to keep their captives as wild as possible, the Crislers rarely imposed their will on the animals. This left the canines a kernel of self-determination, but it placed their caretakers in an uneasy position. They became subordinate members in a pack of wild predators.

The Crislers held an intermediate position among the canines. For many years, Alatna was the dominant animal in the pack. She disliked her subordinates' brawls. She prevented skirmishes and punished aggressors. This included the hybrids that tried to intimidate Lois. Dominance hierarchies change with time, however, and Alatna lost her authority as her pups matured. Alatna's fall altered the humans' place in the pecking order. As Lois walked the pens to feed and "love" her charges, she searched for clues to her shifting social position. A wildlife advocate, she admired and publicized the wolves' communication skills, their peacefulness, and their sense of social responsibility. She downplayed their dominance behaviors. The animals, however, forced her to grapple with the roughness of wolf politics. They often dominated her. They frightened and bit her, and Herb destroyed several wolf-hybrids for assaulting their human packmate.[22]

Ultimately, the Crislers' interspecific social unit unraveled. Not from the animals' hostility, but from the humans' frailty. The Crislers got a divorce. Their emotional attachment foundered as they struggled to maintain their connection to a group of wild creatures. Herb stopped photographing animals and took up gold mining to stay near home and pay for the beasts. The bulk of the wolf care fell to Lois; Herb slowly faded from her life. Near the end of her second memoir, Lois drives to the mine to see him. They cannot resolve their personal differences. They agree to sell the Tarryall property. Lois drives to Colorado Springs. She purchases meat and sleeping pills. After waiting three days, she drugs the animals and shoots them.

Wolves congregate in social units to kill prey species larger than themselves. The Crislers' adventure with a canine gang proved this statement both true and woefully insufficient. After years of intimate contact, the animals still baffled their caretakers. Of course, the humans' biases contributed to their puzzlement. True believers with intellectual blind spots as spacious as Pontiacs, the Crislers thought that wolves exemplified freedom, wildness, and decency in a cruel, people-driven world. Yet every time Lois backed out of the wolves' pen to avoid a confrontation with an aggressive animal, she tacitly acknowledged the ugly side of pack relations. Wolves could be tyrants and bullies too.[23]

Like all observers, the Crislers were captives of their assumptions. Their politics colored their perceptions, as did their species affiliation. The couples' humanity led to a basic misunderstanding about time. Wolves and people inhabit overlapping but fundamentally different lifetimes. They mature at different rates; think at different speeds; and die at different ages. Human lives span decades, whereas wolves are lucky to see their tenth birthdays. These time differentials mark a series of conflict points between the species. Wolves cycle through generations faster than humans, making the social dynamics of their packs appear fluid and cruel to human eyes. The social volatility of wolf packs is an illusion created by humans' temporal frame of reference. People not only expect a generation to rule for a lengthy span of time, but they also want social institutions like families and nations to endure many lifetimes. Longevity shapes humans' perspective of wolf sociality and militates against some people's attempts at integrating themselves into wolf societies. Humans and wolves can trade signals and form emotional bonds, but humans struggle to keep pace with a social order that seems in continuous upheaval as two-year generations jostle for power and reproductive opportunities.

Lupine emotional bonds form and dissolve at a rate unacceptable to most humans. People want the relationships they value most to last, if not forever, at least for a few decades. Homo sapiens can place extraordinarily high expectations on their affectionate ties, and these aspirations for transcendence hint at a paradox: with their large brains, human beings are models of adaptability, but many people use their lithe intellects not to adapt but to preserve the relationships, institutions, and identities they adore. Groups feed, nurture, and educate children, granting them the time to develop minds that can interpret and respond to environmental change. Socialization creates a web of affection as youngsters bond with parents, teachers, and playmates as well as abstract collectives like religious congregations and ethnic groups. The pull of kin and country can somersault the biological rationale for love and culture. Instead of modifying their beliefs, institutions, politics, and property systems to fit their environment, humans enter habitats and alter them to suit their cultures.

In the 1840s the Latter-day Saints ventured into yet another novel environment. Having sojourned in Ohio's Western Reserve, frontier Missouri, and on the banks of the Mississippi River, the Mormons wandered out onto the Great Plains. European colonization had already made the grasslands a site of amazing social and cultural innovation. Horses, introduced from Spain, via Mexico, changed the way some Native Americans hunted bison, which in turn altered wolves' relationships with both humans and herbivores. At mid-century, American colonization added farmers and livestock (as well as miners, hide hunters, teamsters, soldiers, and missionaries) to a nest of mammalian societies that had been undergoing modification for more than a century.

The Mormon immigrants, however, refused to think and behave creatively. Instead of befriending native groups, the Saints fought them. Instead of showing mercy toward noxious animals as Joseph Smith instructed, they shot snakes and clubbed whelps. At every historical juncture where they might have walked a new path, the Mormons chose persistence over adaptation. Why did one of the most inventive social groups in American history, a faith-based community that rewrote the Bible, experimented with polygamy, and flirted with communistic property relations, abandon their imaginative thinking on the Plains?

Compared with the forested East, where colonists heard but rarely spied wolves, the Great Plains was a petting zoo. American immigrants, Mormon and Gentile, saw, heard, smelled, and, in desperate moments of hunger, tasted the predators. At night the animals announced their presence through their howling. "Were regaled all night," wrote Lawson Cooke next to the Republican River in 1858, "with the perfect hell of noise by the wolves." Far from desolate, the moonlit Plains reverberated with grunts, snorts, clicks, yaps, whines, and moans. The racket frustrated weary travelers. Near Fort Elsworth, Kansas, in 1864, G. S. McCain described the noise: "I am entertained every night by the wolves. No need of getting lonesome or sleepy."[24]

Mosiah Lyman Hancock, age fourteen and an aspiring Mormon nimrod in 1848, recalled two howling encounters on the Great Plains. At Winter Quarters, Hancock walked forty miles to retrieve a family cow before their spring departure. He camped in a grove of slippery elm and basswood before heading home. Near midnight, "a dismal noise awakened" the teenager. He scrambled up a tree and waited as a "force" of wolves inspected his campsite. At sunrise the animals departed, and Hancock "tried some praying, for the music in the wolves' choir seemed to introduce in me a desire to feel a little religious." Later that summer, Hancock met another pack along the Platte River. He and a hunting party of four boys had killed their first buffalo. Feeling bold, the gang strolled farther upriver "in quest of other game," but they walked "too far and got surrounded by wolves before [they] got home." The boys escaped, only to be encircled by another pack of fuming mammals at the wagons: their mothers. "We got a severe scolding when we got home," Hancock wrote, "but the howling and massing of the wolves was a great deal worse in my estimation."[25]

Americans traveled into a landscape suited to wolf watching. The absence of forests exposed vast sightlines, and colonists observed wolves at close range for the first time. "Here we saw thousands of buffalo, all along the plains," noted one traveler near the south fork of the North Platte River in 1842. "We also saw packs of wolves, which followed them." In April 1859 Calvin Perry Clark went hunting along the Arkansas River and spotted sixty antelope, "about 8000 Buffaloes," and "40 big grey wolves." He shot at the crowd "but did not hurt them much." Travelers attached a number of descriptors to the region's wild canids, labeling them at different times "western wolves," "lobo wolves," "mountain wolves," "grey wolves," "little wolves," "prairie wolves," "timber wolves," "loafer wolves," "blue wolves," and "coyotes." They needed a range of adjectives to capture the jumble of species, subspecies, body types, muzzle lengths, paw prints, coat markings, hair colors, and social behaviors on display in the canine mobs that trailed the bison. And the howling congregations were enormous, sometimes numbering in the forties and sixties. In 1841 Lewis Gerard watched "a large band of buffaloes running toward the Arkansas [River]." Behind them loped "200 large wolves in pursuit."[26]

Gerard's observation underscored one of the ironies of the American colonization of the region: earlier European conquests had altered the Plains' mammalian societies, fostering economic and ecological innovations, before settlers rolled across grasslands in an attempt to transplant their churches, families, and property systems. Filtering north from Mexico, Spanish horses inspired some native groups along the Mississippi and Missouri Rivers to give up agriculture to become equestrian bison-hunting nomads. Groups of Sioux, Crows, Comanches, Arapahoes, Cheyennes, and Kiowas followed the migrations of the High Plains bison herds, and the area's canine predators trailed along. A formidable prey species, the bison's size and collective defenses put only the weakest herd members within wolves' reach. Equestrian hunters injured healthy adults, orphaned calves, and heightened the stress of entire herds. Wolves learned to associate human hunters with bison vulnerability. Plains wolves lived in large packs; they sought out human hunters instead of running from them; and they let smaller canid rivals live in close enough proximity that human observers could notice the size difference between the species. All these signs seem to indicate a lack of competition among Great Plains predators for the resource they savored most: bison meat. Wolves, coyotes, and humans lived together in peace on the mid-nineteenth-century Plains, and their shared bounty was due to behavioral adaptations to ecological imperialism.[27]

In the late nineteenth century, the wolves' feast years abruptly ended. Euro-American hide hunters shot and skinned hundreds of thousands of bison. Interested only in the leather (industrial factories used buffalo skins as drive belts), they left the corpses to rot. Wolves had always shadowed the bison and their Indian hunters, and as the slaughter intensified they began trailing the American skinners as well. The report of rifles announced a feast, and the wolves ran to the sound. As long as the bison were plentiful, the skinners paid little attention to the wolves. When the bison population crashed, however, the skinners saw the wolves' hides as a new source of income. Hunters shot and skinned the bison as before, but now they laced the corpses with crystals of strychnine. Instead of a bounty of calories, the guns summoned the wolves to mouthfuls of death.[28]

The skinners mounted their poisoning campaigns in the winter, when the pace of work, be it farming, soldiering, or buffalo hunting, slackened. Ranchers at Walnut Creek Crossing, Kansas, destroyed two thousand wolves in the winter of 1856–57. Buffalo hunters wintering at Old Bent's Fort on the southern Plains spent their days poisoning the "thousands" of coyotes and lobo wolves near the fort. Pony Express riders at posts strung between Fort Kearney, Nebraska, and Denver, Colorado, killed wolves in the winter to earn bounty money. According to Justus Conzad, they piled up the skinned carcasses of wolves "like cordwood" next to their stations; some piles measured a "full cord." Near Hutchinson, Kansas, in 1871, buffalo hunters regularly laced bison cadavers with strychnine following a day's kill. The next morning, they would skin the dead canines and dump the bodies in the road across "Swampy Creek." The bones of thousands of wolves supported the colonists' wagons as they rolled through the mire.[29]

Over thousands of years, wolves' intellects helped them survive in a wide range of ecosystems. From Arctic tundra to boreal forests, from high deserts to balmy jungles, wolves established footholds in every environment in the Northern Hemisphere. To do so they modified their behavior, their diets, their territories, and even their bodies. (In general, northern wolves are bigger and maintain larger territories than their southern relatives.) The Great Plains wolves were demonstrating their flair for innovation when they incorporated human bison predation into their hunting practices. This was a smart move. Speedy replies to novel situations underwrote the species' extraordinary success. But the swift acquisition and dissemination of knowledge can lead large-brained creatures toward errors as well as clever adaptations. On the Great Plains in the late nineteenth century, wolves learned to run toward the sound of a lethal weapon fired by a dangerous rival. This blunder makes the slow response rate of flatworms and sponges to environmental change seem judicious.

The Great Plains episode illustrates two lessons about adaptation. First, the context of an action, not the intelligence of the actor, determines that action's brilliance or stupidity. Second, wolves often behaved like imbeciles when a particular group of human beings refashioned the context within which the animals made decisions. Euro-Americans often bewildered the predators. Wolves were intelligent and capable of altering their behavior, so what prevented them from adapting to colonization? Other animals managed it. Coyotes and prairie dogs flourished in the presence of Euro-Americans, much to the conquerors' displeasure. Why did wolves falter while other varmints prospered?

The Mormons' Great Plains experience can help illuminate the wolves' unique predicament. The Latter-day Saints were ironic pioneers. They spearheaded the American conquest of the Plains and Great Basin, expanding a nation that feared and despised them. They were outcasts with suspicious morals, allegiances, and sexual practices. Yet while they represented the creepy edge of American civilization to their many critics, the Latter-day Saints' radicalism did not extend to their dealings with predacious canines and Native Americans. And it could have. The Mormons' avant-garde belief system contained ideas that could have revolutionized the American style of conquest. The migrants remembered and preached Joseph Smith's admonition to treat varmints with compassion. The Book of Mormon taught that Native Americans descended from a lost tribe of Israel, the Lamanites, who received a special visit from Christ in North America following his crucifixion. These notions of interspecific mercy and cross-cultural religious kinship nudged the Mormon colonists toward a sympathetic consideration of wolves and Indians. Other elements of Mormon culture, however, rooted the immigrants to the violent traditions of American colonization. Specifically, their livestock and their vision of eternity kept the Latter-day Saints from seeing and treating their Great Plains rivals differently.

* * *

Unlike Illinois, where the Mormons' religious practices incited riots, beasts, not beliefs, caused the most trouble on the Plains. Following Joseph Smith's murder and the 1844 "wolf hunt," the Latter-day Saints decided to abandon Nauvoo. Brigham Young, after reading explorers' accounts of the region, selected the Great Basin as the Mormons' destination, and in 1846 the migrants began to march their possessions across North America's vast grasslands to reach their new home. Livestock pulled the colonists' wagons, filled their stomachs, and carried their hopes for a better future. The Saints had converted their Illinois farms—sold at cut rates amid violence and persecution —into mobile animal property. During the Plains crossing, bovines, equines, ovines, and porcines would determine the course of America's only home-grown world religion.

The Mormons' livestock battles commenced on the edge of the Plains. From 1846 to 1848, groups of Saints "camped" at points along the trail. They constructed shelters, planted crops, and ranged cattle, building up supplies as they waited for spring. Winter Quarters, near Omaha, Nebraska, was one of the largest and most developed of these way stations. In May 1848, as the last group of migrants prepared to abandon the camp, Brigham Young received a bill from the United States Army. They wanted the church to pay a fee to the Omaha and Otoe Indians for the use of their land during their stay. Flabbergasted, Young replied: "The Indians have killed, I suppose, from three to five thousand dollars worth of cattle. . . . The government ought to pay us." In his opinion, the Mormons had fattened their hosts enough. Stopping along the trail rested legs and increased supplies, but stationary livestock herds quickly exhausted the native grasses. Beasts had to move on the Great Plains, ranging over broad spaces to accommodate the region's slow-to-recover vegetation. The Mormons instigated their first battles by staying still and depleting the Omahas' forage.[30]

West of Winter Quarters, the livestock fights continued. Thomas Bullock recalled a skirmish with a group of Pawnees over some horses. The domestic animals traveling with the Mormons were incorrigible wanderers. Roundups, rescues, and retrievals filled Bullock's journal. In April 1847 the immigrants' horses strayed from the wagons, and a Pawnee rode away with one. The ease of this transaction encouraged a raiding party to try for the rest of the herd the next day. Dressed as wolves (native hunters often donned wolf skins to sneak up on bison), the Pawnees had nearly reached the horses when Porter

FIGURE 13 George Catlin's portrait of Plains Indian bison hunt. Courtesy Denver Public Library Western History Department.

Rockwell fired his rifle at a doglike creature and fifteen armed Pawnees jumped up "ready for a fight." After trading shots and trying to set the prairie on fire to roast the wagons, the Indians departed without their animal prizes.[31]

The Indians' theft of their livestock appalled the Latter-day Saints. Cattle rustling and horse pilfering ranked as high crimes in their moral universe. But the notion that their behavior might trample the Indians' sense of property and decorum never entered the Mormons' minds. Euro-American colonists had been traveling across the Great Plains oblivious to rules that governed the landscape since the migration to Oregon commenced in 1842. Their intrusions angered the tribes along the overland trail, and the U.S. government negotiated treaties, built forts, and requisitioned troops to keep the trespassers safe. To further erode their welcome, the immigrants blew holes in the Indians' livelihood. The wagon trains sent out hunting parties to claim a share of the region's wild creatures. Mormon travelers shot bison, badgers, antelope, snakes, grizzly bears, geese, deer, prairie dogs, and prairie hens. While the Saints' kill paled next to that of the hide hunters who would follow years later, their destruction of wildlife exacerbated a volatile situation.[32]

Mormon snipers also attracted wolves. Hunting parties often set out in the evening after the wagons had stopped for the day. Darkness prevented gunners from collecting all the animals they shot. Wolves ate injured and unclaimed beasts, and packs began to follow the wagons. "Wolves appear to be in greater abundance here," wrote Thomas Bullock in October 1847, "by their tremendous howling all night." Earlier that month "a very musical band of Wolves" had serenaded the travelers "thro' the entire night." Sometimes the howlers appeared near the wagons. In May 1847 the Saints camped next to a bison herd on the trail between Fort Kearney and Fort Laramie. One night, a bison calf walked into the camp and a sentry shot the animal. "Some Wolves," Bullock wrote, "smelling the blood come to get some of it." A member of the pack invaded one human's zone of personal comfort, loping too close "to be social." So the man shot it.[33]

The overland trail punished domestic animals. "The very dry season, the scarcity of grass, the heavy dragging, dusty roads, and inhaling so much of the alkali by breathing, eating and drinking," wrote Brigham Young in 1848, "has been the cause of our losing many of our cattle." Maladies like "bloody murrain," "hollow horn," and "an unusual swelling of the melt" weakened animals, and wolves targeted the sick and the worn-out. "Oxen, when foot-sore or exhausted by fatigue, are left by the emigrants," recalled the guide and memoirist Edwin Bryant, "and immediately become the victims of the wolves, who give them no rest until they fall." On August 14, 1848, William Burton, a clerk in Heber C. Kimball's company, recorded the discovery of Mrs. Long's dead sow near the camp: "The wolves had torn her considerably." That fall an ox belonging to a member of Willard Richard's company perished in the night and "was found in the morning partly eaten by wolves." Like a herd of Moses, hundreds of domestic beasts carried God's chosen people to the edge of the Promised Land only to collapse in a heap at the border. Wolves added a final touch of melancholy to livestock owners' gloom by eating the remains of their investments.[34]

And cow entrails were not the only vestiges upon which the predators dined. The Great Plains wolves robbed human graves, and this activity eliminated the last whiff of sympathy the Latter-day Saints had for the animals. In March 1848 the *Missouri Republican,* a newspaper friendly to the Saints, published a call for concerned Americans to aid the Mormon immigrants wintering on the Plains. Emergency funds ("five thousand dollars, seasonably bestowed") could "save the lives of two or three thousand human beings, whose carcasses must otherwise be left to the prairie wolves." Mountain fever took Esther Ogden Bosworth's father near the Bear River in Utah. Her mother gathered Esther and her siblings together and told them to hunt for rocks to place on the grave. "On top of the stones," Bosworth wrote, "we piled sagebrush . . . until the rocks were covered two or three feet deep, then it was set on fire." The purpose of the flames "was to do away with any odor that would induce an animal to dig [the rocks] up." Mormons who died on the trail were truly lost. Sarah Burbank remembered the burial of her "husband's wife Abby." Abby died from cholera, and her family buried her without a coffin in an unmarked grave by the Platte River. "The wolves were howling" the night of the funeral, and the sadness of the groans coupled with their promise of disinterment underscored the bleakness of the moment. Abby had left her body, and now her family was abandoning it as well. "We had to go on the next morning," Burbank wrote, "and never saw [the grave] again."[35]

The Latter-day Saints lost farms, businesses, temples, family members, church founders, and friends as they moved across the country. On the Great Plains, wolves severed connective tissues and emotional ties. The act of dismemberment overtook the hunt as the focus of the colonists' wolf lore. Euro-Americans had imagined the hot breath of pursuing wolves on the back of their necks for generations. They told travelers' tales that recounted the near-death experiences of innocent wanderers. The Great Plains canids took this humans-as-prey symbolism a step further. The animals' foraging conjured up grisly images of gnawed flesh and body parts disappearing down the gullets of wild beasts. These bodies were beloved, and the sympathy the Mormons felt for their dead relatives and friends squelched any chance of showing compassion to predators. Wolves caused too much pain and loss to be forgiven.

On his deathbed Jedediah M. Grant floated to heaven in a dream. The celestial kingdom was orderly and well governed, filled with "righteous men and women" existing in "perfect harmony." He spotted many people he knew, but only his departed wife, Caroline, spoke to him. She "looked beautiful" and carried the couple's daughter Margaret in her arms. The child had perished during the Mormons' hegira across the Great Plains; wild animals had violated her grave.[36]

"Mr. Grant," Caroline addressed the dreaming president of the Church of Latter-day Saints, "here is little Margaret; you know that the wolves ate her up, but it did not hurt her; here she is all right."

His glimpse into the hereafter doubly comforted Grant. First, the trip reaffirmed the LDS Church's vision of immortality. "Why," he proclaimed,

"It is just as brother Brigham (Young) says it is; it is just as he has told us many a time." Second, the visit with Margaret answered a question that had concerned him since the Plains. The wolves had ripped apart and digested her body on earth; would she be whole in eternity? Grant died in peace a few days later on December 3, 1856, secure in the knowledge that heaven was a pleasant, meticulously "organized" place and that the wolves' fangs had not touched his daughter's spirit.

Jedediah Grant's visit to the celestial kingdom delivers a blow to the theory of evolution. Darwinism presupposes a kind of afterlife, but it reverses the view that immortality waits in an organism's future. Instead of experiencing an out-of-body nirvana, creatures generate transcendence through their offspring. Heaven exists in genes left behind, not paradises to come, and natural selection determines the amount of immortality an individual can achieve.

Human beings are supremely adaptable. Over thousands of years, they have survived in a variety of climates and ecosystems, overcome many reproductive challenges, and withstood a host of cataclysms and upheavals. Humans' intellects aided their survival, and the hallmarks of their large brains —culture, language, and technology—enhanced their speed and flexibility. Jedediah Grant's mental endowment helped him cross the Great Plains and adjust to life in locales as diverse as a muggy river bottom (Nauvoo, Illinois) and a high-altitude desert (Salt Lake City, Utah). Yet instead of a surprising heaven filled with challenge and variety, Grant dreamed of an eternity ruled by order and predictability. His culture worshiped stability, fortitude, and intransigence, not adaptation. The Mormons colonized the Great Basin to practice their religion unmolested by vicious mobs and Gentile politicians. They undertook a radical change of venue to stay the same.

Humans cling to their cultures and fight to preserve them. They have turned an instrument of biological perpetuation into an end in itself, and their conservatism is hardly surprising given the bleakness of evolutionary heaven. In a timescale measured in thousands of years, human culture may indeed encourage the passage of genes, ensuring the perpetuation of the species. But this afterlife, were it to last millions of years, would not be an unchanging, restful existence. Successful biological modifications sometimes reward great-great-great-great-great grandparents with descendants who bear only a fleeting resemblance to them. Adaptation can lead to extinction as well as longevity.

Supposing humanity responds to every upcoming environmental crisis with aplomb, the species' future may still be dark, strange, and even dramatically unhuman. Evolution cares nothing for the categories, ideologies, and allegiances of particular organisms. This is the ambivalence of life on earth: creatures survive by changing, but adaptation can bring about a sort of death as beings shift forms, shed behaviors, and reorganize anatomies to match their surroundings. In the enormous spans of biological time, immortality and oblivion merge into the endless and amoral project of continuation.

In the end, human beings' longing for cultural transcendence—their struggle to reproduce their ideas, possessions, social structures, churches, communities, families, and political organizations as well as their genes—is a feverish dream. To endure, humans must change, and every deviation threatens the persistence of cultural forms. Life will eventually kill everything particular groups of humans hold dear.

Wolves dug up this conundrum with the bodies of dead immigrants along the overland trail. Colonization demanded a wagonload of personal and social adjustments. Conquerors entered new environments and adapted their diets, clothing, shelter, and economies to survive in them. Yet many pioneers left their home territories for conservative reasons. They longed for persistence; radical change was their hell. Wolves chewed through the tethers of sentiment that bound together households, congregations, and civilizations through eternity. Americans' hatred of the predators grew out of their love for one another.

CHAPTER EIGHT

Call It a Coyote

HOW TO EXTERMINATE WOLVES IN COLONIAL UTAH

"'TWAS IN THE MIDDLE of the winter," and the families around Plain City, Utah, wanted to throw a party. They sent word to Uncle Tom, the local fiddler, to come to town and supply the music. On the night of the dance, Tom finished his chores late and started walking toward Plain City in the dark. Snowdrifts blocked the main road, so he cut across the frozen Weber River. The howls caught him on the ice. Tom scrambled up the riverbank. He spotted the shack where the McFarland boys boiled their molasses and hurried inside. The wolves surrounded the cabin and tried to enter through a broken window. Frantic, Tom tucked his fiddle under his arm and climbed up the chimney and out onto the roof. A search party found the musician there, perched atop the molasses shack charming the wolves into docility with a rendition of "Turkey in the Straw."[1]

So far, this legend, collected by the Utah folklorist Austin Fife, adheres to the conventions of the besieged travelers' tale type and mimics the "Old Dick" fiddler tale from Kentucky. Wolves accost a lone wanderer at dusk. The victim runs only to be trapped at the brink of destruction by his pursuers. To survive he offers a sacrifice—a dance tune this time rather than children, picnic leftovers, or a leg of lamb. The community arrives. Hunters surround the wolves, destroy them, and everyone celebrates.

The fiddler legend ended differently, though, with a reference to memory, not revenge. The "boys," including the McFarland brothers, rescued Uncle

Tom by shooting at the wolves. They killed one, but the other sixteen marauders escaped. Following the ordeal, Uncle Tom nearly died from pneumonia, and the skin from the slain wolf covered the floor in front of the stove at Robert McFarland's house for years.

Instead of focusing on the spectacle of a rural community seizing control of a natural environment, this narrative highlighted the remembrance of the conquest. The key figure in this shift is the dead wolf. Robert McFarland keeps the wolf hide, an item that disappears in most travelers' tales. After the rescue, the hunters in the stories skin their victims and trade the hides for bounty money. Dead wolves become currency, and their bodily remains vanish when town constables bury them to prevent swindlers from claiming multiple prizes. This transformation—predators to rewards—completes the agrarian fairytale. The farmers not only exterminate a rival predator, they turn the ultimate discommodity, an animal that devours property, into the supreme article of exchange: money. Handing in a wolf carcass for a bounty was, for frontier agriculturalists, akin to spinning gold out of straw, and they celebrated the sweetness of this conversion in their folktales.

As told to Fife, the Utah legend bypasses the magical climax when cash-poor agrarians realize their dream of changing nature into legal tender. Instead, Robert McFarland, a farmer on the outskirts of the American market economy, turns his wolf skin into a rug. Perhaps McFarland's assets were unusually liquid for rural nineteenth-century Utah and he did not need the money; perhaps the authorities had suspended Weber County's bounty prizes the year of the fiddler incident; or perhaps Mrs. McFarland enjoyed the feel of wolf hair on her bare toes as she scrambled eggs in the morning. Perhaps it does not matter why he kept the skin. The crucial decision maker in the fiddler legend was not McFarland but his niece, Fife's informant. She chose to end the story with the hide she remembered on her Uncle's floor, and her decision revealed the link between wolves and memory that distinguished the Utah Mormons' wolf lore from its eastern antecedents.[2]

The Mormons' wolf legends privileged the conquest of time over the conquest of territory. Wolves belonged to the immigrants' past. The animals marked the line separating a history filled with suffering from an orderly and prosperous future. The timeframe of the fiddler legend was as important as the triumph over nature, and the wolf skin rug helped Robert McFarland's niece turn a Utah in which beasts attacked strolling musicians into a fading memory.

Once in the Great Basin, the Latter-day Saints labored to turn folklore into history. Many American communities tried to achieve this alchemy in the late nineteenth century. In New England local historians resurrected travelers' tales and wolf anecdotes to distinguish a staid present from a wild past. Wolves belonged to a colonial epoch of violence, fear, and struggle, and the authors of town histories, county almanacs, and state gazetteers collected shards of folklore to titillate and instruct their readers. Wolf tales and hunting rituals took on new meanings; they became colorful remnants from a bygone era instead of cultural forms used by living people. History, genealogy, and geography connected the residents of nineteenth-century New England towns to the region's first European colonists. Wolf stories stretched these connections, distancing local historians and their audiences from their vermin-slaying progenitors. Wolves helped create a time period—colonial history—by exempting the readers of gazetteers and reminiscences from the work of conquest.[3]

The Mormon colonists in nineteenth-century Utah wanted to live a similar distance from their colonial past. After decades of violence and removal, they desired a safe gathering spot to build farms and grow families. They sought a place to remember hardships, not experience them. They wanted a Promised Land, but the Great Basin proved a rambunctious Eden. The Saints' battles with wolves demonstrated that building a Zion required more than hard work and social cohesion. It also required a measure of accommodation and self-delusion.

The Great Basin's wild canids posed an interpretive dilemma to groups of colonists searching for signs of progress. Large wolves roamed Utah's mountain valleys, but smaller canines inhabited the desert flats. These "prairie wolves" puzzled American observers. Scrawny, yapping creatures, could they be wolves? The Mormons solved the taxonomic problem with a linguistic ploy. They called the smaller predators wolves until it became obvious that the prolific species had no intention of disappearing. The small wolves adjusted to colonization and flourished in rural landscapes under intense human predation, the precise circumstances that stymied their larger relatives. If the Mormons wanted to leave wolves in their past, they would have to change their canine definition scheme. And they did exactly that; over time prairie wolves became coyotes, and the Mormons held onto their notions of progress by adapting their culture to their surroundings.

The presence of coyotes in postpioneer Utah contradicted the message of the fiddler's legend: it was not clear even in the late nineteenth century that wolves and the hardships they embodied were a fading memory. Rather than preserve the faithful, spatial mobility threatened to pull apart their community as hungry pioneers looked into the future and glimpsed not improvement but more Gentile persecution, Indian raids, locust plagues, and wolf-eaten livestock. Church leaders battled these grim forecasts with narratives that built a wall between a woeful past and a promising future.

The Latter-day Saints were miserable conquerors. Not defective invaders, just glum ones. They performed most of the jobs of colonization with skill. They crossed the Plains, sowed crops, fought Indians, built temples, dug irrigation canals, shot bears, and raised babies. Yet they were physically uncomfortable and emotionally distraught while accomplishing these tasks. They arrived in the Great Basin tired and hungry, and once they unpacked their gear, rain flooded their homes; wolves and Native Americans attacked their livestock; crickets devoured their crops; and grizzly bears invaded their corncribs. The Great Basin difficulties joined a string of melancholy incidents: mob attacks, Joseph Smith's murder, Nauvoo farms sold for pennies, and dead family members abandoned on the Plains. The Latter-day Saints rallied their communities around the memories of past suffering, and their folktales declared that setbacks and privations only helped them achieve their colonial aspirations. They had traveled hundreds of miles to farm, raise livestock, parent children, and practice their religion without interference. The Mormons wanted freedom and stability, and pioneer hardships tested their resolve to build and preserve an earthly paradise.

The Mormons immortalized their first years of settlement in thousands of personal narratives. Families collected histories, memoirs, and reminiscences. Mormon elders recalled the pioneers' struggles in their Sunday lectures, and folk songs remembered the immigrants' suffering in their lyrics. The LDS church archived hundreds of pioneer diaries, and the Daughters of Utah Pioneers published hard luck tales and pain-laden anecdotes in newsletters and books. The pioneer hardship story became a tale-type variant, a regional folk legend that transmitted information critical to the survival of the Mormon community. The tales helped the Latter-day Saints indoctrinate children and converts who missed the exodus and the early years in the Great Basin. Their first lesson: those who had never tasted a thistle or gnawed a wolf's hide in the first years of settlement had no right to protest the discomforts that continued to dog Utah communities years after their founding.

FIGURE 14 Mormon family, Salt Lake City, 1868. Courtesy Yale Collection of Western Americana, Beinecke Rare Book and Manuscript Library.

The Mormons escaped the howling mobs only to confront their growling stomachs in Utah. The journey across the Great Plains devoured energy. Wagon trains rolled into Salt Lake City with empty larders and skinny livestock. An arid region with none of the botanical lusciousness of the Mississippi Valley, the Great Basin looked sparse, daunting, and inedible. The wagon trains reached the Salt Lake Valley in the fall, too late to cultivate the kinds of plants that delighted the travelers' tastes. After the colony's first harvest, old settlers aided new arrivals. Food supplies, however, were short for years.[4]

In an 1853 sermon, LDS President Orson Hyde recalled the first year in Salt Lake settlement. "When [the pioneers] arrived here," he reported, "all they had to subsist upon . . . was in their wagons." Their cattle wandered "to and fro" like "skeletons," and, in the spring, the insects stripped the fields bare. Men "labored hard under the pangs of hunger to put up a little adobe cabin" and sent their wives and children, "pale with want," into "the hills and benches to find thistles and roots to eat, which [they] boiled in the milk of the remaining cows the wolves had not eaten." In an 1855 sermon Heber C.

Kimball expanded the menu of the early settlement years: "When we first came here, and lived on thistle roots, segos, wolf skins, and like articles of food, we considered that we were doing well." Claude T. Barnes, in a memoir titled *The Grim Years,* remembered eating bowls of "salt mess" as a child in the Utah settlements: "They would put some bread in a bowl, add salt, pepper and a little butter; and then pour boiling water over it." "I guess we had other things to eat," he wrote, "but not much." Bran held a special place in the child-hood memories of Margaret McNeil Ballard and Daniel Leigh Walters. Both recollected eating bran bread at every meal for entire winters, a riot of fiber that may have pleased the children's intestines but curdled their taste buds.[5]

One of more extreme culinary incidents in Mormon history occurred in 1856 back on the Great Plains. That winter the Martin Handcart Company, an experiment in an oxen-free Plains crossing, foundered in the snow of Wyoming. The handcart immigrants have become icons of pioneer suffering. Their belongings piled in wheelbarrows, the men and women in the cart companies looked pitiful and exposed compared with the robust stereotype of musclebound oxen hauling Conestoga wagons along the overland trail. Oxen, however, were expensive and more fragile than they appeared. Brigham Young endorsed the handcart venture to save cash and free migrants from the burden of finding grass for domestic beasts. Several wheelbarrow compa-nies reached Salt Lake City without incident, but the Martin Company de-parted Winter Quarters late in the summer, and fall snowstorms punished the travelers for their eagerness to reach Zion. Young learned of the immi-grants' trouble and sent out a rescue party. Of the 1,076 men and women who started out with their carts, 200 died on the road. The rescuers guided the survivors to Salt Lake City, leaving behind a guard at Devil's Gate fort to protect the company's cattle and carts through the winter. The suffering of the handcart pioneers made them legends, but the men left at Devil's Gate endured a season in hell that rivaled the cart pushers' pain while garnering none of their fame.[6]

They did not begin to eat skin until late winter. By then the herd of more than two hundred bovines under the guard's care had died. With no grass, the beasts had weakened and collapsed, attracting "droves of prairie wolves." The Mormons shot "over a hundred," skinned them, and stacked their "fat carcasses" next to the fort. As the weeks passed, the cow corpses migrated across the edibility frontier. Drool-inspiring rump roasts became vomit-inducing lumps of carrion. Their beef rotted, the men tried eating a cow skin "without any seasoning and it made the whole company sick." They then soaked, scorched, and scraped the hides repeatedly until they created "a jelly" they could stomach with a little sugar. Skins gone, they devoured the leather "wrappings from the wagon-tongues, old moccasin-soles, . . . and a piece of buffalo hide that had been used for a foot mat for two months." Finally, the starving band eyed the pile of wolves that by now "looked very much like nice fat mutton." But they could not bring themselves to ingest the predators' flesh. They would wait for "a good clean supper of healthy food" and trust that God would provide it.[7]

You might not expect men hungry enough to swallow their shoes to be finicky eaters. The Mormon colonists, however, turned down many of the delicacies offered by their new home. They refused, for example, to eat bugs. The Goshutes and Paiutes living near the Great Salt Lake harvested grasshoppers. In 1846 the non-Mormon adventurer Edwin Bryant witnessed three Indian women hauling baskets filled with "a substance, which, upon examination, we ascertained to be service-berries, crushed to a jam and mixed with pulverized grasshoppers." After the mixture dried it hardened into "what may be called the 'fruitcake' of these poor children of the desert." To Bryant and the Mormon colonists that followed him to the Great Basin, eating insects revealed the poverty and ugliness of the region's native inhabitants. The Indians' diet summed up their wretched existence. Yet the Euro-Americans ensured their own misery by refusing to enjoy the few sources of easy calories available in the Great Basin. The colonists adhered to an energy policy of reproduction. Instead of adapting to their surroundings, they struggled to reproduce the calorie sources they left behind. They fought to grow the food they liked to eat in an environment filled with fast-adapting rivals who quickly developed a taste for the Mormons' comestibles.[8]

The colonists declined the food the West handed them, but the region's aboriginal residents devoured the energy grown by the Saints. The Great Basin adapted to the Mormons faster than they adapted to it. Wolves ate imported livestock, bears attacked cornfields, and native groups raided horse herds. The conquerors bled calories. They fed everyone but themselves, and they turned to God and wolf folklore to reverse this unnatural order.

As soon as the Mormons announced their presence in the Salt Lake Valley in 1848, the residents of the Great Basin began exploiting them. On winter nights, reported Thomas Bullock, wolves "made things hideous with their continuous howls," and the teeth through which these dreadful moans passed soon touched the hindquarters of livestock. In March, Salt Lake City's High Council assessed the state of the settlement's cattle: "Our expectations as to the number of teams we should send back [to Winter Quarters] in the spring are somewhat clipped from the loss of cattle by mire holes, springs, wolves and Indians, also." The crickets arrived a few months later. In June 1848 Isaac C. Haight described the infestation of the Mormons' plants. "The crickets," he wrote, "have destroyed some of the crops and are still eating the heads of the grains as soon as it heads out." The situation grew so dismal that "many of the Saints begin to think of leaving the Valley for fear of starvation." The survival of the Mormon colony depended on keeping its food out of the jaws and pincers of aboriginal pests, and the Latter-day Saints deployed their hunters, their children, their communities, and their God to defend their cuisine.[9]

Divinely inspired gulls solved the colonists' insect troubles. "There must have been thousands of them," wrote John R. Young in June 1848, "their coming was like a great cloud; and when they passed between us and the sun, a shadow covered the field." The massive flocks from the Great Salt Lake swept the cricket hordes before them, leaving enough grain for the colony to survive its crucial first year. The gull incident became the founding myth of Mormon Utah. A last-second miracle, the birds' intercession confirmed not only the Saints' status as a chosen people but also their ability to select the right gathering spot. The Great Basin was the Promised Land, and, while he would continue to test them, the Lord would not let a plague of locusts destroy his pilgrims.[10]

Wolves escaped the hand of God to be cast down by the trigger fingers of vengeful mortals. During their second winter in the Great Basin, the residents of the Great Salt Lake City organized a community hunt to stop "so much annoyance from wolves howling at night and depredations committed by foxes, catamounts, ravens, and other animals." The colony's men divided themselves into two teams. John D. Lee captained one team, John Pack the other. The captains agreed to bring in a tally of their teams' kill after two months of hunting. The side with more points (large pests like bears were worth more than crows) would enjoy a dinner and dance hosted by the other side.[11]

On March 1, 1849, Lee and Pack gathered at Thomas Bullock's office to total their scores. The counts were impressive. Lee's team destroyed 84 wolves, 65 foxes, 4 eagles, 130 magpies, and 340 ravens, while Pack's hunters shot 2 wolverines, 247 wolves, 151 foxes, 10 mink, 5 eagles, 377 magpies, and 558 ravens. This triumph for all those humans who savored bread and beef, however, soon degenerated into a spat. Lee, protesting that only a portion of his team's kills had been brought in, wheedled a four-day extension out of the hunt's referees. He came back with a tally that included 2 bears, 783 wolves, and 1,026 ravens. The dispute heated up as each side accused the other of inflating body counts and employing Indians to perform most of the hunting. The dance and dinner never took place. Instead of bringing order, the 1849 vermin hunt exposed the colony's fault lines.[12]

The winter of the vermin hunt, the Mormons' second in the Basin, proved more unsettling than the first. The snow drifted higher, and so did the piles of dead cattle. After Christmas, bands of Utes raided the settlement's herds. While the militia battled raiders, Brigham Young fought back the gold rush. The discovery of gold at Sutter's Mill in 1848 attracted thousands of fortune seekers from around the globe, and many Utah colonists wanted to try their luck in the diggings. Young saw California as moral quicksand. The gold fields, he argued, "would do nothing for" the migrants except give them time for "idleness, drunkenness, or riding horses to death, instead of laboring to prepare to raise grain." Now that his people had arrived in Utah, Young tried to stop additional migrations, seeing physical mobility as a threat to the church's survival. Snowed in, surrounded by predators and horse thieves, their social bonds strained by the pull of easy money, the Salt Lake Valley settlers could have used a rousing communal event in the winter of 1849, but the wolf hunt only daubed more woe on a bleak season.[13]

Today a gull statue decorates Salt Lake City's Temple Square, but no artwork commemorates the great vermin hunt of 1849. The absence of a bronze heap of crow claws, eagle skulls, wolf skins, and bear paws in the sacred locus of Mormondom is not surprising. It was a ghastly scene, a pile of dismembered bodies that exposed the fractiousness of the pioneer community. Still, while the vermin hunt had none of the grace of a miraculous winged intervention, the events did share a common outcome. Neither settled the Mormons' pest problems. Energy thieves continued to attack the immigrants' food, and the Utah Saints continued to declare victory over the Great Basin's noxious beasts even though their foes never surrendered.

In 1868 Brigham Young attended a Pioneer Day celebration in Provo. John Nuttal entertained the crowd with a song, "'Tis Utah's Natal Day," written by Samuel Jones. The ditty included a verse about settlers and pests:

FIGURE 15 Gull monument in Temple Square, Salt Lake City.
Courtesy Denver Public Library Western History Department.

We'll not forget today,
To applaud the pioneer,
Who stared grim famine in the face,
Met trails without fear,
And served the crickets, wolves, and snakes
That once resided here
With notices to quit the vales of Utah.

In June 1870 the *Salt Lake Herald* ran an advertisement that challenged the
past tense of Jones's song. "The most effectual way," read the ad, "to destroy
grasshoppers [is to] buy your custom made boots and shoes at Dunford and
Sons Mammoth Shoe and Hat Sale." The sound of exoskeletons mashed beneath soles of bug-squishing boots contradicted the conquest melodies sung
on Pioneer Days. The Saints wanted to commit their struggles with crickets,

wolves, and snakes to history. After decades of hardships, they wanted a peaceful and permanent home. The Basin's pests, however, did not fade into history. They bit back. The Saints answered with new methods of destruction. They reclassified some opponents as they eradicated others. They discovered that language could extinguish unwanted lives in ways miracles, hunting competitions, and insecticidal footwear could not.[14]

The Mormons killed thousands of wolves. In 1850 the General Assembly of the State of Deseret passed a bounty of "three dollars for each large mountain wolf" and "one dollar for each small prairie wolf." The next year Utah's auditor (the government name change reflected the region's admittance as a territory of the United States) reported an expenditure of $2,233.00 "for sundry Wolf certificates." Wolf bounties claimed nearly 15 percent of the territory's $16,021 budget. Only the 1850 Indian wars ($3,457.87) cost more. The bounties' expense alarmed Brigham Young. In his 1851 governor's address, Young asked the legislature to repeal the wolf bounty law. The county governments could pay for scalps if they wanted, but the territorial government was through with the skin trade.[15]

Mormon bounty hunters were so deadly that they nearly bankrupted the territory. Two factors explain their proficiency. First, they owned powerful firearms and aimed them well. The Saints had been collecting rifles and training with them since the dark days of Joseph Smith's murder. Second, they targeted large wolves. The higher bounty on "mountain wolves" encouraged hunters to shoot big canines. These animals, however, may have kept the region's coyote population in check. Wolves grow bigger and travel in larger packs than coyotes. When coyotes intrude on wolves' territories, they usually die. Utah hunters may have created as many "wolves" as they destroyed by helping opportunistic coyotes invade wolves' territories.[16]

The Mormon pioneers were not taxonomists. They acquired a size-based canine categorization scheme on the Great Plains and applied it to the Great Basin. Brush, loafer, or prairie wolves belonged on the smaller side of the size gradient, while timber, mountain, or "large gray wolves" resided on the big end. Slighter wolves—females, yearlings, animals glimpsed at a distance —could easily be categorized as brush or prairie variants, just as a robust coyote could be mistaken for a timber or mountain wolf. Euro-American naturalists and explorers were just beginning to use the Spanish term *coyote* to describe the species of western canids that lingered between foxes and

wolves. The naturalist Thomas Say first employed the name in 1823 for speci-
mens he collected in Nebraska. The Mormons, however, lumped every wild
canine into a familiar category. Thus all doglike predators in the Great Basin
were wolves, but only for a while. The Latter-day Saints soon discovered that
if they wanted to rid their Zion of the infernal beasts that had been harassing
them since Illinois, they would have to rethink their categories. Coyotes liked
the changes the Euro-Americans made in their home. Indeed, they responded
to the colonists' destruction of wolves by mounting their own conquest of
North America. Before 1900 no coyotes lived east of the Mississippi River.
Today, they prowl the suburbs of Boston.[17]

Compared with wolves, with their matinee-idol charisma, coyotes seem
miscast as conquering heroes. They have puny skulls with sharp facial features; they yip-yip instead of howl; and they feed on a buffet of medium- and
small-sized beasts instead of restricting their diet to the mightiest herbivores.
Because they are food generalists, coyotes require neither large nor permanent packs. Sometimes they form groups to kill deer and calves, but these
cadres remain transient and permeable. Whereas wolves despise unknown
rivals, coyotes warm to strangers quickly. Their social malleability, coupled
with their variable diets and reproductive prowess (juvenile coyotes reach
sexual maturity at age one; juvenile wolves at twenty-two months), has made
coyotes a formidable counterpunch to ecological imperialism.[18]

In Utah, Euro-American colonists met a wild canine species with the
diet and the procreative exuberance to withstand losses by gun, trap, and
strychnine bait. In 1888 the state legislature resurrected Utah's vermin bounties, and these records combined with county documents spotlight the amazing resiliency of coyotes. From 1888 to 1895 Utah's state auditor collected
bounty reports from eighteen counties. Neither systematic nor comprehensive, the reports offer only a glimpse—albeit a striking one—into varmint
killing in turn-of-the-century Utah. In eight years Utah hunters turned in
4,055 coyote scalps. The height of the destruction was 1890 (1,146 coyotes
taken); and the low was 1889 with 105 rewards claimed. Bounty records from
Cache and Wasatch Counties track the death toll into the twentieth century.
Between 1909 and 1921 Cache County officials recorded 3,007 coyote deaths,
while Wasatch County tallied 4,934 from 1911 to 1930. Coyote populations
endured terrible losses, yet they managed to coexist with Euro-American
predators for eighty years.[19]

Wolves, on the other hand, faded. If the high number of coyotes killed by Utah hunters merits a raised eyebrow, the pitiful number of wolves slain warrants an ogle of wonder. The 1890s state auditor's records included only fifty-one wolves. Wasatch County paid bounties for thirty-six wolves, and not a single wolf entered the bounty book in the Cache County Courthouse between 1909 and 1921. Three sources, two sample decades, 11,926 dead coyotes, and 87 dead wolves: these numbers describe a canine environment far different from the one portrayed in 1850 territorial legislature. That year, Utah spent $2,233.00 on bounties for two kinds of wolves and nothing for coyotes. Thirty-eight years later, wolves were nearly gone from the records and coyotes had overrun the Great Basin.[20]

The prime culprit for wolves' fall and coyotes' ascendancy was language, not violence. The Utah colonists dropped the canine categorization scheme they had picked on the Great Plains. The question is not why the Mormons killed more of one species than another but why they stopped calling smaller doggish predators "prairie wolves" and start calling them "coyotes." They could have stuck with the "prairie wolf" designation and continued their running battle with a species both familiar and symbolically resonant. Instead, they chose to adopt a new category for smaller canines and abandon the bête noire that had followed them from Nauvoo to Salt Lake City.

Pioneer hardship tales can help explain why Utah colonists turned to a linguistic trick to escape an old adversary. Lorenzo Clark arrived in Salt Lake City in 1853, a few months after his first birthday. As a child Clark worked as a herder, looking after cows with the other neighborhood boys from early spring to late autumn. One evening, the boys heard a "wolf howl and, thinking it was a coyote," they walked toward the animal with their hunting dogs, Lion and Bess, in the lead. As they approached the howler, Lion and Bess "put their tails between their legs and ran for home as fast as they could." The boys faced "the largest wolf [they] ever saw" alone. The animal eyed the quaking prepubescent gang and "in no hurry" slowly retreated. The boys, knowing better "than to run," fought the urge to sprint all the way home. From that day forward, Lorenzo Clark "knew a wolf's howl from that of a coyote."[21]

Clark recounted his wolf incident in a short memoir published by the Daughters of Utah Pioneers (DUP). The predator belonged to a scrapbook of childhood memories that included ceaseless work—hauling wood and water, running errands, feeding chickens and pigs—fights with bugs, and living on two pieces of cornbread a day whenever the insects bested the family. In pioneer Utah, a boy learned to "kill crickets and grasshoppers on sight with sticks" as well as to tell the difference between a wolf and a coyote. But recognizing the nuances of canine vocalizations became a quaint skill as the pioneer generation grew up. While Utah herders might still hear a howl well into the twentieth century, they need not fear the howlers. Only coyotes survived the pioneers.[22]

The DUP preserved Clark's anecdote and countless other pioneer childhood stories to remind readers of the historic sacrifices that made their lives easy. The Mormons created their past through the hardship tales. They marked time, erecting a boundary between historical suffering and contemporary comfort. Thomas Irvine summarized the narratives' moral in 1924. "All of us lived pretty skimp sometimes," Irvine told the Logan *Journal.* "But for all our poverty we were cheerful and happy and had lots of fun in a way. We were all on a level in the same condition, and I think there was more of a spirit of sociability than there is now." Hard times may strengthen social bonds, but nostalgia for hard times rallied communities without subjecting their members to hunger, violence, and persecution.[23]

The nomenclature shift from prairie wolves to coyotes helped the Latter-day Saints feel secure in a landscape that battered and upset them. The pioneers' anxieties threatened to pull their community apart. "We found it somewhat difficult," wrote Patriarch John Smith in 1848, "to establish order, peace and harmony among the Saints after so much mobbing, robbing, and traveling through a dreary country." Instead of feeling cheerful, the residents of Salt Lake City "became restless, not having much faith, the fear of starving, etc. came upon them." The Great Basin tested the immigrants' patience. They wanted food and solace. If Utah could not provide these necessities, perhaps California could. Brigham Young fought to keep his flock from dispersing in search of greener Zions. To hold their movement together, the Saints needed a sense of history, and the eradication of wolves announced the end of the pioneer era.[24]

But the prairie wolves would not die. They not only clung to their Great Basin niche, they expanded it as large wolves perished. In order to terminate their relationship with real and symbolic wolves, the Mormon colonists had to learn to tell a *Canis latrans* from a *Canis lupus*. Lorenzo Clark explained the difference: pioneer boys ran toward a coyote and away from a wolf. Coyotes were small and safe; wolves might eat you. The Latter-day Saints reached an accommodation with coyotes that, given their history, was impossible with wolves. After using real and metaphoric wolves to strengthen their social bonds from Nauvoo to the Great Basin, the Mormons consigned the beasts to history in a similar effort to safeguard their communities. They adapted to the canid realities of the Great Basin to create the illusion of progress and prevent their movement from splintering; they changed in order to stay the same. They slaughtered coyotes in the thousands to protect their sheep and poultry, but they abandoned the notion that all doglike predators must die to make Utah a paradise. The Mormons claimed their wolfless Promised Land even as the animals formally known as prairie wolves continued to nibble the colonists' bounty.

PART FOUR THE FEDERAL GOVERNMENT

CHAPTER NINE

Annihilation and Enlightenment

THE CULTURAL EXTINCTION OF NORTH AMERICAN

WOLVES

THE SHOT ECHOED off the rimrock. The bullet tore an artery, clipped a lung. Perhaps the hurtling metal demolished a kidney. Whatever the injury, it dropped the wolf. She lay in the dust sucking air. Her killers walked up and watched her die. As the high desert sunshine played across her corneas for the last time, she bled out. Many years later, this scene, filtered through memory and infused with symbolism, would help save wolves from oblivion. That bullet whistling through the New Mexican air brought death and insight.

In his 1944 essay "Thinking Like a Mountain," Aldo Leopold traced the birth of his environmentalist land ethic to the killing of a wolf. Trained in forestry at Yale University, Leopold spent the early part of his career trying to manage the game herds in New Mexico's Gila National Forest. Predators had no place in U.S. Forest Service lands. USFS employees destroyed the animals in order to maximize the number of deer, a resource coveted by recreational hunters. In "Thinking Like a Mountain," Leopold recounted how he and a group of rangers happened upon a pack of wolves chasing a deer. The men fired on the pack from a distance. They hit the leader, a female, and Leopold "reached the old wolf in time to watch a fierce green light dying in her eyes." The sight changed him. Young and "full of trigger itch," he had assumed "that because fewer wolves meant more deer, . . . no wolves would mean a hunters' paradise." "But after seeing the green fire die," he "sensed that neither the wolf nor the mountain agreed with such a view." Killing predators endangered Edens rather than creating them. Wolves protected the mountain's foliage by stomaching the overabundant leaf nibblers.[1]

Extinction and enlightenment: the drama in Leopold's wolf story comes from the pairing of these warring notions. He was not the first writer to match a fade into eternity with the dawn of an idea. Throughout American history, dead animals inspired reflection. In 1653 the historian Edward Johnson noted the transformation of New England from "hideous Thickets" where "Wolves and Beares nurst up their young from the eyes of all beholders" into "streets . . . full of Girles and Boys sporting up and downe." In 1821 Timothy Dwight described a Connecticut environment in which "hardly any wild animals remain[ed] besides a few small species of no consequence." Neither Johnson nor Dwight felt bad; they celebrated the disappearance of wolves and bears. Nonetheless, both understood the eradication of a species as a denouement worth pondering.[2]

In 1855 Henry David Thoreau contemplated New England's mammal-deficient woods. "When I consider," he wrote, "that the nobler animals have been exterminated here,—the cougar, panther, lynx, wolverene, wolf, bear, moose, deer, the beaver, the turkey, etc., etc.,—I cannot but feel as I lived in a tamed, and, as it were, emasculated country." Thoreau's sentiments would have puzzled (appalled) Edward Johnson and Timothy Dwight. They saw a world improved by the death of feral creatures, whereas Thoreau read their absence, in the words of William Cronon, "as a sign of declension in both nature and humanity." Yet the transcendental hermit and the upright Protestants shared more than any of them would care to admit. All three used the local extinction of charismatic mammals to reflect on the consequences of ecological imperialism. European colonization altered the New England environment. Johnson and Dwight enjoyed the renovations; Thoreau abhorred them. But all three exploited the cultural moment of extinction to pass and to dramatize their judgments.[3]

From 1900 to 1950 American wolf hunters cleared the animals from every region in the temperate United States in which a human could grow a marketable plant or animal. (Remnant packs survived in a swath of forest in northern Minnesota and Michigan.) This achievement, however, required that livestock owners accept a partner they would come to resent. To eradicate the last wolves, state governments and livestock growers associations in the American West joined forces with the federal government. The predator-

FIGURE 16 Wolf in leghold trap. Courtesy Denver Public Library Western History Department.

control unit in the Department of Agriculture's Biological Survey took over the job of wolf killing. Instead of vengeful farmers with their pit traps or local nimrods with their hounds and axes, degree-toting bureaucrats hired professional wolf hunters to deliver the final blow.

The ramifications of this switch in killers at the climax of European agriculturalists' centuries-long struggle with wolves were not immediately apparent. Except for the wolves, everyone seemed happy. Domestic beasts frolicked in predator-free landscapes; livestock owners delighted in the profitable offspring conceived by frolicsome beasts; and the federal exterminators enjoyed the favorable publicity dead wolves generated. They needed the advertising. Western congressmen, state governments, and livestock associations all wanted the Department of Agriculture to destroy vermin, but none of them wanted to pay for the service. The predator-control unit survived on a small appropriation from Congress and voluntary contributions from state governments and growers associations. In order to secure this cash flow, the bureaucrats publicized the unit's handiwork. They displayed wolf and coyote pelts in department store windows and at state fairs, and, like the agriculturalists before them, the biologists and hunters in the predator control program told stories about the animals they killed. Unlike the farmers, however, the civil servants depicted wolves as doomed-yet-heroic desperados. They created laudable vermin to make their department look good, and, by infecting wolf lore with nostalgia, the government men began to erode the cultural consensus that underwrote Americans' loathing of wolves.

The heroes of the bureaucratic folktales were the last wolves. Prodigious killers, these outlaws bit livestock and swallowed fame. They slaughtered hundreds of domestic animals and ascended to the heights of celebrity when ranchers and cowpokes tried to punish them for their dietary transgressions. The animals' shiftiness was legendary. Ranchers swore that the wolves knew how far a rifle bullet could travel and that they danced just out of reach. Cow herders set steel traps and dumped strychnine-laced hunks of beef along game trails, but the last wolves detected every snare, sniffed every trick. Defeated, livestock owners turned to the Department of Agriculture. The federal government sent out hunters. These men and women (three female hunters were on the federal payroll) specialized in predator eradication. Trained and equipped by the Biological Survey, the government hunters received a salary and were assigned districts. Among the stipulations in their contracts: accept no bounties. State and local bounties actually preserved the smartest and most destructive wolves. Apprehending a celebrity wolf took months of tracking, trap setting, and waiting. Amateurs refused to expend all that unpaid time trailing a wily outlaw when the skins of dimmer animals brought the same reward. The government hunters plugged the hole in the bounty system through which the worst offenders passed, and their duels with the last wolves provided fodder for a new kind of wolf tale.[4]

The men in charge of federal predator control would have vigorously denied that their outfit was part of a legend-generating folk group. They possessed a vivid self-image, but it was hardly folksy. They considered themselves enlightened professionals, fighting both noxious beasts and inane practices. They disliked wolf bounties, they displayed little patience for outlandish travelers' tales, they did not torture captive wolves with small dogs, and they certainly never smeared bear grease on one another at the office Christmas party. It is odd, therefore, that these sophisticated professionals authored such corny wolf stories. The names of the last wolves exemplified the bureaucrats' romanticism. Before the federal takeover of predator control, the wolves in American folktales remained anonymous. The government's wolf slayers broke this tradition. The last wolves sported homespun titles like Old Whitey,

Old Three-Toes, Old Lefty, and Old Rags the Digger. The "old" epithet held a double meaning. It signaled both affection—as in "good ol' boys"—and advanced age. Due to their superior intelligence, the celebrity wolves loped into their golden years. Wizened, they battled time as well as human civilization, capitalist property relations, American colonization, and modern state bureaucracies. The civil servants' fondness for the wolves arose from the animals' impossible situation. They were endearing because they were doomed.

This brings us back to the cultural moment of extinction. Like Aldo Leopold, Edward Johnson, Timothy Dwight, and Henry David Thoreau, the storytellers in the Bureau of Biological Survey seized upon the death of animals as an opportunity for reflection. Standing over the bodies of the last wolves, the bureaucrats could do nothing but ruminate. The inexorable forces of private property, territorial expansion, and human progress had cornered the wolves. Their fate was inescapable. Freed from the responsibility to act on their sentiments, the wolf killers expressed tender feelings that would have shocked their forebearers. They saluted the last wolves. Sure, they devoured property, but they did so with enthusiasm and panache. The animals had to die, but the humans felt nostalgic about their passing.

This was the cultural logic that guided the birth and the spread of the last-wolf folktales. Numerous and often confused, the motives behind these stories included the installation and promotion of a federal bureaucracy. The deaths of the last wolves publicized the work of the Department of Agriculture's predator-control unit. But there was a price to be paid for good advertising. The authors of the last-wolves stories wallowed in the cultural moment of extinction long before wolves reached the biological point of no return. In union with state governments and livestock associations, the predator-control unit pushed wolves to the brink of elimination in the continental United States by 1950. Yet as early as the 1920s, civil servants were spinning stories about doomed-yet-heroic outlaws. They assumed the inevitability of wolves' demise, and this assumption liberated the humans to feel wistful. The nostalgia, however, when coupled with the scientific studies of wolves performed by the same government bureaucracies, laid the groundwork for a new ambiguity in Americans' relationship with wolves. Nostalgia and ecology worked like water frozen in the crags of a rock. Eventually, they broke a solid mass of antiwolf sentiment into blocks of mixed emotions. Americans completed their journey from unanimity to ambiguity with an ironic twist:

the federal bureaucracies that once shouldered the task of wolf extermination now served as the species' chief protectors.

Like grim Siamese twins, extinction and colonization marched across North America in tandem. The arrival of European colonists signaled the departure of a parade of wild species. Great auks, monk seals, bison, Townsend buntings, passenger pigeons, Tecopa pupfish, Carolina parakeets, Goff's pocket gophers, Louisiana voles, Labrador ducks, and Penasco chipmunks vanished. Many more species experienced drastic cuts in their numbers. The list of threatened and endangered creatures reads like a catalog of waste and destruction: American crocodiles, green sea turtles, northern spotted owls, snail darters, grizzly bears, cougars, humpback whales, ocelots, Dismal Swamp shrews, black-footed ferrets, gray and red wolves, all nearly gone. Europeans hit the beaches and animals perished in the millions. The die-off was real, and the reverberations of this loss of life continue to haunt the continent.[5]

The colonization of North America was a profoundly zoological event. The muscles of dead beasts nourished European bodies as the skins of slain mammals filled European boat holds. The disappearance of native fauna eased the dispersal of European people, livestock, and plants across the continent. The conquest dripped animal gore. While visions of God, country, and treasure motivated the invaders' actions, the bones of aboriginal creatures serve as reminders of the physicality of the colonial experience. Any story of colonization must account for the flesh in the humans' teeth as well as the thoughts in their heads.

The story of North American extinctions combined biology and ideology. Culture influenced extinction in two ways. First, the European colonists belonged to a culture that divided the living world into categories. They organized an array of creatures with similar morphological, behavioral, and genetic characteristics into distinct orders, families, genera, species, subspecies, and varieties. The survival of a species depended on how European migrants categorized them, as well as how harshly they treated them. Second, colonists used biological extinctions as opportunities for cultural introspection and innovation. Before their group's brush with eternity, wolves had to be conceptualized as a group, and the story of wolf categorization reveals the impossibility of separating biological extinctions from cultural definitions.

The classification of organisms is an intellectual briar patch. Arguments for and against definition schemes—whether the species concept is natural or imagined, whether species evolve like individuals or groups, whether sub-species and variations are meaningful distinctions or not—have grown ever more tangled and thorny over centuries of debate. Biologists still use the categories deployed by Linnaeus in 1751, but they do so more out of habit than shared conviction. The controversies over taxonomy reflect a duality at the heart of evolution: the notion of difference emerging from sameness. Linnaeus based his species classification system on the idea of group essences. Sets of organisms, like tigers and mulberry bushes, remained stable and co-herent because God distributed the essence of tigerdom and bushiness ac-cording to his own unwavering plan. Darwin's theory of a few species evolv-ing through natural selection into many species undermined the certainty of the Linnaean taxonomy. Instead of strict boundaries separating organisms, groups mingled and merged on their frontiers. Instead of uncovering divine essences, scientists imposed categories on spectrums of changing beings. Instead of basking in peaceful conformity, scholars have been wrestling over the definition and significance of biological classes ever since.[6]

Wolves illustrate the dilemmas of animal classification. They have a long history of shifting shape, size, color, and behavior. Fossils record the species' two hundred million–year journey from an ancestral protomammal. These beasts, called *Creodonts,* rummaged through the early Mesozoic, epochs be-fore the dinosaurs. As time passed, doggish creatures surfaced in an array of morphological guises. *Dissacus,* a mammal living forty million years ago, ran on hooves but snapped jaws filled with teeth similar to wolves'. Ten mil-lion years later, a creature appeared with wolflike teeth and a weasel's bendable torso. This animal, *Cynodictus,* produced several genetic lines, including those of wolves and raccoons. *Tomarctus,* a Miocene mammal, looked more hyena than wolf, but today's wolves and foxes evolved from this creature. *Tomarctus* disappeared ten million years ago. A final spurt of evolutionary exuberance three hundred thousand years ago created two North American wolf species —gray wolves and dire wolves. *Canis dirus,* larger than *Canis lupus,* ranged from Oregon to Indiana. Dire wolves vanished during the wave of Pleis-tocene extinctions that emptied the continent of its spectacular megafauna. Scientists have discovered the remains of dire wolves along-side those of wooly mammoths and saber-toothed cats in Rancho La Brea's tar pits.[7]

Wolves, bears, civets, raccoons, foxes, dogs, hyenas, coyotes, and cats evolved over millions of years from a common ancestor. This shared history reflects the magic of descent through modification: organisms are at once distinct and connected. Few people would mistake a bear for a house cat, but only sex and time separate a grizzly and a tabby. The relatedness of species makes their differences meaningful.

Taxonomists struggle with the duality of sameness and variation all the time. After Darwin, they have been asked to draw boundaries that bind as well as divide. Categorizing organisms over vast time spans using a scatter-shot record of fossilized impressions is tough enough, but pigeonholing living creatures brings as many challenges. While maddeningly incomplete, evolutionary histories at least point out meaningful variations. Every step along the journey from *Creodont* to wolf, for example, represented a success-ful adaptation. At one time, beings with doglike teeth and weasel-like bodies out-reproduced, say, catlike dogs with goatlike feet. Yet the value of canine carnassials and bendable torsos—the characteristics that defined *Cynodictus*—is apparent only in hindsight. Biologists confront a living world that varies horizontally through space as well as vertically through time, and they are constantly being asked by politicians, environmental activists, and property owners to indicate which differences matter.

North American wolves provide a case study in the shifting definitions of meaningful variance. Classifiers have segmented the continent's wolf population into as many as twenty-four subspecies. These geographic sub-groups represent variants on a theme. All North American wolves behave in similar ways. They all hunt in packs, form affective bonds, and erect so-cial hierarchies. They create and defend territories. They disperse, hunt, fight, mate, play, and snooze. They sometimes look different, however, and cosmetic variations form the boundaries of most wolf subspecies. For example, nearly all wolf taxonomists, whether enthusiastic splitters or unapologetic lumpers, draw a subspecies divide along the Mississippi River. The eastern wolves, *Canis lupus lycaon,* differ in size and color from their Great Plains brethren. Smaller in stature, lighter in color, the western wolves, *Canis lupus nubilus,* are also distinguished by their close relationship with one prey species: bison. Nineteenth-century travelers noted the difference between the eastern and the western subspecies, calling the Great Plains variant "loafers" or "buffalo wolves." Early taxonomists based their organization schemes on these anec-dotes, and more recent classifiers, armed with DNA tests rather than travel narratives, have retained the *lycaon* and *nubilus* boundary while rejecting most other North American subspecies. The slight differences between tim-ber and plains wolves, they theorize, may indicate two separate invasions of

North America by Eurasian wolves. *Nubilus* arrived later than *lycaon*, pushing the older settlers east and south. Perhaps the cosmetic differences that struck American colonists in the nineteenth century were remnants of an ancient wolf conquest.[8]

Yet these subspecies boundaries may be more significant to history than to biology. Wolves are chronic boundary crossers. Dispersers break down physical and social barriers, traversing hundreds of miles to find unguarded territories, willing mates, and friendly hunting partners. Wolves' wanderlust creates taxonomic havoc. Geographic isolation promotes speciation. Splintered into insular units, the closest of relatives can move along such vastly divergent evolutionary paths that they not only look different from one another but wildly unattractive to one another as well. When the former members of a species diverge through geographic isolation to the point where they can no longer have sex, combine genes, and produce offspring, then the groups have reached an evolutionary milestone. One species has become two. In North America highly mobile wolves prevented evolutionary splitting. Instead of a landscape dotted with isolated and distinct gene puddles, wolves swam in an ocean DNA that stretched across a continent. Sex and travel kept wolf populations vital and related, but the genetic mixing that served the animals so well tormented their human classifiers. Wolves mated across subspecies boundaries, and, sometimes, they traded DNA with neighboring dogs and coyotes too. Their dips into these gene pools marked wolves as transgressors of a higher order.[9]

Species boundaries throw up reproductive obstacles only a few organisms try to circumvent. In general, different species refrain from sexual intercourse. This may seem obvious. It is plainly true that mice and musk oxen, pelicans and pigs, humans and hamsters possess neither the appetite nor the equipment to mingle chromosomally. Closer relatives, however, sometimes connect accidentally across less precipitous species boundaries. The social and biological restraints that keep species from intermingling sometimes break down. Horses and donkeys often swap genes, and their progeny exemplify the price of such couplings. Horses and donkeys, of course, beget mules, a sterile hybrid. (Actually, only female horses and male donkeys produce these brawny but infertile offspring; male horses and female donkeys produce hinnies, feeble beasts that can sometimes reproduce.) Interspecific fertilizations often end badly, and the production of infertile offspring, stillborn infants, and malformed youngsters halts most amorous adventures across species.

Mating mistakes, however, do have their upsides. Every so often, oddly matched pairs accidentally hit the procreative jackpot: they introduce a gene with a competitive advantage into the world. They produce a baby with a quirk that enhances rather than retards the spread of their DNA. Instead of withering, the hybrid thrives and blesses the entire population with its originality.[10]

Wolves' movements over land and across species boundaries, undertaken for reasons that had nothing to do with DNA, nonetheless helped the animals achieve genetic variation. Over millions of years, the species' wandering paws and roaming passions aided the dispersal of genes. No doubt, wolves' intercourse with dogs and coyotes generated its share of travesties. Just as dispersing wolves risked starvation and dismemberment, coyote-courting wolves risked parenting sickly pups mired in genetic dead ends. But these mating mistakes proved invaluable. Wolves protected their station as one of the Northern Hemisphere's top predators by constantly adapting, and sex with distant relatives was an engine of adaptation. Mixing genes fostered novelty as well as abnormality, and the continual exchange of alleles underwrote the long-term health and geographic success of the species.[11]

Scientists, however, discovered wolves' penchant for hybridization only after the animals had entered the twilight of their golden age. European colonization dethroned wolves as the continent's top predator. As wolf numbers plummeted, small populations clung to existence in safe havens—frosty places unsuitable for agriculture and "wild" places under the protection of federal governments. These refuges forestalled extinction, but their isolation raised serious problems. Wolves need space to hunt, establish territories, and disperse. Long-range travel is essential to the species' survival: rambling not only alleviates population pressures, it aids genetic variability. With European colonization a species that had grown accustomed to milling about a continent was crowded onto patches of land surrounded by hundreds of miles of hostility. Individuals with new genes rarely left or entered these islands of tranquility, and this procreative isolation could prove as deadly to the last wolves as snares, bullets, and strychnine pellets.[12]

As human predators, livestock fences, and four-lane highways stymied the exchange of genes across space, wolves fell in with relatives distant in time. Wolves and coyotes split from a common ancestor a million years ago. While different in size and social behavior, the species can reproduce, and wildlife biologists have observed the conditions that foster their reunions.[13]

Coyote alleles have appeared in DNA tests conducted on gray wolves in

Ontario's Algonquian Provincial Park. John B. Theberge, an ecologist who has studied the Algonquian wolves for more than a decade, describes the park as "a fortress held by wolves, under siege by coyotes." The larger predators keep their smaller relatives out of the park, but the packs living just outside the refuge's boundaries have been overrun. They mate with coyotes and then disperse into the park, spreading the coyote DNA. Smaller, friendlier to strangers, and practitioners of coyote-like "split-pack" hunting, the interbred perimeter wolves become more *latrans* and less *lupus* every year. Theberge theorizes that spatial fragmentation and human predation explain the inter-mixing on the park's borders. Logging roads and commercial trappers have kept wolf populations small and isolated. As the large predators disappeared from the region around the park, smaller predators took their place. Coyotes invaded the wolves' territories. Smart and fecund, coyotes have overtaken wolfless spaces throughout North America. Coyotes have thrived in colonial landscapes, and the packs on the fringe of Algonquian Park may be trying to exploit the smaller animal's resilience. An emergency reserve of novel DNA, coyotes may give the besieged wolf population time to rebound. If the wolf numbers do bounce back, Theberge imagines that the canines will re-turn to their old arrangement. Wolf packs will attack the slighter interlopers, and the coyotes' amorous forays will stop. If, however, the perimeter wolves fail to recover, then the park could eventually become home to a new species, a hybrid wolyote.[14]

The prospect of coyote genes swamping remnant wolves alarms many of the charismatic predators' human supporters. Hybridization would tarnish wolves' attractive physique, diminish their hunting prowess, and disrupt their social structures. The smaller canines have displayed a talent for surviv-ing in colonized environments. If wolves hope to inhabit a world filled with national parks, logging trucks, and suburban backyards, they need to become more like coyotes. Hybridization may help wolves survive, but interspecific mingling violates the cultural values twentieth-century humans have attached to the taxonomic categories "wolf" and "coyote." Americans marked wolves for oblivion early in the century. Seen as doomed, the one-time wasters and destroyers gained a measure of goodwill as remnants of wilderness in an in-dustrial age. They also received legal protection as an endangered species. Neither the court of law nor the court of public opinion offered coyotes much respite. Unlike wolves, they extended their numbers and expanded their territory in the face of fierce opposition by farmers and ranchers. They too obtained better press as North American societies became more urban and industrial, but coyotes never approached wolves' popularity, a disparity in charm explained in part by the larger predators' closer proximity to extinction.[15]

Hybridization threatens wolves' purity as cultural symbols as well as their integrity as genetic entities. With the behavioral ticks and physical features of their less-glamorous relatives, wolves may lose their cachet as icons of freedom, nobility, and wilderness. They may also lose their legal protections. Coyote sex could be wolves' ruin. The question is: should we feel bad about this? Species die all the time. Wolves' evolutionary past is replete with both endings and beginnings. Vaguely mammalian organisms gave way to creatures with weasel torsos that gave way to animals with hyena heads. The wolf is but a morphological and behavioral way station in a journey that began millions of years ago. Who are we to judge the course of evolution?

We judge because our sense of ourselves—our culture—compels us. Alone among the planet's organisms, humans impose both categories and values on their fellow living creatures. Dividing organisms into groups is a uniquely human preoccupation. Some naturalists argue that the categorization of living beings forms the basis of human cognition. Human brains learned to think, they assert, by wrestling with the differences and similarities between animals. This fascination with pigeonholing appears early in childhood, when, as toddlers, humans learn to sort the pigs that go oink from the cows that go moo. The handiwork of evolution fascinates us. We are transfixed by the sameness and variation animals display. But humans not only organize creatures into groups, they invest these clusters with values. Some animals are smarter, nobler, or more useful than others, and, of course, the most value-laden group boundary of all is the one humans draw to segregate themselves from the rest of the planet's creatures.[16]

The story of colonists and wolves in American history challenged people's understanding of natural order. Wolves continually transgressed geographic, biological, and taxonomic boundaries. Their activities exposed human classification schemes as imperfect descriptions of a living world. Evolution created spectrums of organisms at once distinct and connected. Humans imposed categories on these spectrums, erecting divisions that highlight differences and downplay similarities. The focus on difference reflected the values humans place on biological categories. Throughout their tenure on the planet, humans have displayed a preference for clear and robust species boundaries, and they have punished creatures that refused to stay in their groups. Take bats, for instance. Bats' association with all kinds of infernal nastiness is due in part to the creatures' nebulous position betwixt birds and rodents. Pigs' reputation for uncleanliness arises from an ancient boundary transgression. Unlike their cloven-hoofed brethren who ate only grass, pigs devoured a rainbow of edibles from honey to excrement. They deviated from their class of animals, a grouping some people believed God established. Thus several cultures deemed the animals unholy and the eating of their flesh taboo. Among its many purposes, taxonomy is a cultural project that reinforces people's notions of their place in a natural order. Homo sapiens classify organisms as much to understand themselves as to understand nature, and the history of wolves in America shows how the values people attach to animal categories can change with their self-conceptions.[17]

In the early twentieth century, Americans began to reform their opinions about wolves. A new ambiguity crept into their vision of the beasts. Agriculturalists continued to emit animosity toward the predators, but as the century progressed, there were fewer agriculturalists. The United States became more urban and industrial, and huge forces transformed Americans' relationships with animals. A host of intermediaries inserted themselves into a beast's journey from the field to the plate. Butchers, veterinarians, stockyard workers, truck drivers, steroid salesmen, and maitre d's lengthened a process that once spanned the ax handle farmer Jones swung to turn Bossy into dinner. Urban Americans lost the tactile experience of raising food. They neither heard the squeals, nor smelled the offal, nor saw the blood, nor tasted the rage when predators swallowed a cherished investment. A seismic shift in Americans' daily interactions with animals underwrote their changing ideas about wolves.

The transformation of the United States from a rural into an urban society helped save wolves from extinction. But this transformation only created a sympathetic constituency, an audience open to new ideas. Someone had to mobilize this crowd, introduce them to a different kind of wolf. Beginning in the 1920s, one of those people, along with wildlife biologists like Adolph Murie and natural philosophers like Aldo Leopold, was a government bureaucrat named Stanley Paul Young.

Born and raised in Astoria, Oregon, Young joined the Bureau of Biological Survey in 1917. Hired as a trapper, he destroyed predators and rodents in southern Arizona. Smart, politic, and credentialed (he held a master's degree in biology from the University of Michigan), Young rode the range for only a short while. In 1919 he won a desk job and spent the rest of his career pushing papers instead of poisoning animals. In 1921 he oversaw predator control in the Bureau's Colorado-Kansas District. In 1928 he moved to Washington, D.C., and took over as the chief of economic investigations. In 1934 he became head of game management. Two years later, he reached the apex of his career, as chief of the Division of Predator and Rodent Control in the Bureau of Biological Survey. To vermin throughout the United States, Paul Stanley Young was the high priest of obliteration. He served in this post for two years. In 1939 he transferred to the research department, and his career wound down there.[18]

All this time, Young wrote. He wrote articles for academic journals and stories for hunting magazines. He wrote how-to manuals for killing vermin and memoirs of his youth along the Columbia River. He wrote books; he wrote bulletins. Anyone who leafed through the *World Book Encyclopedia* in the 1950s searching for information about furry mammals sampled Young's work. He composed the entries for bears, beavers, capybaras, chinchillas, chipmunks, deer, gophers, hedgehogs, lemmings, marmots, porcupines, rabbits, and woodchucks, among others. His bibliography included three opuses—*The Wolves of North America*, *The Puma: Mysterious American Cat*, and *The Clever Coyote*—as well as a host of minor works including "Señor Yip Yap" and "If Waterfowl Could Read." Young's literary endeavors yielded nearly a dozen books and more than a hundred articles, leaflets, reviews, and editorials.[19]

Young published his first book in 1929. Cowritten with Arthur H. Carhart, *The Last Stand of the Pack* was a collection of wolf stories from his tour as head of predator control in Colorado. Young teamed with Carhart, an experienced author, to reach a popular audience. Carhart served as the adjectives man, peppering Young's bureaucratic prose with florid descriptors. He also added plot and drama to Young's accounts, borrowing liberally from the inventor of the heroic-yet-doomed-outlaw-wolf short story, Ernest Thompson Seton. While eerily similar, Seton's stories differed from Carhart's and Young's in one respect: they sold. *The Last Stand of the Pack* hit the market like a wet sponge tossed against a brick wall. Instead of breaking through to the masses, the book sank along with a host of commercial enterprises during that bleak economic time.[20]

Largely unread and wholly unoriginal, *The Last Stand of the Pack* pales in comparison to Young's later contributions to wolf literature. His *Wolves of North America* (1944) stands as the first history of the species' relationship with Euro-Americans. Others have rightly challenged, revised, and expanded *The Wolves of North America*, but the book remains an important repository of wolf lore and hunting tactics. In contrast, *The Last Stand of the Pack* advanced humanity's understanding of wolves nary an inch. The book misled, exaggerated, and anthropomorphized. It ripped off Seton and the government hunters that actually performed the deeds Young and Carhart romanticized. Yet despite its many problems, we are going to delve deeply into the production of this shallow book.

The stories in *The Last Stand of the Pack* deserve considered attention not for the truths they expose about the nature of wolves but rather for the insights they offer into the culture of twentieth-century Americans. The tales represented the coming together of science and folklore in a modern state bureaucracy, a bizarre coalescence that produced a new species: the sympathetic wolf. Stanley Young did not invent the last-wolf story form, but he did use it to justify and celebrate the work of federal predator control. Young's colleagues at the Bureau of Biological Survey aided and abetted his literary escapades. And their support requires an explanation. Instead of balking at the hackneyed portrayal of wildlife, the college-educated civil servants in a government department dedicated to the rational conservation of animal resources embraced the legends. To understand why these progressive scientists and managers welcomed a vision of nature rooted in fantasy rather than fact, we need to understand the conventions of the last-wolf folktales. We need to visit Lobo, the King of Currumpaw.

Ernest Thompson Seton killed Lobo on January 31, 1894. A few months later, he resurrected the animal in a short story published in *Scribner's Magazine*. Heart-wrenching and credulity-stretching, the tale followed the exploits of Lobo and his pack, an outlaw gang of archpredators who terrorized the rangelands along the Currumpaw River in northern New Mexico. Lobo's pack "scorned all hunters, derided all poisons." As the bodies of cows, sheep, and horses piled up, the bounty on Lobo's scalp grew into the thousands of dollars. In 1893 a friend of Seton's living in the valley asked the writer to try to destroy the wolf. A hunter in his youth, Seton accepted the challenge and trailed the pack for the next year. Lobo refused every bait, avoided every trap until Seton discovered the monster's weakness: love. He caught and slaughtered Lobo's

FIGURE 17 Three tiers of canine predators—coyotes mostly—near Wamsutter in Sweetwater County, Wyoming, 1921. Courtesy Denver Public Library Western History Department.

mate, Blanca. He staked her corpse on a wolf runway and ringed the body with traps. Overcome with grief, the mighty predator, "who never ceased to search for his darling," walked into the ring and four steel mouths closed on his paws. Seton lugged his demoralized captive to camp, and the animal died of "a broken heart" later that night.[21]

Hunters, biologists, and naturalists cringed at the sentimental schlock and anthropomorphic fluff that oozed from Seton's short stories. A pack of critics led by Theodore Roosevelt, William T. Hornaday, and John Burroughs denounced him as a "nature faker." Yet despite the hoopla surrounding Seton's imaginative renderings, his stories did contain some brutally honest moments. A starry-eyed portrayer of beasts, Seton cast humans in less dappled light. In "Lobo, King of Currumpaw," he described the techniques of wolf hunting in accurate and excruciating detail. He recounted the making of a strychnine-laced bait: "I melted some cheese together with the kidney fat of a freshly killed heifer, stewing it in a china dish, cutting it with a bone knife to avoid the taint of metal." He recalled the trap set that caught Blanca: "I killed a heifer . . . cutting off the head. . . . I set it a little apart and around it placed two powerful steel traps properly deodorized and concealed with the utmost care." And he relived Blanca's death: "We each threw a lasso over the neck of the doomed wolf, and strained our horses in opposite directions until

FIGURE 18 Two wolves killed by biological survey hunters
hang from wooden pole on the Diamond Bar Ranch outside
Silver City, New Mexico. Courtesy Denver Public Library
Western History Department.

the blood burst from her mouth, her eyes glazed, her limbs stiffened and
then fell limp." He may have sentimentalized animals, but Seton did not
sentimentalize people. In his world, animals burst with feelings while hunters
operated in an emotional void.[22]

Seton's wolf stories pulled in opposite directions. They were at once

FIGURE 19   Man and two girls among predator pelts. Part of predatory animal catch for January and February 1916. Courtesy Denver Public Library Western History Department.

hardboiled and softhearted, and only the concept of doom kept the narratives from being torn apart by their contradictions like a wolf strung between cow-ponies. Fate justified the wolf hunters' treatment of their prey. Civilization had the animals in its teeth. Cruel or humane, the manner of death mattered little, for the wolves were already dead. Hopelessly out of place in rangelands dedicated to the growing of livestock, their extinction was unavoidable. Seton mustered only a tinge of regret for Blanca's horrid sendoff because her death, however gruesome, was an "inevitable tragedy." So too was Lobo's. After capturing the King, Seton spoke to the prostrate beast: "Grand old outlaw, hero of a thousand lawless raids, in a few minutes you will be a great load of carrion. It cannot be otherwise." He later wrote: "The life of a wild animal *always has a tragic end*" (his emphasis). This sense of doom permeates the last-wolf folktales, and the inevitability of wolves' demise combined with the realistic portrayal of wolf killing explains the stories' acceptance among the civil servants of the Bureau of Biological Survey.[23]

Unlike the generation before them, the conservationists in the USBBS displayed a fondness for sentimental wolf stories. The reasons for their literary tastes were twofold. First, the last-wolf tales advertised the survey's work in predator control much like gangster dramas promoted the FBI's crime busting activities. Wolf stories helped the agency win public, political, and financial support. Second, animal control was a euphemism for drowning, poisoning, shooting, trapping, stabbing, strangling, and dismembering living creatures, many of them cute and fuzzy. Animal conservation was a bloody business, and wolf stories helped mitigate the gore. Government hunters were not stone-cold killers. They felt for the beings they destroyed, but the march of civilization demanded the beasts' removal. The government spearheaded a historic movement—the dispersal of Euro-Americans with animal property across the continent. To denounce predator control was to denounce American progress. The last-wolf stories gave USBBS employees, nicknamed "gopher chokers" by their critics, a moral high ground upon which to stand as the corpses piled up.

The last-wolf legends served the needs of an emergent folk group that included federal bureaucrats, professional wolf hunters, and western stockmen. It may seem strange to characterize this collection of twentieth-century Americans as folk. They wore suits, Stetsons, and cowboy boots, after all, not peasant blouses and clogs. And their ideas were as modern as their garb. Folklorists, however, have long abandoned the Brothers Grimm stereotypes of the folk. Illiterate serfs create and repeat legends, myths, jokes, and songs, but so do college freshmen, professional bowlers, and systems analysts. Any group can generate and transmit lore.[24]

The letters and reports Stanley Young used as sources for the renegade wolf stories in *The Last Stand of the Pack* illustrate the role folk legends played in the formation of a modern social group. The documents show that the last-wolf stories were a collaborative enterprise. Long before he teamed with Carhart, Young accumulated coauthors. Ernest Thompson Seton provided the template for the last-wolf narratives, while government hunters and livestock owners applied this template to the tracks and kills left by remnant wolf packs. The hunters and stockmen transformed their encounters with a biological competitor into stories with beginnings, endings, and messages. Instead of receiving unvarnished accounts, Young gathered wolf anecdotes already touched by active imaginations. He tweaked the stories further, giving shape to tales that promoted group cohesion and expressed shared aspirations. The last-wolf legends were a cooperative invention that helped invent a cooperative. They cemented an antivermin alliance, and they gave this alliance

FIGURE 20 Rancher James Shaw holding female wolf pelt and skull near Thatcher, Colorado, 1922. Courtesy Denver Public Library Western History Department.

an identity. By portraying remnant wolves as doomed-yet-heroic outlaws, the stories placed wolf killers at the cutting edge of history. They improved vast landscapes, securing them for commercial agriculture. They were the executioners of American progress.

Human fingerprints covered the last wolf folktales. A crowd of people manipulated the stories. Stock growers and government hunters singled out certain wolves—usually the ones with the largest or strangest pawprints—for heroic treatment. Stanley Young gathered their reports, blended them into a master narrative, and forwarded them to Washington, D.C., in his monthly reports. Later, he and Arthur Carhart used these reports to create even more fantastic legends. The last-wolf stories grew so outrageous that it is easy to forget that the tales described actual biological encounters. In the early 1920s human predators attacked a series of wolf packs in Colorado. These packs were the remnants of a wolf population that had feasted on the herds of tasty ungulates (bison, antelope, deer) that roamed the plains and plateaus at the feet of the Rocky Mountains. Glimpsing the besieged animals through the fog of legend is daunting. The wolves' human enemies block our lines of sight. Did the remnant packs truly munch livestock at the rate stockowners reported? Did the wolves learn to avoid traps, baits, and bullets? Were these animals extraordinary or desperate? Wrapped in their authors' biases, the folktales offer few clear answers.[25]

The last-wolf legends tell more about the humans who wrote them than about the animals that inspired them. They are best read as cultural artifacts, not ethological observations. Yet separating human fantasies from animal realities is not easy. Biology and culture clung to one another in the legends. The storytellers incorporated wolves' physical characteristics and behavior patterns into their narratives. Indeed, details like missing toes and trap wariness confirmed a wolf's status as an exceptional renegade. These characteristics and behaviors were real, even if the legend makers' interpretation of them tended toward the fanciful. The folktales distorted a biological situation to suit the needs of an emergent social group—the antivermin alliance among professional hunters, western stockowners, and federal bureaucrats. But the legends preserved clues that suggest an alternative history. Instead of doomed-yet-heroic outlaws, the stories portray a species trapped in a corner of fear, pain, and death.

Livestock owners in Colorado trapped, poisoned, shot, and dragged wolves to death long before they turned to the federal government for help in the 1920s. Amateurs killed thousands of wolves in the state, leaving only a few packs on the southeastern rangelands and the western slope of the Rocky Mountains for the government experts to eradicate. Coyotes surrounded these remnant groups. In a typical month government hunters exterminated a dozen coyotes for every wolf they destroyed. Livestock associations and county governments continued to pay huge bounties for wolf scalps, sometimes offering a hundred dollars for an adult and fifty bucks for a whelp. The price on wolves' heads indicated the general belief that large predators, not diminutive coyotes, were responsible for most cattle depredations.[26]

But the lush bounties did not yield outlaw scalps. Amateurs slaughtered litters of pups in their den every spring, but the wide-ranging adults grew harder to catch as they learned to avoid poorly laid traps and clumsy poison stations. These last wolves survived, but they clung to a bleak existence. Den hunters slaughtered the group's future while steel traps and strychnine baits turned their homes into lethal obstacle courses. The animals struggled against constant predation, and their bodies exhibited the toll of this fight.[27]

The last wolves carried the marks of their beleaguered existence on their extremities. Newhouse traps claimed toes, paws, tails, and teeth. Old Lefty, the largest wolf killed during Young's time as head of predator control in Colorado, lost his foot escaping from a steel trap in 1913. Following his recapture in 1921, Lefty's pursuers inspected his old injury, finding "a well formed stump [that] was protected by a tough layer of calloused skin." The missing foot, Young reported, "might have been amputated by an up to date surgeon of repute." In the spring of 1922 H. A. Roberts, a government hunter, destroyed a pack north of Grand Junction, Colorado. The group's leader was Bigfoot, the Terror of Lane County. Roberts trapped Bigfoot's cadre after discovering their den. He crawled into the hole and grabbed the pack's youngsters. He slaughtered them and extracted their scent glands for an attractant. The puppy-scented traps snagged Bigfoot and his mate, an alpha female with three legs. Like Old Lefty's truncated limb, the she-wolf's stump exemplified the relentless harassment the last wolves endured.[28]

The missing toes of other famous outlaws served as their badges of persecution. Old Three Toes and the Unaweep Wolf left digits in traps. Their damaged paws enhanced their legends. Mangled pads left distinctive tracks, and stockmen and government hunters read unique prints as indicators of an animal's fortitude, intelligence, and leadership. A creature that snapped off a toe to escape a trap truly valued her liberty, and the jaws of Newhouse traps taught harsh lessons. The near-death experience "educated" the wolf; she would be hard to catch again. Smart and iron-willed, the animals with clipped toes must have been the leaders of their packs. Thus trail-reading humans turned injured animals into legendary outlaws.[29]

Ranchers and trappers built their understanding of wolves on slim evidence. They rarely spotted the beasts. They never saw Bigfoot command his troops or hamstring a calf. They read his tracks and kills and extrapolated. Pawprints and kill sites inspired leaps of imagination, and the tracks of female wolves roused especially broad jumps. Old Three Toes' impressions left "no doubt" that she was Old Whitey's mate and that her consequent tryst with a ranch dog signaled her loneliness following Whitey's death. The Unaweep Wolf displayed "the mother instinct of protection—caution—etc., to a greater degree than any female taken by us in this district." Tracks left near the body of a poisoned pup signified her motherliness. In *The Last Stand of the Pack*, Carhart and Young described the Unaweep Wolf's reaction to her fallen offspring: "Whining, upset beyond comprehension, torn by fear and mother love, Unaweep moved cautiously toward her dead son." All this drama from pawprints left on a dusty trail.[30]

The guiding emotions in the last-wolf folktales were grief, anger, vengeance, and love. Intended to cultivate feelings of loss and longing, the stories preyed on the sentiments of nostalgia. But the last-wolf episodes described in the hunters' correspondence and Young's monthly reports to Washington, D.C., highlighted another emotion. They reeked of fear, not sadness. As we have seen, fear was a vital force in wolves' lives. Warning howls fostered anxiety, creating space between rival packs. Subordinates cringed under the glare of alpha animals. Fear arranged wolf spaces and societies. The storytellers were right; wolves were emotional creatures. But the legend makers buried the sentiments that wolves actually expressed under torrents of human melodrama. The last wolves did not die brokenhearted, longing for open fields and meaty prey. They died afraid, biting at steel contraptions or vomiting strychnine. Far from wistful, the deaths of the last wolves were spasms of terror that capped lifetimes of anxiety.

The death of Old Whitey captured the blind panic that accompanied a last wolf's termination. Government hunters snared Whitey near Bear Springs, Colorado, in the fall of 1920. The hunters knew they had a monster when they spied the drag marks. (Wolf traps were not pinned to the ground. Instead, trappers attached a dragline, a long chain with a cumbersome object—sometimes a log, usually a grappling hook—at the end of it. The drag would tangle in the vegetation, exhausting the animal and preventing long chases.) The tracks led into a cedar thicket. There a small bush had caught the drag hook, sparking a "terrific battle." "It looked as though a small elephant had been picketed temporarily at this point." Whitey had pummeled the shrub, tearing its branches and gnawing its trunk. The ferocious effort broke him free, but Whitey did not run far. The hunters found him a hundred yards from the bush in a patch of torn-up dirt. He was "securely fastened with each front foot in a trap, badly tangled."[31]

Gray hair covered the ground where Whitey had rolled and rubbed trying to extract himself from the traps. The scene reminded Stanley Young of a hog scaling, so many follicles littered the earth. Skin protruded from patches of missing fur. Blood seeped from the animal's mouth. Whitey, Young wrote, had "fought the traps in such a terrific manner that his teeth were badly broken as a result." The hunters lassoed him, wired his muzzle shut, and carried him alive to the ranch of Jim Shaw, the local stockman who had requested the federal wolf hunters. Whitey volunteered little entertainment: "His spirit was broken and he refused during these days all offer of food and water—

his expression was one of absolute doom. At the end of the third day Whitey died evidently from nothing other than a broken heart."[32]

The last wolves' killers endowed the animals with a host of emotions, talents, and virtues. The beasts embodied strength, cunning, determination, ruthlessness, and leadership. The story of Old Whitey, however, undermined the predators' legendary bravado. Whitey was terrified. The traps snapped and he panicked. He demolished foliage, shredded his coat, and cracked his teeth in wild fear. Following his capture, Whitey grew passive. Like the wolf John Josselyn brought into his Maine living room in the 1660s or the wolves cornered in the Ohio Valley farmer's pit trap in the 1820s, Whitey sank before his conquerors. He advertised his submission, but the hunters wanted to dispatch a worthy foe rather than execute a cringing subordinate. They interpreted the gestures to fit their vision. They saw stoicism in the beast's passivity, not fear. Unlike Josselyn or Audubon's farmer, Stanley Young read wolf meekness as a sign of comprehension rather than cowardice. At the moment of their passing, the last wolves realized the truth of their situation. They could not live in a world with cows. They were doomed to extinction.

Ranchers, hunters, and bureaucrats authored the last-wolf folktales to build an antivermin alliance with a purpose loftier than destroying vermin. Stanley Young hoarded renegade wolf anecdotes to impress western livestock owners and state legislators. The federal government's partners in "cooperative control" required constant prodding to keep their wallets open. The last wolves served this purpose beautifully. They devoured property and evaded capture, exposing the impotence of amateur hunters and the scalp bounties that motivated them. Only professionals with government training, equipment, and sponsorship stood a chance against the outlaws. And Young made sure Colorado stockmen and politicians knew this. He issued press releases and solicited letters of recommendation from ranchers. Following the killing of Old Lefty, for example, the "Stockmen of Castle Peak Ranges" wrote, "It is a big relief to us to know that 'Old Lefty' is a thing of the past. . . . We breath a sigh of keen satisfaction, and fully realize the capture of 'Old Lefty' was truly a job for you government men who study out these things and apply methods no ordinary amateur can touch." Young's mission as an agent of a fledgling bureaucracy was the redirection of local funds. He wanted livestock associations and county governments to stop paying bounties to amateurs and start contributing to the salaries of professional hunters. The last-wolf

FIGURE 21 Old Three Toes, legendary renegade wolf,
caught. Courtesy Denver Public Library Western History
Department.

legends justified the federal takeover of the resources agricultural communities
dedicated to predator eradication.[33]

But the stories did more than hasten the decline of amateur wolf killing.
They linked the death of noxious beasts to the advancement of humanity. The
bodies of slain wolves marked the end and triumph of American colonization.

Young's comments on the death of the Greenhorn Wolf demonstrated how the last wolves embodied the close of a colonial epoch:

> Here lay a big symbol. The West of the old days was passing. A new day was coming. In it there would be no naked red men riding in warring parties toward white settlements. There would be no big herds of bison that spread for acres over the open prairies. The Pony Express was but a memory, a tradition. The old stage coach was now crowded out by high-powered gas wagons. The longhorn cow had given way to grade and purebred white-faces. Even the old type of man that trod the open spaces was giving way to a business man of the New West.

"And in all this," Young concluded, "the gray wolf had no place." Predacious canines, Native Americans, buffalo, mounted letter carriers, unruly cattle, and tough men found no refuge in a modernizing America. Caught in a wave of extinctions, wolves succumbed to history.[34]

As the length of Young and Carhart's roll call of doom suggests, Euro-American colonists found ample opportunities to mull over many types of extinctions. They buried peoples, landscapes, towns, ages, and social processes. Frederick Jackson Turner interred the frontier in 1890, while James E. Fraser sculpted his vision of Indian termination, a bronze statue of a mounted warrior slumped over the edge of oblivion, in 1915. James Fenimore Cooper bemoaned the passing of the forested wilderness of upstate New York in the 1820s, while Edward Abbey lamented the destruction of the desert canyons along the Colorado River in the 1960s. Euro-Americans colonized and pondered the wreckage of colonization nearly simultaneously. They sought out moments of awesome finality—points in time that signaled the downfall of a species, a culture, a place, or a historic age—and they used them to mark time and express regret. Often these fits of grief and reflection included a hard lesson. The ruminators grasped the significance, value, or beauty of the thing lost only at the instant of its passing. The last wolves can help us understand these bouts of thoughtfulness at the crossroads of extinction and conquest.[35]

Stanley Young and Arthur Carhart luxuriated in the extinction moment, and their death scenes often featured the acquisition of wisdom at the last second of life. The brains accumulating the insights, however, belonged to the wolves, not the humans. Bill Caywood shot Rags the Digger as the monster wolf

charged toward him. The animal, moving fast despite having a trap clamped
to one leg, dropped at the hunter's feet. As "life flickered feebly," the wolf
rose one last time "to reach the feet of wolfer Caywood, his master." With
his snout nuzzled against Caywood's boot, the outlaw finally admitted the
truth: humans were his masters. Other wolves realized the absurdity of resist-
ing their fate as the darkness loomed. Caught in a trap, Three Toes quit fighting and "lay panting, as docile as a dog" after seeing that "fate, inevitable,
certain, unavoidable, had followed [her] for months." Old Lefty discovered
the meaning of fear as H. A. Roberts wired his muzzle shut, while Bigfoot
"acknowledged defeat when he was finally trussed up." The Greenhorn Wolf
learned to recognize the "ripping and tearing" sensation of strychnine as the
"bitter death potion" brought her the knowledge of extinction. The "last loner
wolf" in Colorado stole a final glimpse of "the old range of her ancestors
spreading for miles in every direction without one vestige of her kind in that
whole vast empire." With that thought, the "soul of the wolf left the stiffening
body and galloped away into that farther land where there are no traps, no
guns, no poisons, no enemies." And, one hopes, no sappy biographers.[36]

For Young and Carhart, death brought the knowledge of inescapable
loss. The government men glimpsed the wisdom in the dying wolves' eyes,
and the glassy orbs foretold the hunters' own extinction. The modern West
had no room for professional killers, be they men or beasts. The government
hunters approached the end of their usefulness with each scalp taken. Sharing
the same fate, the hunters empathized with their foes. The last-wolf legends
concluded not with an animal's death but a hunter's lament. "I kinda' hate
to do it," Young and Carhart have H. A. Roberts say after killing the Bigfoot's
three-legged mate, "They're just the knowin'est brutes on four legs. Sometimes
they're almost human . . . actually, I sometimes feel sorry for them, wipin' out
whole families this way." In the end, death and "knowin'" produced regret.[37]

Young and Carhart exploited the local extinction of a charismatic predator
to reaffirm American progress and express remorse for the necessity of wip-
ing out entire families of animals to ensure human advancement. They
thought this combination of sentiment, doom, and brutality would sell books.
The dramatic re-creation of the last wolves' enlightenment represented the
authors' attempt to introduce the lessons of the bureaucratic folktales to a
mass audience. Beginning in 1925 Young and Carhart gathered together
nine last-wolf tales, dressed them up in flowery prose, and tried to sell them
as a package to magazines and book publishers. In 1927 the stories began

appearing in *Red-Blue Book* magazine. Sears and Company published the stories as *The Last Stand of the Pack* in 1929. By this time Young had moved to Washington, D.C., as head of the Biological Survey's economic division. Carhart remained in Denver, where he labored as a landscape architect, a wilderness advocate, and a weekend writer. The pair's correspondence has survived, and their letters express their hope and disappointment as a topic they had imagined hot found a chilly reception.

Born as narratives to promote cooperation among ranchers and civil servants, the last-wolf folktales did not appeal to a broader public. By 1932 Young's annual residual check totaled four dollars and five cents, and Carhart joked: "Guess we should have devised some hot sex stuff to cram in somewhere." Young and Carhart never found out whether an audience existed for literature depicting frisky interactions among ranchers, hunters, and wolves, but they proved that American book buyers had little appetite for collections of stories about livestock owners bringing in professional killers to slaughter wild animals.[38]

Carhart blamed the publisher for the book's failure. "Sears," he wrote, "could have pushed *The Pack* to a better sale. . . . They have never put out sufficient publicity." But Carhart's market analysis was as overblown as his writing style. Young had ensured that *The Pack* had quite an elaborate publicity campaign. He had requisitioned the skulls and hides of the last wolves stored in Denver. With the addition of some enlarged photographs and a few Newhouse traps, he assembled a traveling bookstore-window display. Sears paid for the shipping and the insurance, and the remains of Old Lefty and Rags toured the country in support of a product that celebrated their deaths.[39]

The Last Stand of the Pack had plenty of "whoopee," Carhart's term for media promotion. What the book lacked was a fan base. The last-wolf folktales, with their realistic violence and persistent fatalism, struck a chord with ranchers and federal employees, but eradicating animals in the name of progress made less sense to people who lived in cities where no livestock roamed. In a society growing ever more urban and industrial, fewer people inhabited landscapes or engaged in occupations troubled by wolves. Few people knew or repeated community hunting rituals and wolf legends. Indeed, by the early 1920s the agriculturalists who continued to battle wolves delegated the fight and the lore to professionals. The federal takeover of wolf killing was a by-product of the enormous historical trends that were transforming Americans' relationships to the animals. Many Americans still loathed

FIGURE 22 Canine carcasses and car. Courtesy Denver Public Library Western History Department.

wolves; others sympathized with the marauders. Worse for Young and Carhart, a sizable chunk of the population neither cared nor thought about the animals. Wolves no longer touched their lives as thieves or symbols.

Readers' responses to *The Last Stand of the Pack* reflected the changes in American society. A. E. Gray, a friend of Young's in Oklahoma City, "devoured" the book "with the same avidity" as a wolf swallowing "a [poisoned] magpie bait," but he wondered why the Greenhorn Wolf had to fall for the strychnine lure "after all the years she had evaded traps and poison." Carhart worried about readers' desire to see a few outlaws lope into sunsets rather than buried in shallow graves. "We have a barrier against these stories that is plumb awful," he wrote in 1927. "In animal stories the hero animal should solve his problem and continue to live more happily after it is solved." People "like to see the animal succeed and like to see man and animal working together harmoniously." Instead, Young and Carhart offered impasses resolved in the most unharmonious fashion imaginable. Government hunters brutally killed the character that readers identified with and then posed for a snapshot with the bodies. In one rejection letter, the editor of *True Western Stories Magazine* found the photographs Young sent with a draft of "Old Whitey" too gruesome: "The pictures are a bit morbid including the skulls and carcasses." For centuries Euro-American colonists beheld wolf scalps and heads as tokens of conquest worthy of display and celebration. In 1927 the same items made some Americans uneasy.[40]

Young and Carhart unleashed their wolf stories on a fractured audience. Their vision of wolves succumbing to history entertained some Americans, but the book-buying masses stayed away. The federal government, however, nurtured another storyteller who succeeded where Young and Carhart failed. In 1944 Aldo Leopold penned a wolf story that not only sold paperbacks but helped launch a social movement as well.

"Thinking Like a Mountain," a short essay sandwiched in the middle of *A Sand County Almanac,* distilled Leopold's environmental philosophy to a tale that combined death and insight. As Leopold's biographer Curt Meine recounts, the author reluctantly included the story to symbolize his own intellectual journey. The tale was an allegory of personal enlightenment. It was also a last-wolf legend. While you would need a bus to transport the historians who have investigated the development of Leopold's ecological ideas, a skateboard would suffice for the number intrigued by his use of bureaucratic folklore. But "Thinking Like a Mountain," a fable of a new thought entering a young head, was not itself an original idea. Leopold borrowed the story form from Ernest Thompson Seton and the alliance of sport hunters, ranchers, and civil servants that sought the elimination of wolves through cooperative predator control. An early advocate of wildlife conservation, Leopold had helped invent the concept of cooperative control. His ecological she-wolf sprung from the same intellectual and occupational environment that produced Stanley Young's doomed renegades.[41]

Watching the "fierce green fire" die in the she-wolf's eyes, Aldo Leopold rejected the conservationist notion that equated the destruction of "useless" animals with progress. The wolf was not a renegade hopelessly out of place in human landscapes. Wolf hunters were the outsiders, disrupting ecological systems in which predators played a vital role. Leopold inverted Young's wolf stories, but he accomplished this flip with wolf legends and scientific ideas that grew out of federal agencies. "Thinking Like a Mountain" arose from the same government bureaucracies and conservationist traditions the essay critiqued.

A publicity stunt from the 1920s summarized the utilitarian philosophy of animal control Leopold rebelled against. The predator elimination unit in the Bureau of Biological Survey sponsored traveling promotional exhibits that featured animal body parts. Wolf, coyote, and mountain lion skins hung from black felt panels. Skulls of predators and rodents sat on tables next to steel traps of various sizes. In Arizona a display included panels of photographs and captions that summarized the agency's two-pronged mission. A gopher panel showed the destruction of a useless beast, while a jackrabbit panel depicted a useful animal's transformation into a stylish commodity. (Viewers saw the rabbit's skin ripped from its body and remade into a flapper's hat.) Eradicate the useless; encourage the useful: this was the message of the display and the goals of federal animal conservation.[42]

Aldo Leopold believed in this mission for most of his professional life. A pioneer in game management, he labored to maximize the number of useful animals (beasts hunters could shoot) and minimize the useless ones (creatures who ate the beasts hunters enjoyed shooting). During his career in the United States Forest Service, he advocated the destruction of wolves, bears, and mountain lions. As the historian Susan Flader explains, Leopold's attitudes toward predators changed as his confidence in game management dipped. Manipulating environments to favor utilitarian animals did not work. Groups of herbivores were as manageable as hopped-up movie stars. Wild animal populations erupted, crashed, and whipsawed independent of human efforts to control them. To his credit, Leopold admitted his mistakes and searched for the deeper causes of wildlife fluctuations. This search led him to his "land ethic." "A thing is right," he wrote in A Sand County Almanac, "when it tends to preserve the integrity, stability and beauty of a biotic community. It is wrong when it tends otherwise." By changing his definition of conservation, Leopold ended his career (cut short by a heart attack in 1948) with a far different mission from the one with which he began.[43]

Whereas Leopold's intellectual journey arced from the conventional to the innovative, Stanley Young's thought processes chugged around a familiar circuit. In 1970 Macmillan published Young's final book, The Last of the Loners, posthumously. The book dug up the Colorado wolves for one last encore, this time without Arthur Carhart. Beyond the disappearance of their coauthor, the wolf tales had changed little in fifty-one years. Once again, the government hunters brought down the cunning renegades, and as the professionals mopped up the predators, a sense of loss crept into their work. When the Greenhorn Wolf—the last last wolf—perished, so did the period of American history that needed tough men to master wild beasts.[44]

Stanley Young identified with the doomed men and animals in his stories. An office dweller for most of his career, Young portrayed himself as a hunter. He wore the two years he spent killing coyotes in New Mexico as a badge of honor, authenticity, and identity. The book jacket to *The Last of the Loners* introduced him as "Stanley P. Young, himself a government hunter, [who] was personally involved in the necessary control of certain renegade wolves." Young also identified with wolves. The animal was his personal icon. A gold wolf letterhead decorated all his correspondence. In 1954 he printed a small booklet containing a list of all his publications. The bibliography included articles on gophers and books on mountain lions, but an image of a wolf graced the pamphlet's cover. He admired the animals. Unlike the amateur wolf slayers who preceded him, Young did not hate wolves. "No reason is apparent to me," he said in a 1947 radio interview, "why they should not always be tolerated and even given a permanent place in the fauna of the continent." Wolves could live unmolested in the remoter regions of North America, he theorized. Still, in the areas where predators clashed with human interests, "there, undoubtedly, rigid control might have to be applied." Civilization and predation were antithetical. Young "supported" wolves, but, unlike Leopold, he struggled to imagine a place for them in a modern world.[45]

The persistence of Young's opinions is astonishing given the scientific research that passed under his nose. To accomplish its mission, the Bureau of Biological Survey sponsored thousands of animal studies. Biologists examined eternal questions like how to feed weaned minks and safeguard commercial blueberry farms from herring gulls. They investigated the use of table salt as a curative for cannibalism among game birds in captivity, and they probed the mysteries of the care and feeding of pet chameleons. They sought out the best traps, poisons, and hunting techniques for destroying injurious animals, and they searched for the keys to the propagation of beneficial ones. Stanley Young served in the bureau's research department from 1939 until he retired in 1961. For ten years he was the department's head. He oversaw the studies of blueberry defense and chameleon nurturance, and, every so often, he encountered information that could have rearranged his understanding of the world. If he had been so inclined.[46]

In 1955 the regional director of the Fish and Wildlife Service in Juneau, Alaska, wrote Young to pass on an eyewitness account of a wolf pack killing a caribou. A bush pilot working for the FWS landed his plane "near the big sand dunes out of Kubuck." He spotted five wolves chasing a "large adult caribou." The wolves fanned out and quickly pulled down the beast. "They did not hamstring the animal," the pilot reported, "but rather attacked it in the neck and head." Here was evidence that contradicted one of Young's cardinal beliefs: that wolves chewed heel tendons to disable their prey. But wolves' hunting practices intrigued Young less for the light they shed on ecological relationships than the pall they cast on the predators' future. Hamstringing signaled the animals' doom. It was part of wolves' repertoire of cruelty that included bobtailing (gleefully biting the tails off prey), udder munching, and evisceration. When the predators applied their dastardly techniques to livestock, they "signed their [own] death warrant in the blood of cattle." Contradictory evidence never led Young to question his understanding of wolves. Why should it? His world moved in fixed grooves. Wolves brutalized herbivores, humans exercised control, and history lurched forward. Stanley Young's fatalism hamstrung his curiosity.[47]

Yet while his preference for hunting lore over fieldwork crippled his wolf research, Young's legends contributed to the survival of North American wolves as much as any scientific study. They freed Americans to feel nostalgic for a despised animal. The bureaucratic folktales returned continually to the moment of extinction. The awesome finality of termination liberated wolf killers to try out new ideas and emotions. They expressed admiration and regret without having to alter their behavior to match their sentiments. Convinced that impersonal and irreversible forces had dragged the animals toward the precipice, the humans applauded the last wolves as they shoved the beasts into the darkness.

And Young was hardly the only American writer fascinated by dead animals. The promise of oblivion attracted artists of all kinds. Extinction inspired people to shed old ideas and audition new ones without the onus of acting on their inventions. The artist arrived to observe, reflect, and report on death, not prevent it. They might celebrate or criticize the causes of extinction, but they could neither advance nor remedy a historical process that had run its course. Yet despite this fatalism, the cultural representations of dying species did affect the organisms they portrayed. The extinction moment intrigued artists so much that they often showed up early. They anticipated the death of species and mourned their departure prematurely. Wolves experienced this phenomenon, and it may have saved them.

Stanley Young predicted the death of wolves in the 1920s. He hoped the animal would survive in wild areas "where its presence is not in conflict with human welfare." But when airplanes opened the remotest Alaskan tundra to sport hunters, the likelihood of wolves' finding a landscape uninteresting to humans dropped to zero. As people multiplied, cities expanded, roads grew, and planes flew, the spaces wolves might inhabit dwindled. By 1941, when the United States government stopped destroying wolves on federal lands for lack of targets, the legends seemed prophetic. Colonizing humans had pushed wolves to the fringes of the continent. Packs survived on ice in Canada and Alaska, but temperate North America was a *Canis lupus* wasteland. Hundreds of thousands of wolves had died, clearing the way for cornfields and shopping malls.[48]

Yet on the way to continental dominance, a strange attitude adjustment befell segments of the colonizers. Young city dwellers embraced wolves as symbols of their alienation from nature. On the brink of extinction, wolves became the poster beasts for an environmental movement. Aldo Leopold's "Thinking Like a Mountain" demonstrated wolves' usefulness as icons of nature. Leopold combined nostalgia and ecology. He mixed loss and longing with diversity and interrelatedness, turning the bureaucratic folktales on their heads. Humans were out of place in the wolves' world, not the other way around. The predators belonged to a natural order. They ate herbivores, protecting habitats from overgrazing. Aggressive and unthinking humans, on the other hand, disrupted ecological systems. If they wanted to restore balance to a land knocked off-kilter by centuries of colonization, then people had better find a place for wolves.

Leopold's last-wolf story located the germ of his ecological thinking in the "fierce green light" dying in the wolf's eyes, and his story of personal enlightenment has blossomed into an origin myth for the modern environmental movement. But the story describes an ending of a life as well as a start of an idea. An animal's death brought on Leopold's fit of self-scrutiny. Like so many Americans before and since, Leopold saw extinction as a moment of truth. Alas, knowledge gained from death was a cheerless prize. For Leopold, the fading green light symbolized the end of nature, wildness, and balance. In order to comprehend their true value, the forester had to watch them die in the wolf's eyes. Leopold's "land ethic" would continually strive to restore the natural harmony lost at the violent moment of its birth.

Reintroduction

ON APRIL 24, 1995, Chad McKittrick, an underemployed lover of guns, beer, and bear hunting, shot an animal he hoped was a wolf outside of Red Lodge, Montana. McKittrick and his associate, Dusty Steinmasel, hiked to the canid sprawled in the mud. The scene—two hunters standing over a beast leaking from a high-caliber wound—qualified as a cliché in this portion of the American West. Montanans had been pumping bullets into wild things for more than a century. This killing, however, elicited none of the customary reactions. Instead of "nice shot" or "he's a keeper," the situation warranted an exclamation more along the lines of "oh, shit."[1]

Two red United States Department of Fish and Wildlife tags dangled from the wolf's ears. The black alpha male labeled R-10 (r for red) belonged to the "experimental-nonessential population" of eight Canadian wolves released in Yellowstone National Park in January 1995. R-10 had wandered out of the preserve with his mate, R-9, in search of a denning site. The fight over reintroducing wolves into Yellowstone had raged for years, and the communities around the park buzzed with wolf talk. McKittrick and Steinmasel knew the red tags signaled trouble, and Steinmasel nearly convinced his associate (they, he insisted, were not friends) that they might avoid thousands of dollars in fines and jail time if they reported the incident immediately to a Fish and Wildlife agent. This was good advice. The "experimental-nonessential" designation voided the harshest penalties of the 1969 Endangered Species Act, giving hunters and livestock owners a pass if they killed a wolf by accident or in the act of slaughtering a domestic animal. All McKittrick had to do was notify the proper authorities within twenty-four hours, say the shooting was an accident, and he could have escaped without punishment. But he had other plans.

He wanted a trophy and would risk federal prosecution to keep the wolf's skull and hide. The men hauled the cadaver into the woods. They strung the body up with bailing twine, sliced off the skin, and lopped off the head. The choice remains of R-10 traveled to McKittrick's cabin in a garbage bag. Steinmasel took charge of the animal's radio collar, tossing the device in a road culvert near his home. The still-transmitting collar (broadcasting in "mortality mode" since the wolf had stopped moving) led the Fish and Wildlife officials to Steinmasel. He led them to McKittrick. The killer of R-10 received a six-month jail sentence and a ten thousand–dollar fine. He also won a prominent place in Red Lodge's Fourth of July parade, waving to the crowd on horseback, attired in a T-shirt that declared his allegiance to the "Northern Rockies Wolf Reduction Project."[2]

The transplanting of Canadian wolves onto American soil unleashed a flood of news reports, articles, books, and documentaries. (The writer, rancher, and conservationist Thomas McNamee tells the story of R-10's murder in his book about the first year of the Yellowstone reintroduction.) The predators sparked a debate over Americans' relationship to their environment, their national parks, their hamburgers, and their government. The Environmental Impact Statement that preceded the reintroduction garnered 160,000 written public comments: 100,000 for the plan, 60,000 against. Mammoth environmental organizations like the Sierra Club and the National Audubon Society entered the fray. The plan infuriated local ranchers, and conservative politicians like Wyoming's Alan Simpson and Idaho's Helen Chenoweth used rural outrage to blast the Endangered Species Act. As Chad McKittrick discovered, the days when shooting a wolf in the American West required as much forethought and carried as many consequences as blowing one's nose were gone. At the close of the twentieth century, the animals existed in a whirlwind of lawsuits, policies, jurisdictions, agencies, ideologues, and media.[3]

Far from fading into oblivion, wolves staged a comeback in the waning decades of the millennium. Americans had degrees of latitude to thank for their second chance at living with the animals. Exterminated in the rangelands and farming regions of the United States, the species survived in the frosty reaches of Canada and Alaska and in the portions of northern Minnesota and Michigan that hugged the international border. In 1995 Canada hosted a *Canis lupus* population that numbered between 50,000 and 70,000. An additional 6,000 to 7,000 wolves lived in Alaska, and 2,000 inhabited the Great Lake states.[4]

Bringing predators back to ecosystems overrun with herbivores may improve habitats, giving browse perennially clipped by elk teeth time to recover. But reintroduction will not save a species. North American wolves are not dead; they are just overwhelmingly Canadian. Wolf restoration is a symbolic act as much as a biological necessity. Few Americans would endure the monetary expense and civic trauma of wolf reintroduction to protect wild shrubbery. A majority, however, would open a checkbook and shout down a neighbor to safeguard their wilderness fantasies, to listen to a howl from their Winnebago, or to wash the animal blood from their notion of a civilized society.

Americans have many good reasons to support and oppose predator reintroduction, few of them scientific. Despite a mountain of hard data, the wolf controversy has dredged up and often turned over symbols, myths, and behaviors that would have struck an ax-wielding nimrod or a trench-digging Puritan as familiar. A sixteenth-century resident of Providence, Rhode Island, for example, would have understood Chad McKittrick's decision to keep R-10's skull. Providence wolf killers displayed their victims' heads in public after collecting their bounties. The head symbolized the community's resolve to punish livestock thieves and control their environment. It was a token of power. A jobless laborer in a Montana town racked by the fickle economies of ranching and tourism, McKittrick collected mementos of power. R-10's skull entered a stockpile of masculine totems—guns, skins, and antlers—that helped a small man feel big.

Both the opponents and advocates of reintroduction exhumed old wolf symbols, folktales, and rituals to bolster their cause. The battle over the species' future turned into a fight over America's past. As the sides debated wolves' proclivities—Did the animals lust for bovine blood? Or were they shy recluses who ate wild meat whenever possible?—they asked a second round of human-related questions. Were the pacifiers of agricultural landscapes heroes or villains? Did wolves' crimes deserve extreme retribution? Or did the United States go too far in its predator-control efforts? The restoration of wolves resurrected Americans' history of colonization.

Transporting sedated animals across international boundaries to satisfy an endangered-species law signed by Richard Nixon may seem a peculiarly modern activity, but wolf reintroduction linked the past and the present in ways that help illuminate Americans' long colonial history. The story of wolves spotlights the violent interaction of three chronologies—biological, folkloric, and historical. Wolves reveal the vital connection between natural history, cultural history, and the history of European colonization, and if the animals are to have a future in the United States, Americans need to reckon with the grip that genes and folktales, domestic animals and communal rituals still hold on their attitudes and behaviors.

After skinning R-10 and hacking off his head, McKittrick and Steinmasel left the animal's torso in the woods. Shot, dismembered, abandoned in a heap of baling twine and body fluids, R-10 epitomized the brutal sameness of wolf killing in American history. Whether shot by a 7mm Ruger or brained by a log, wolves not only perished in great numbers throughout American history, but they died in some of the most atrocious ways imaginable. Euro-American colonists trapped wolves to protect livestock, expand markets, combat evil, and collect bounties. Some of their motives were comprehensible. But once they caught their animal foes, why did they beat, bait, torture, and humiliate them? What explains the pleasure so many found in wolf abuse?

One answer: human nature. They may smile, hug, rescue kittens, write thank-you notes, and attend support groups, but people are vicious at the core. Human beings' track record offers little hope for a soft center of goodness. Too many wars, famines, massacres, holocausts, and acts of daily unpleasantness mar the species' past. Wolf killing confirms people's knack for generating pain and suffering. From John Josselyn's wolf baiting in the 1690s to ranchers waving pelts like battle flags in the 1990s, extreme violence defined Euro-Americans' relationship with wolves. Yet while rife with cruelty, the history of humans and wolves in America was not predetermined by the essential character of either species. Neither had a core, heinous or cheery. Rather, the history demonstrated the contingency of people's morality and wolves' behavior. The methods and meaning of wolf killing traveled through folktales and hunting rituals. People transported their hatred in stories and traditions, not their souls.

Travelers' tales and circle hunts epitomized the ways culture preserved and spread animosity toward wolves. The stories and the rituals worked in tandem. The narratives described an inverted natural order. In the tales, wolves assaulted lonely travelers; the hominids became the hunted. The circle hunts attacked this unnatural hierarchy, reclaiming the apex of the food pyramid for predators that wielded guns, owned livestock, and tended plants. As Richard Slotkin has argued, frontier cultural forms that stressed regeneration through violence excused all kinds of nasty behavior. The myth freed colonists to chop heads, fire villages, and torture animals. This was wholesome, conservative brutality: atrocities committed in the name of order, authority, and decorum. Travelers' tales and circle hunts made wildlife abuse socially acceptable.

Regeneration through violence rested upon the assumption (many times the delusion) of powerlessness. Wolves never threatened humans physically, but they devoured livestock, and colonists identified with their animal property. They often saw themselves as sheep surrounded by ravening foes. Destroying predators, therefore, became a metaphor for overturning many types of weakness. Farmers in Ohio's Western Reserve encircled wolves to protest absentee landlords and economic isolation; Mormons shot wolves to secure their Zion and end decades of persecution and hardship; and new western ranchers waged a publicity campaign against wolf reintroduction, portraying themselves as besieged victims of power-mad bureaucrats, touchy-feely environmentalists, and clueless urbanites. For wolves, the most dangerous animal on the planet was a livestock owner feeling surrounded, exploited, and impotent.

Vulnerability not only accounted for the ferocity of colonists' wolf loathing, it also explained wolves' susceptibility to human predation. While ugly and pervasive, Euro-Americans' bad attitudes did not exterminate wolves. The species' ecological vulnerability did. Wolves inhabited a niche—a group-hunting predator specializing in large herbivores—that collapsed under pressure. Reckless killers who sought out encounters with scary, top-tier beasts like wolves, bears, and panthers, Euro-Americans killed wild animals and transformed habitats. This combination of predation and environmental change proved too much for wolves. The species needed to behave more like coyotes, but there was not enough time to switch to smaller prey, adopt flexible pack structures, or increase fertility. Wolves' niche trapped them as much as invading agriculturalists did.

The concept of vulnerability linked biology, folklore, and colonization. Wolves' biological vulnerability, combined with their killers' sense of powerlessness, created a bizarre and dangerous situation: a predator that imagined itself prey attacking a predator that could not imagine itself prey.

Euro-Americans' cruelty was not timeless. There was nothing natural or pre-destined about their behavior. The interaction of folklore and history explained the longevity and intensity of colonists' wolf hatred. Euro-Americans arrived in North America equipped with animal legends, metaphors, and hunting rituals. They performed this wolf lore in specific historical circumstances, generating new meanings while preserving old motifs and tale types. Coloni-zation—driven by historical causes as diverse as national conquest, expanding markets, religious persecution, and growing farm families—introduced Americans to novel environments and different kinds of wolves. At each mo-ment, the colonists could have invented new behaviors, adopted new attitudes. Eons of evolution had given the species brains capable of quick adaptations. Humans not only could change, they could change faster than any animal on earth. The quandary then is why did Euro-American colonists, a group willing to change their place of residence, fight other types of environmental adjustment so fiercely?

Euro-Americans struggled to pass down cultural, economic, political, and religious legacies to their offspring. They wanted cattle herds, farms, churches, and governments to transcend individual lives. They wanted the possessions, relationships, and institutions they valued most to linger for centuries, not years or decades. These dreams of transcendence often crashed against the realities of colonization. Livestock foundered in unfamiliar habi-tats; children died on the trail; and locusts devoured crops. Wolves ingested property, and they also served as symbols of regeneration. They were ecological rivals and cultural icons, and they perished in multitudes as Euro-Americans tried to harmonize their movement through space with their culture's move-ment through time.

And this was a biological movement as well. Transcendence linked bi-ology, folklore, and history. Indeed, transporting ideas and possessions across time would be inconceivable without biology. Sexual reproduction under-pins the very concept of social and cultural regeneration. Without future generations to own property and remember stories, there would be no im-mortality. Nature and culture share an obsession—perpetuation over time —and they share a process—persistence through adaptation. Evolution

WAITING FOR A CHINOOK

FIGURE 23 Charles Russell's "Waiting for a Chinook." The watercolor captures the emotional bond between livestock owners and their animals as well as wolves' threat to both humans and bovines. Used with permission of the Montana Stockgrowers Association, Helena.

influences the transmittal of objects, values, and ideas across generations, not by determining which items or beliefs survive, but by shaping the people who will perform and cherish the inheritance. As time stretches, the common thread binding history, folklore, and biology wears to the thinness of a filament. The connection between years and eons grows weaker as biology slowly overwhelms culture.

Persistence through adaptation works for genes, but humans place conditions on immortality. They not only want cultural institutions like nations and religions to endure, they want these institutions to resemble the ones they know and love. Yet in the fullness of biological time, the values human beings place on existence are destroyed by existence. To survive millennia, forms, whether cultural or biological, must change. Life forms adapt to shifting environmental conditions, while cultural forms mutate as they interact with the specific historical contexts that give them meaning. Transcendence is a dream of a large-brained species with high expectations.

FIGURE 24   Female wolf in wire muzzle. Courtesy Denver Public Library Western History Department.

*   *   *

The reintroduced gray wolves in Idaho, Montana, Wyoming, Arizona, and New Mexico inhabit a cultural landscape radically different from the one that exterminated their cousins. Americans' opinions of nature, food, and domestic animals have changed to match their historical environment. Today, enormous multinational corporations fatten, slaughter, package, and market animal protein. The typical American steer leads a life bizarrely different from his pioneering forebearers'. A product of artificial insemination, he enters a world designed to maximize his muscle weight and the profits of the company that owns him. Antibiotics allow him to grow big eating corn, a diet that would normally kill his grass-eating species. This animal's ancestors spear-headed the colonization of North America. They were valued for their mobility. Modern bovines move as little as possible. Trucks transport them from one feedlot pen to another until a mechanized killing device begins the disassembly process.[5]

Human predation has become so technical and abstract that the consumers of animal protein no longer feel emotionally connected to the beasts they ingest. Americans used to empathize with their meat. They placed their aspirations for a pleasant and lucrative future in their herds. When predators attacked their livestock, they responded passionately. Animal blood and human sentiment flowed together. The ranchers opposed to wolf reintroduction maintain the historic link between emotion and livestock ownership, but they are antiques. Massive feedlot and packing enterprises control the price of beef, pork, and poultry in the United States (if not the world), and these corporations have been using their power to keep prices low, bankrupting the small operators who care deeply about the welfare of animal property up to the moment they sell them for slaughter. As sentimental pastoralists, wolves' traditional enemies, struggle to survive the turn of the millennium, the predators' new allies—disconnected consumers—have expanded their influence.

The beneficiaries of American society's movement away from small-scale agrarianism, reintroduced wolves have thrived in a cultural environment that accepts the scientific extermination of millions of domestic animals but rejects violence toward handfuls of wild creatures. Breathtaking in its hypocrisy, this situation would be unfathomable without some understanding of American wolf history. Industrial livestock production killed the stories, the symbols, and the traditions attached to domestic animals. Euro-American colonists were not only fond of their herds, they identified with them. Christianity and colonization worked in tandem to produce a string of pastoral narratives and associations. In a world of steroid injections and genetic engineering, however, the language of shepherds and flocks seems quaint and inapplicable. Few Americans want to see themselves in the mooing and bleating masses headed to the slaughterhouse, and the special affinity they once felt for their food supply is nearly gone.

Unlike livestock, wolves became more storied as the twentieth century wore on. They retained their dark connotations: werewolves bit coeds in movies; Nazi submarines gathered in "wolf packs"; and lupine predators assaulted Red Riding Hoods in forums as diverse as children's literature, women's magazines, and XXX pornography. Wolves continued to be bad, aggressive, and sexy. But they also accrued reputations as noble, endangered, and ecological creatures. Modern wolves exist in a network of stories that flatter and defame, and both the positive and negative portrayals are critical to their recovery. Wolves need their patina of wickedness to stay imperiled. At present, 3,500 wolves live in the upper Midwest, while around 700 live in the Rocky Mountains. Their numbers have rebounded so well that their legal status may soon change from "endangered" to "threatened." Then, if their robust growth continues, they will be "delisted" completely. When this happens, the federal government will turn over the management of wolves to state fish and wildlife departments, a scenario that has some state legislatures salivating. Wyoming's draft management plan designates wolves as predators outside of national parks, giving hunters and trappers the freedom to kill the animals at will.[6]

Yet in a strange way, the vision of wolf-loathing ranchers and elk hunters turning the areas outside of parks into free-fire zones may be the predators' best protection. Since their reintroduction in 1995, wolves have flourished in a cultural environment that depicts them as both threatened and threatening. Ranchers and hunters portray the animals as incurable vermin and ruthless killers. (Wyoming stockgrowers reported 89 sheep and 54 cattle killed by wolves between 1999 and 2002.) Wildlife advocates use the vehemence of this animus to protest any alteration in wolves' federal protection. Strip wolves of the environmental laws that guard them, they warn, and the ugly days of extermination will return. The passions wolves inspire keep them endangered even as their numbers climb. The animals have finally discovered a safe haven in a climate of public opinion that mixes love, hate, and indifference.[7]

As folkloric beasts and enthusiastic molesters of private property, wolves loped through the breadth of American history. The animals connect Lois Crisler and Roger Williams, Brigham Young and Stanley Young, Israel Putnam and Aldo Leopold. They provide a historical bridge far more sturdy than the concepts scholars lay down to span the gaps in the past. Cobbled-together ethnic identities like Euro-American or abstract processes like colonization often fail to make the linkages they imply. Were the Latter-day Saints who settled in Utah's Great Basin engaged in the same conquest as the farmers who plowed rocks in Vermont? Does the term *Euro-American* mean anything when people as diverse as John Winthrop and Chad McKittrick fall into the category? Historians work to come up with synthetic concepts that sew together vast time periods and address the continent's past as a whole. The prime lesson of wolf history is this: life and history create their own connections. Genes bind generations; folktales cross thousands of miles; and wolves integrate the American past through the synthesis of biological, folkloric, and historical time.

Wolves help Americans understand their past, and historians might be able to help wolves in return. The best reason for letting wolves repopulate the United States may be historic rather than ecological. Wolves may heal ecosystems overrun with herbivores; they may bring a sense of wildness to national parks; their presence may even brighten the human soul. But wolf reintroduction will most certainly preserve a species that united Americans through a long, brutal, and vital colonial past. Americans spend millions of dollars to safeguard historic treasures and monuments. Tax dollars, foundation grants, and visitor donations safeguard the constitution, polish the Vietnam Memorial, and keep Richard Nixon's birthplace from crumbling to the ground. Wolves tell a story longer than any nation's, larger than any war's, and more significant than any president's. They push history beyond the confines of humanity to include the creatures and biological processes that shaped the past. Wolves are living reminders of the legacies of colonization, and when the likes of Chad McKittrick shoot the animals to possess their skulls, the rituals and symbols of colonization thunder back from the distant past to enliven wildlife debates in postmodern America. The predators continue to fire imaginations, ignite controversies, and elicit savage behavior; their grip on American culture remains fierce. They embody an unbroken history of conquest worth pondering and protecting.

NOTES

INTRODUCTION

1. The date of this episode is a guess based on Audubon's statement that it occurred two years after another wolf incident in the Ohio River Valley that had taken place twenty-three years before. Audubon, however, never says twenty-three years from when. I have counted back, then forward from the publication date of the third volume of the *Ornithological Biography* in which the wolf pit story first appeared. John James Audubon, *Ornithological Biography, or, An Account of the Habits of the Birds of the United States of America,* vol. 3 (Edinburgh: A. and C. Black, 1835), 338–41.

2. Scott Russell Sanders, ed., *Audubon Reader: The Best Writings of John James Audubon* (Bloomington: Indiana University Press, 1986), 51.

3. Ibid. The farmer described the killing of wolves as a sport, and Audubon seemed to accept this designation: "He would beyond a doubt shew me some sport rarely seen in those parts."

4. Stephen Kellert et al., "Human Culture and Large Carnivore Conservation in North America," *Conservation Biology* 10 (August 1996): 977–89.

5. Barry Holstun Lopez, *Of Wolves and Men* (New York: Simon and Schuster, 1978), 139, 140; L. David Mech, *The Wolf: The Ecology and Behavior of an Endangered Species* (Minneapolis: University of Minnesota Press, 1970), 348, 335. Nonhistorians have dominated the writing of wolf history, producing fine works that examine wolf eradication according to the questions and concerns of various disciplines. See L. David Mech and Luigi Boitani, eds., *Wolves: Behavior, Ecology, and Conservation* (Chicago: University of Chicago Press, 2003); Michael A. Nie, *Beyond Wolves: The Politics of Wolf Recovery and Management* (Minneapolis: University of Minnesota Press, 2003); Peter Steinhart, *The Company of Wolves*

(New York: Vintage, 1995); Hank Fischer, *Wolf Wars: The Remarkable Inside Story of the Restoration of Wolves to Yellowstone* (Helena: Falcon, 1995); and Stanley P. Young and Edward A. Goldman, *The Wolves of North America* (Washington, D.C.: Wildlife Institute, 1944). Historians have only recently turned to wolves as monograph subjects. Karen R. Jones tells the story of wolf persecution and protection in the national parks of the Rocky Mountains in *Wolf Mountains: A History of Wolves Along the Great Divide* (Calgary: University of Calgary Press, 2002); Timothy Rawson investigates the management of wolves in an Alaskan national park in *Changing Tracks: Predators and Politics in Mt. McKinley National Park* (Anchorage: University of Alaska Press, 2001).

6. Lopez, *Of Wolves and Men*, 63. For uplifting works see Rick McIntyre, ed., *War Against the Wolf: America's Campaign to Exterminate the Wolf* (Stillwater, Minn.: Voyageur, 1995); Robert Busch, ed., *Wolf Songs: The Classic Collection of Writing About Wolves* (San Francisco: Sierra Club, 1994); R. D. Lawrence, *Secret Go the Wolves* (New York: Holt, Rinehart and Winston, 1980); and Farley Mowat, *Never Cry Wolf* (New York: Bantam, 1963). Standout works in wolf biology include Adolph Murie, *The Wolves of Mt. McKinley* (Washington, D.C.: U.S. Government Printing Office, 1944); Mech, *The Wolf*; Durward Allen, *The Wolves of Minong: Their Vital Role in a Wild Community* (Boston: Houghton Mifflin, 1979); and Douglas Pimlott et al., *The Ecology of the Timber Wolf in Algonquin Provincial Park* (Ontario: Ontario Ministry of National Resources, 1969).

7. For the violence of wolf killing see Young and Goldman, *The Wolves of North America*; McIntyre, *War Against the Wolf*; Hampton, *The Great American Wolf*; and David E. Brown, ed., *The Wolf of the Southwest: The Making of an Endangered Species* (Tucson: University of Arizona Press, 1983). Lopez describes humans (Russian aristocrats, specifically) hunting wolves with eagles in *Of Wolves and Men*, 155–57. Wolf hooks described in John Josselyn, *New-England's Rareties Discovered* (London: G. Widdows, 1672; rpt., Boston: Massachusetts Historical Society Picture Books, 1972), 7. Lopez entitled his chapter dealing with wolf killing "An American Pogrom," *Of Wolves and Men*, 167–99; other authors have compared predator control campaigns in the United States to the Holocaust; for examples of this metaphor at work see McIntyre, *War Against the Wolf*, 17; and Donald Worster, "Other People, Other Lives" in *An Unsettled Country: Changing Landscapes of the American West* (Albuquerque: University of New Mexico Press, 1994): 70.

8. Robert Darnton, *The Great Cat Massacre and Other Episodes in French Cultural History* (New York: Vintage, 1984), 4, 5.

9. These timeframes echo Fernand Braudel's trisection of history into geographical, social, and individual time. I happily acknowledge my debt to Braudel for this scheme, but time works somewhat differently in this book than in his classic works. I have substituted evolution and biological adaptation for geography as my *longue durée*, and I try not to privilege one timeframe over another. Instead of the slow, nearly imperceptible actions of the environment directing the course of human events, I posit that biology, folklore, and history create one

another's "destiny" (Braudel's term) through their interaction. See Fernand Braudel, *The Mediterranean and the Mediterranean World in the Age of Philip II*, vol. 1 (Berkeley: University of California Press, 1995), 21; Fernand Braudel, *On History*, trans. Sarah Matthews (Chicago: University of Chicago Press, 1980), 26–27.

10. For reproduction's role in history, ecology, and culture see Carolyn Merchant, *Ecological Revolutions: Nature, Gender, and Science in New England* (Chapel Hill: University of North Carolina Press, 1989): 17–19; and Marshall Sahlins, *Islands of History* (Chicago: University of Chicago Press, 1985), 144. I want to compare and contrast (not conflate) wolves' and humans' struggle to pass down inheritances in the midst of chaotic historical circumstances. I argue that biology and culture share a goal—the conquest of time—and a method to achieve this goal —persistence through adaptation. Still, despite this common ground, culture and biology remain starkly dissimilar in other ways. Ambivalence, for example, lurks in many human efforts to reproduce their cultures. To endure, cultural forms must adapt to new situations. Yet change endangers the very notion of persistence. Cultural reproduction is fraught with anger, frustration, and regret, whereas biological change simply happens. For far bolder arguments about evolution, culture, and human history see Edward O. Wilson, *Sociobiology: The New Synthesis*, 25th anniversary ed. (Cambridge: Harvard University Press, 2000); Robert S. McElvaine, *Eve's Seed: Biology, the Sexes, and the Course of History* (New York: McGraw-Hill, 2001); Walter Burkett, *Creation of the Sacred: Tracks of Biology in Early Religions* (Cambridge: Harvard University Press, 1996); and Jared Diamond, *Guns, Germs, and Steel: The Fate of Human Societies* (New York: Norton, 1997). For wolf population recovery see Mech, *The Wolf*, 60.

11. Charles Darwin, *The Origin of Species* (New York: Bantam Classic Edition, 1999), 55; Stephen Jay Gould, *Ever Since Darwin: Reflections in Natural History* (New York: Norton, 1977), 11.

12. For wolf evolution see Mech, *The Wolf*, 18–20.

13. See Daniel C. Dennett, *Darwin's Dangerous Idea: Evolution and the Meanings of Life* (New York: Touchstone, 1995); Steven Pinker, *The Blank Slate: The Modern Denial of Human Nature* (New York: Viking, 2002); and E. O. Wilson, *On Human Nature* (Cambridge: Harvard University Press, 1988).

14. For species competition see Paul Colinvaux, *Why Big Fierce Animals Are Rare: An Ecologist's Perspective* (Princeton: Princeton University Press, 1978), 136–49.

15. For an overview of European and English demography and economic history in this time period see Ralph Davis, *The Rise of the Atlantic Economies* (Ithaca: Cornell University Press, 1973), 16–17; and Keith Wrightson, *English Society, 1580–1680* (New Brunswick: Rutgers University Press, 1982), 122–23.

16. For biology and colonization see Alfred W. Crosby, *Ecological Imperialism: The Biological Expansion of Europe, 900–1900* (Cambridge: Cambridge University Press, 1986); and Diamond, *Guns, Germs, and Steel*.

17. Thomas Morton, *New English Canaan* (Boston: The Prince Society, 1883), 208.

18. For the persistence of Euro-American colonizers' self-perception of innocence

see Patricia Nelson Limerick, *Legacy of Conquest: The Unbroken Past of the American West* (New York: Norton, 1987), 35–54.

19. For settlers' environmental frustrations and the brutal narratives generated by them see Alan Taylor, "'Wasty Ways': Stories of American Settlement," *Environmental History* 3 (July 1998): 291–310.

20. Lopez cites 1942 as the end point for wolf killing in the lower forty-eight states. That is when the federal government stopped funding PARC and its professional hunters. Lopez, *Of Wolves and Men*, 187.

21. For wolf recovery see Nie, *Beyond Wolves;* Gary Ferguson, *The Yellowstone Wolves: The First Year* (Helena: Falcon, 1996); Rick McIntyre, *A Society of Wolves: National Parks and the Battle over the Wolf* (Stillwater, Minn.: Voyageur, 1993); Hank Fischer, *Wolf Wars: The Remarkable Inside Story of the Restoration of Wolves to Yellowstone* (Helena: Falcon, 1995); Thomas McNamee, *The Return of the Wolf to Yellowstone* (New York: Henry Holt, 1998); Roland Smith, *Journey of the Red Wolf* (New York: Penguin, 1996); Rick Bass, *The New Wolves: The Return of the Mexican Wolf to the American Southwest* (New York: Lyons, 1998); and John Elder, ed., *The Return of the Wolf: Reflections of the Future of Wolves in the Northeast* (Hanover: University Press of New England, 2000).

1. HOWLS, SNARLS, AND MUSKET SHOTS

1. The yell in this episode comes from *A Relation or Journal of the Beginning and Proceedings of the English Plantation Settled at Plymouth in New England* (London, 1622; rpt. as *Mourt's Relation*, Boston: John Kimball Wiggin, 1859), 53. William Bradford also recorded the incident in Bradford, *Of Plymouth Plantation*, ed. Samuel Eliot Morison (New York: Knopf, 1952), 69–70.

2. Bradford, *Of Plymouth Plantation*, 70, 62.

3. For animal communication see W. E. Lanyon and W. N. Tavolga, eds., *Animal Sounds and Communication* (Washington, D.C.: American Institute of Biological Sciences, 1960); and R. G. Busnel, *Acoustic Behavior of Animals* (New York: Elsevier, 1963). For a definition of territory see Edward O. Wilson, *Sociobiology: The New Synthesis*, 25th anniversary ed. (Cambridge: Harvard University Press, 2000), 256–76.

4. For a comparison of human and animal communication see Wilson, *Sociobiology*, 177. For the role of miscommunication in colonization see Stephen Greenblatt, *New World Encounters* (Berkeley: University of California Press, 1993); Tzvetan Todorov, *The Conquest of America: The Question of the Other* (New York: Harper Perennial, 1982); and Jill Lepore, *The Name of War: King Philip's War and the Origins of American Identity* (New York: Knopf, 1998).

5. See L. David Mech and Luigi Boitani, eds., *Wolves: Behavior, Ecology, and Conservation* (Chicago: University of Chicago Press, 2003), 11–19; Nathaniel Valière et al., "Long-Distance Wolf Recolonization of France and Switzerland Inferred from Non-Invasive Genetic Sampling Over a Period of Ten Years," *Animal Conservation* 6 (2003): 83–92; L. David Mech, Steven H. Fritts, and Douglas Wagner, "Minnesota Wolf Dispersal to Wisconsin and Michigan," *American Midland*

Naturalist 133 (April 1995): 368–70; and L. David Mech, *The Wolf: The Ecology and Behavior of an Endangered Species* (Minneapolis: University of Minnesota Press, 1970), 13, 159.

6. Mech and Boitani, *Wolves*, 13–14. Mech's Minnesota wolf story is retold in Peter Steinhart, *The Company of Wolves* (New York: Vintage, 1995), 99. Scientists do know one of the prime benefits of dispersal: genetic diversity. See Pär K. Ingvarsson, "Conservation Biology: Lone Wolf to the Rescue," *Nature* 420 (5 December 2002): 472. Diane K. Boyd et al., "Transboundary Movements of a Recolonizing Wolf Population in the Rocky Mountains," in L. N. Carbyn, S. H. Fritts, and D. R. Seip, eds., *Ecology and Conservation of Wolves in a Changing World* (Edmonton: Canadian Circumpolar Institute, 1995): 135–40.

7. For wolf eating habits see Mech, *The Wolf,* 170.

8. Paul Colinvaux, *Why Big Fierce Animals Are Rare: An Ecologist's Perspective* (Princeton: Princeton University Press, 1978), 177.

9. Thomas J. Meier et al., "Pack Structure and the Genetic Relatedness Among Wolf Packs in a Naturally-Regulated Population," in Carbyn, Fritts, and Seip, *Ecology and Conservation of Wolves,* 301.

10. See M. W. Fox, "A Comparative Study of the Development of Facial Expressions in Canids: Wolf, Coyote and Foxes," *Behaviour* 36 (1970): 49–73; Mech, *The Wolf,* 82; and Randall Lockwood, "Dominance in Wolves: Useful Construct or Bad Habit?" in Erich Klinghammer, ed., *The Behavior and Ecology of Wolves: Proceedings of the Symposium on the Behavior and Ecology of Wolves* (New York: Garland, 1979), 225–41.

11. Rolf O. Peterson, et al., "Leadership Behavior in Relation to Dominance and Reproductive Status in Gray Wolves, Canis Lupus," *Canadian Journal of Zoology* 80, no. 8 (2002): 1405–12.

12. G. B. Rabb, J. H. Woolpy, and B. E. Ginsburg, "Social Relationships in a Group of Captive Wolves," *American Zoology* 7 (1967): 305–11. See Mech, *The Wolf,* 114.

13. For scent marking see Mech, *The Wolf,* 93–95; and C. S. Asa and L. D. Mech, "A Review of the Sensory Organs in Wolves and Their Importance to Live History," in Carbyn, Fritts, and Seip, *Ecology and Conservation of Wolves,* 289–90.

14. For an overview of howling see John B. Theberge and J. Bruce Fall, "Howling as a Means of Communication in Timber Wolves," *American Zoologist* 7 (1967), 331–38; Z. J. Tooze, F. H. Harrington, and J. C. Fentress, "Individually Distinct Vocalizations in Timber Wolves, Canis Lupus," *Animal Behavior* 40 (1990), 723–30; Erich Klinghammer and Leslie Laidlaw, "Analysis of 23 Months of Daily Howl Records in a Captive Grey Wolf Pack," in Klinghammer, *Behavior and Ecology of Wolves,* 153–81. Fred H. Harrington and L. David Mech, "Wolf Howling and Its Role in Territory Maintenance," *Behaviour* 68 (1979), 239–41.

15. "The Visit of Verrazano," in Howard M. Chapin, ed., *Documentary History of Rhode Island,* vol. 2 (Providence: Preston and Rounds, 1919), 1, 2.

16. Ibid., 3, 4.

17. For Poutrincourt's visit to southern New England see Samuel de Champlain, *The Works of Samuel de Champlain,* vol. 1, ed. H. P. Bigger (Toronto: Champlain

Society, 1922; rpt. ed., 1971), 407–31; and Neal Salisbury, *Manitou and Providence: Indians, Europeans, and the Making of New England* (New York: Oxford University Press, 1982), 63–66. Salisbury describes the sand-flinging episode, 66.

18. Bradford, *Of Plymouth Plantation*, 25. John Underhill, *Newes From America* (London, 1638; rpt. in *Collections of the Massachusetts Historical Society*, vol. 6, 3d ser., Boston: American Stationers' Company, 1837), 15. William Hubbard, *The Present State of New England*, vol. 1, ed. Samuel D. Drake (Roxbury, Mass.: Eliot Woodward, 1865), 205. Amy Schrager Lang, ed., "A True History of the Captivity and Restoration of Mrs. Mary Rowlandson," in William L. Andrews, ed., *Journeys in New Worlds: Early American Women's Narratives* (Madison: University of Wisconsin Press, 1990), 33.

19. For dogs as warriors see Marion Schwartz, *A History of Dogs in the Early Americas* (New Haven: Yale University Press, 1997), 162–63. For modern mastiffs see Dee Dee Andersson and Luana Luther, *The Mastiff: Aristocratic Guardian* (Phoenix: Doral, 1999). Harriet Ritvo discusses the shifting definitions of breeds in *The Animal Estate: The English and Other Creatures in the Victorian Age* (Cambridge: Harvard University Press, 1987). William Morrell, *New-England or A Briefe Enarration of the Ayre, Earth, Water, Fish, and Fowles of that Country* (Boston: Club of Odd Volumes, 1895).

20. George Parker Winship, *Sailors Narratives of Voyages along the New England Coast, 1524–1624* (Boston: Houghton Mifflin, 1905), 61, 57.

21. Ibid., 61, 62.

22. Ibid., 122, 127.

23. See William Wood, *New England's Prospect* (London: Thomas Cotes, 1634), 20.

2. BEASTS OF LORE

1. *Mourt's Relation* (Boston: John Kimball Wiggin, 1859), 75, 77, 79.

2. For an excellent survey of European wolf lore see Barry Lopez, *Of Wolves and Men* (New York: Touchstone, 1978), 203–70.

3. For the discipline of folklore see Roger D. Abrahams, *Deep Down in the Jungle: Negro Narrative Folklore from the Streets of Philadelphia* (Chicago: Aldene, 1970); Jan Brunvand, *The Study of American Folklore: An Introduction*, 4th ed. (New York: Norton, 1998); Dan Ben Amos, "Towards a Definition of Folklore in Context," in Americo Paredes and Richard Bauman, eds., *Towards New Perspectives in Folklore* (Austin: University of Texas Press, 1972): 3–15; and Burt Feintuch, ed., "Common Ground: Keywords for the Study of Expressive Culture," *Journal of American Folklore* 108 (Fall 1995): 391–551. For the research methods of folklore see Kenneth S. Goldstein, *A Guide for Field Workers in Folklore* (Hatboro: Folklore Associates, 1964). For an excellent example of a scholar engaged in this struggle see Henry Glassie, *Passing the Time in Ballymenone: Culture and History of an Ulster Community* (Bloomington: Indiana University Press, 1982). For the relationship between history and folklore see Richard Dorson, *American Folklore and the Historian* (Chicago: University of Chicago Press, 1971); Henry Glassie, "The Practice and Purpose of History," *Journal of American History* 81 (Decem-

ber 1994): 961–68; and Henry Glassie, "Tradition," in Feintuch, "Common Ground," 395–412.

4. Photograph in Jennifer Westwood, *Albion: A Guide to Legendary Britain* (London: Grafton Books, 1985), 152.

5. Ibid.

6. Lopez, *Of Wolves and Men*, 203–70.

7. Ibid., 219.

8. Quotations from Matthew 10:16, Matthew 7:15, Genesis 49:27, and Habakkuk 1:8, respectively.

9. Quotations from John 10:11 and Acts 20:29, respectively.

10. See Increase Mather, *Early History of New England*, ed. Samuel G. Drake (Boston, 1864), 78; and Nathaniel Morton, *New-England's Memoriall* (Boston: Club of Odd Volumes, 1903), 140.

11. J. Franklin Jameson, *Johnson's Wonder-Working Providence* (New York: Scribner's, 1910), 112.

12. Cotton Mather, *Little Flocks Guarded Against Grievous Wolves* (Boston: Benjamin Harris and John Allen, 1691).

13. John Eliot, *The Indian Grammar Begun: Or, an Essay to Bring the Indian Language to Rules* (Cambridge: Marmaduke Johnson, 1666), 5.

14. Letter from Rev. Solomon Stoddard to Gov. Joseph Dudley, October 22, 1703, in *New England Historical and Genealogical Register*, vol. 24, 269–70.

15. Daniel Gookin, *Historical Collections of the Indians in New England*, rpt. in *Collections of the Massachusetts Historical Society, Volume I* (Boston: Massachusetts Historical Society, 1792), 164.

16. Ibid., 165.

17. Gookin, *Historical Collections*, 164, 165; see also James Axtell, *The Invasion Within: The Contest of Cultures in Colonial North America* (New York: Oxford University Press, 1985), 172–73.

18. Gookin, *Historical Collections*, 164, 165.

19. Bruce Hampton, *The Great American Wolf* (New York: Henry Holt, 1997), 43.

20. Lopez, *Of Wolves and Men*, 111–12.

21. Denise Casey and Tim W. Clark, *Tales of the Wolf: Fifty-one Stories of Wolf Encounters in the Wild* (Moose: Homestead, 1996), 46–49.

22. Hampton, *The Great American Wolf*, 53.

23. Lopez, *Of Wolves and Men*, 120, 105.

24. Roger Williams, *A Key into the Language of America* (Bedford: Applewood; rpt., Providence: Rhode Island Tercentenary Committee, 1936), 174–75, 105.

25. Thomas Morton, *New English Canaan* (1637; Boston: Prince Society, 1883), 209.

26. L. David Mech, *The Wolf: The Ecology and Behavior of an Endangered Species* (Minneapolis: University of Minnesota Press, 1970), 16.

27. See Calvin Martin, *Keepers of the Game: Indian-Animal Relationships and the Fur Trade* (Berkeley: University of California Press, 1978); Colin G. Calloway, *The Western Abenakis of Vermont, 1600–1800: War, Migration, and the Survival of an Indian People* (Norman: University of Oklahoma Press, 1990), 49–50; and

Adrian Tanner, *Bringing Home Animals: Religious Ideology and Mode of Production of the Mistassini Cree Hunters* (New York: St. Martin's, 1979).
28. Williams, *A Key into the Language of America*, 172.
29. Ibid., 171–73.
30. Ibid., 76.
31. Edward Johnson, *A History of New-England* (London: Nathaniel Brooke, 1654), 4.

3. WOLF BULLETS WITH ADDERS' TONGUES

1. Thomas Weston, *History of the Town of Middleboro, Massachusetts* (Boston: Houghton, Mifflin, 1906), 351.
2. Exotic wolf-killing devices mentioned in "Pincheon Papers," *Collections of the Massachusetts Historical Society,* vol. 2, 2d series (Boston: John Eliot, 1818), 229.
3. C. C. Lord, *Life and Times of Hopkinton, New Hampshire* (Concord: Republican Press, 1890), 271. For wolf haunts see Josiah H. Temple, *History of Framingham, Mass., 1640–1885,* new ed. (Somersworth: New England Press, 1988; orig. pub. 1887), 24; Esther M. Swift, *West Springfield, Massachusetts: A Town History* (West Springfield: West Springfield Heritage Association, 1969), 266. Wolf place names in E. Carpenter, *History of Amherst, Massachusetts,* vol. 2 (Amherst: Press of Carpenter and Morehouse, 1896), 33–34; *Fairfield, Connecticut, Town Records,* vol. B, *Town Meetings, 1661–1826, April 28, 1687* (Hartford: Connecticut State Library, 1929); Sarah Loring Bailey, *Historical Sketches of Andover* (Boston: Houghton Mifflin, 1880), 38; Betsey D. Keene, *History of Bourne from 1622 to 1937* (Bourne: Bourne Historical Society, 1975), 173; Simeon L. Deyo, *History of Barnstable County, Massachusetts* (New York: H. W. Blake, 1890), 275.
4. For descriptions of thriving livestock see William Wood, *New England's Prospect* (London: Thomas Cotes for John Bellamie, 1634), 10–11; and Samuel Maverick, *A Briefe Description of New England and the Severall Townes Therein together with the Present Government Thereof* (1660; Boston: Press of David Clapp and Son, 1885), 26. English herding traditions described in Terry G. Jordan, *North American Cattle-Ranching Frontiers: Origins, Diffusion, and Differentiation* (Albuquerque: University of New Mexico Press, 1993), 42–55. For New England herding practices see Virginia Dejohn Anderson, *Creatures of Empire* (Oxford: Oxford University Press, forthcoming); William Cronon, *Changes in the Land: Indians, Colonists, and the Ecology of New England* (New York: Hill and Wang, 1983), 128–32; and Howard S. Russell, *A Long, Deep Furrow: Three Centuries of Farming in New England* (Hanover: University Press of New England, 1976), 75. For examples of animal misbehavior see Judith Maureen Adkins, "Bodies and Boundaries: Animals in the Early American Experience," Ph.D. diss., Yale University, 1998, 213–19.
5. "Pincheon Papers," 229. John Josselyn, *New England's Rarities Discovered* (London: G. Widdows, 1672; rpt., Boston: Massachusetts Historical Society Picture Books, 1972), 7. Edward Howes to John Winthrop Jr., April 1634, in *Collections of the Massachusetts Historical Society,* vol. 6, 4th series (Boston: Massachusetts Historical Society, 1912), 498.

6. For a description of a wolf pit see Weston, *History of Middleboro*, 351; for livestock
pens see Henry S. Nourse, ed., *The Early Records of Lancaster, Massachusetts* (Lancaster: Published by the Town, 1884), 21; for gun traps see Franklin Bowditch
Dexter, ed., *Ancient Town Records*, vol. 1 (New Haven: New Haven Historical Society, 1917), 92. For bounties, monopolies, and hired hunters see James Merrill,
History of Amesbury and Merrimac, Massachusetts (Haverfill: F. P. Stiles, 1880),
30; Dexter, *Ancient Town Records*, 1: 73. Livestock owners built a fence across
the neck of Nahant, Massachusetts, in 1637. See Alonzo Lewis, *History of Lynn,
Essex County, Massachusetts* (Lynn: George C. Hubert, 1890), 132; and Keene,
History of Bourne, 79.

7. Joseph B. Felt, *History of Ipswich, Essex, and Hamilton* (Cambridge: Charles
Folsom, 1834), 42–43.

8. Last bounties in *Second Report of the Record Commissioners of the City of Boston;
Containing the Boston Records, 1634–1660* (Boston: Rockwell and Churchill,
1881), 140; *Watertown Records* (Watertown: Fred G. Barker, 1894), 59; Dexter,
Ancient Town Records, 1: 407; Henry M. Burt, ed., *The First Century of the History
of Springfield: The Official Records from 1636 to 1736*, vol. 1 (Springfield: Henry M.
Burt, 1898), 442; *Journal of the House of Representatives of Massachusetts*, vol. 51,
part 1 (Boston: Massachusetts Historical Society, 1982), 232; Edward Rowe
Snow, *A Pilgrim Returns to Cape Cod* (Boston: Yankee, 1946), 99–100; Charles
Boardman Howes, *Gloucester by Land and Sea: The History of a New England
Seacoast Town* (Boston: Little, Brown, 1923), 27; Julius H. Tuttle, ed., *Early
Records of Dedham, Massachusetts, 1706–1736* (Boston: Transcript, 1936), 153;
and *History of the Town of Amherst, Massachusetts* (Amherst: Carpenter and
Morehouse, 1896), 108.

9. For examples of payment boundaries see Burt, *History of Springfield*, 189; *The
Town Records of Topsfield, Massachusetts*, vol. 1 (Topsfield: Perkins, 1917), 63; and
Records of the Town of Plymouth, vol. 1 (Plymouth: Avery and Doten, 1889), 31.

10. For the colonists' hunting practices see Daniel Justin Herman, *Hunting and the
American Imagination* (Washington, D.C.: Smithsonian, 2001), 27–36; Patrick
M. Malone, *The Skulking Way of War: Technology and Tactics Among the New En-
gland Indians* (New York: Madison, 2000), 60–64; and E. Alexander Bergstrom,
"English Game Laws and Colonial Food Shortages," *New England Quarterly* 12
(December 1939): 681–90. Simplicities in William Wood, *New England's Pros-
pect* (London: Thomas Cotes, 1634), 31. Joint bounty law of 1745 described in
Lamson, *History of Manchester*, 57.

11. Merrill, *History of Amesbury and Merrimac*, 30–31.

12. Dexter, *Ancient Town Records*, 1: 73, 74, 92. For set guns see William Dutcher,
"Old-Time Natural History," *Forest and Stream* 28, no. 6 (1887): 105–6. Stanley
P. Young and Edward A. Goldman, *The Wolves of North America* (Washington,
D.C.: American Wildlife Institute, 1944), 302; and Bruce Hampton, *The Great
American Wolf* (New York: Henry Holt, 1997), 75.

13. Merrill, *History of Amesbury and Merrimac*, 86. Dexter, *Ancient Town Records*,
1: 113.

14. For English hunting traditions see Matt Cartmill, *A View to Death in the Morning: Hunting and Nature Through History* (Cambridge: Harvard University Press, 1993); and Malone, *The Skulking Way of War*, 52–54. For examples of New England hunting see Wood, *New England's Prospect*, 21, 29, 30, 31; and Frances Higginson, *New-Englands Plantation* (London: T. Cotes and R. Cotes, 1630), 9–10.

15. Nathaniel Morton, *New-England's Memoriall 1668* (Boston: Club of Odd Volumes, 1903), 28.

16. John Russell Bartlett, ed., *Records of the Colony of Rhode Island*, vol. 1 (Providence: Knowles, Anthony, 1856), 125, 116, 107, 108, 80.

17. Nathaniel B. Shurtleff, ed., *Records of the Colony of New Plymouth in New England*, vol. 3 (Boston: William White, 1856), 212–13. J. Hammond Trumbull, ed., *The Public Records of the Colony of Connecticut* (Hartford: Brown and Parsons, 1850), 14; Nathaniel B. Shurtleff, ed., *Records of the Governor and Company of the Massachusetts Bay in New England*, vol. 2 (Boston: William White, 1853), 252. *Early Records of the Town of Providence*, vol. 9 (Providence: Snow and Farnham, 1893), 191, 201.

18. For examples of these procedures see Joshua Coffin, *A Sketch of the History of Newbury, Newburyport, and West Newbury, from 1635 to 1845* (Boston: Samuel G. Drake, 1845), 42; Shurtleff, *Records of Massachusetts Bay*, 2: 103; and Robert J. Dunckle and Ann S. Lambert, *The Town Records of Roxbury, Mass., 1647–1700* (Boston: New England Historic Genealogy Society, 1997), 19.

19. *Early Records of Providence*, 9: 9, 191.

20. Shurtleff, *Records of the Massachusetts Bay*, 1: 81, 5: 453. Trumbull, *The Public Records of the Colony of Connecticut*, 4: 367. Bartlett, *Records of the Colony of Rhode Island*, 4: 574.

21. John Underhill, *Newes from America*, in *Collections of the Massachusetts Historical Society*, vol. 6, 3d series (Boston: American Stationers' Company, 1837), 15. William Hubbard, *The Present State of New England*, vol. 1, ed. Samuel D. Drake (Roxbury, Mass.: Eliot Woodward, 1865), 205. Amy Schrager Lang, ed., "A True History of the Captivity and Restoration of Mrs. Mary Rowlandson" (1682), in William L. Andrews ed., *Journeys in New Worlds: Early American Women's Narratives* (Madison: University of Wisconsin Press, 1990), 33. Letter from Rev. Solomon Stoddard to Gov. Joseph Dudley, October 22, 1703, in *New England Historical and Genealogical Register* 24 (1870): 269–70.

22. Increase Mather, *Early History of New England*, ed. Samuel G. Drake (Albany: J. Mansell, 1864), 233.

23. Edward Winslow, "Winslow's Relation," in Alexander Young, ed., *Chronicles of the Pilgrim Fathers of the Colony of Plymouth from 1602 to 1625* (Boston: Little and Brown, 1841), 343.

24. Underhill, *Newes from America*, 16–17. Roger Williams to Gov. John Winthrop, February 28, 1637/38, in Glenn W. LaFantasie, ed., *The Correspondence of Roger Williams*, vol. 1 (Hanover, N.H.: Brown University Press/University Press of New England, 1988), 146.

4. PREDATOR TO PREY

1. Paul J. Lindholdt, ed., *John Josselyn, Colonial Traveler: A Critical Edition of Two Voyages to New England* (Hanover, N.H.: University Press of New England, 1988), 60.

2. Ibid.

3. Ibid., 61.

4. Stanley Paul Young, "Den Hunting as a Means of Coyote Control," leaflet 132 U.S. Department of Agriculture ([Washington, D.C.]: United States Government Printing Office, 1937), 7–8; Young describes using a similar method for wolf pups in Stanley Paul Young and Edward A. Goldman, *The Wolves of North America* (Washington, D.C.: American Wildlife Institute, 1944), 97, 319.

5. For hunting wolves from airplanes in Alaska see Bruce Hampton, *The Great American Wolf* (New York: Henry Holt, 1997), 228–39.

6. See Alan Taylor, "'Wasty Ways': Stories of American Settlement" *Environmental History* 3 (July 1998): 291–310.

7. *Prey vulnerability* is a term that appears repeatedly in the scientific literature on wolf predation. See L. David Mech, *The Wolf: The Ecology and Behavior of an Endangered Species* (Minneapolis: University of Minnesota Press, 1970), 246–63; L. David Mech et al., "Patterns of Prey Selection by Wolves in Denali National Park, Alaska," in L. N. Carbyn, S. H. Fritts, and D. R. Seip, eds., *Ecology and Conservation of Wolves in a Changing World* (Edmonton: Canadian Circumpolar Institute, 1995), 135–40; and William C. Gasaway et al., "Interrelationships of Wolves, Prey, and Man in Interior Alaska," *Wildlife Monographs* 84 (July 1983): 40. For a discussion of the predator-prey relationship in wolf evolution see John B. Theberge, *Wolf Country: Eleven Years Tracking the Algonquin Wolves* (Toronto: M and S, 1998), 98–114.

8. See Alan A. Barryman, "The Origins and Evolution of Predator-Prey Theory," *Ecology* 73, no. 5 (1992): 1529–35; H. Resit Akcakaya, "Population Cycles of Mammals: Evidence for a Ratio-Dependent Predation Hypothesis," *Ecological Monographs* 62, no. 1 (1992): 119–42; François Messier, "Ungulate Population Models with Predation: A Case Study with the North American Moose," *Ecology* 75, no. 2 (1994): 478–88. For a discussion of the shortcomings of animal population models see Daniel B. Botkin, *Discordant Harmonies: A New Ecology for the Twenty-First Century* (New York: Oxford University Press, 1990), 27–51.

9. For a perfect example of a hunter misreading kill sites see Theodore Roosevelt quoted in Stanley P. Young and Edward A. Goldman, *The Wolves of North America* (Washington, D.C.: American Wildlife Institute, 1944), 265.

10. *History of Medina County and Ohio* (Chicago: Baskin and Battey, 1881), 163.

11. For wolves' killing techniques see Mech, *The Wolf*, 217.

12. Adolph Murie, *The Wolves of Mount McKinley* (Washington, D.C.: United States Government, 1944; rpt. 1971), 104.

13. Ibid., 124.

14. Alexander Ross quoted in Young and Goldman, *The Wolves of North America*, 270–71. Feminine wiles and cannibalism ibid., 105, 250.

15. For the story of the early years of the Isle Royale study see Durward L. Allen, *Wolves of Minong: Their Vital Role in a Wild Community* (Boston: Houghton Mifflin, 1979). Rolf O. Peterson, *The Wolves of Isle Royale: A Broken Balance* (Minocqua, Wis.: Willow Creek, 1995), 117.

16. Mech, *The Wolf,* 196–203. For locating prey see Peterson, *The Wolves of Isle Royale,* 127; also see Roger Peters, "Mental Maps in Wolf Territoriality," in Erich Klinghammer, ed., *The Behavior and Ecology of Wolves: Proceedings of the Symposium on the Behavior and Ecology of Wolves held on 23–24 May 1975* (New York: Garland, 1979), 119–51. Tooth rot in Peterson, *The Wolves of Isle Royale,* 122.

17. Mech, *The Wolf,* 213–14.

18. Ibid., 210–11. Peterson, *The Wolves of Isle Royale,* 123.

19. For an introduction to island ecology see David Quammen, *The Song of the Dodo: Island Biogeography in an Age of Extinctions* (New York: Scribner's, 1996). For the ups and downs of the Isle Royale wolves see Adolph Murie, *The Moose of Isle Royale* (Ann Arbor: University of Michigan Press, 1934); L. David Mech, *The Wolves of Isle Royale* (Washington, D.C.: U.S. Government Printing Office, 1966); Allen, *Wolves of Minong;* Peterson, *The Wolves of Isle Royale;* and Botkin, *Discordant Harmonies,* 27–49.

20. D. H. Pimlott, J. A. Shannon, and G. B. Kolenosky, *The Ecology of the Timber Wolf in Algonquin Provincial Park* (Ontario: Ministry of Natural Resources, 1969), 87. Michael E. Nelson and L. David Mech, "Deer Social Organization and Wolf Predation in Northeastern Minnesota," *Wildlife Monograph* 7 (July 1981), 32.

21. Nelson and Mech, "Deer Social Organization," 33–37.

22. Ibid., 36.

23. For the spectrum of wolf-prey dynamics see Dale R. Seip, "Introduction to Wolf-Prey Interactions" in Carbyn, Fritts, and Seip, *Ecology and Conservation of Wolves,* 179–86. For surplus killing see Glenn D. DelGuidice, "Surplus Killing of White-Tailed Deer by Wolves in Northcentral Minnesota," *Journal of Mammalogy* 79 (February 1, 1998): 227–35; and L. David Mech, ed., *The Wolves of Minnesota: Howl in the Heartland* (Stillwater, Minn.: Voyageur, 2000), 86.

24. Peterson, *The Wolves of Isle Royale,* 118–19.

25. Wildlife biologists are beginning to publish their findings about predation in Yellowstone National Park following the reintroduction of wolves in 1995. Yellowstone has proven a magnificent place to watch wolves kill. Scientists have witnessed more kills in the past few years than in the previous sixty. See Jim Robbins, "'The Real World, Yellowstone': Wolves on View All the Time," *New York Times,* July 22, 2003, D3. So far, the Yellowstone wolves have followed the pattern of wolves targeting vulnerable prey. See Douglas W. Smith, Rolf O. Peterson, and Douglas B. Houston, "Yellowstone after Wolves," *Bioscience* 53 (April 2003): 330–40; John W. Laundré, Lucina Hernández, and Kelly B. Altendorf, "Wolves, Elk, and Bison: Reestablishing the 'Landscape of Fear' in Yellowstone National Park, U.S.A.," *Canadian Journal of Mammalogy* 79 (2001): 1401–9; and Douglas W. Smith et al., "Wolf-Bison Interactions in Yellowstone National Park," *Journal of Mammalogy* 81 (November 1, 2000): 1128–35.

26. W. B. Ballard et al., "Accuracy, Precision, and Performance of Satellite Telemetry for Monitoring Wolf Movements," in Carbyn, Fritts, and Seip, *Ecology and Conservation of Wolves*, 461.

27. While it is true that wolves feast mainly on large prey, they will also eat beavers, ground squirrels, berries, and human garbage. For wolves' diet see L. David Mech and Luigi Boitani, eds., *Wolves: Behavior, Ecology, and Conservation* (Chicago: University of Chicago Press, 2003), 104–11.

28. For large carnivores' place in the food chain see Paul Colinvaux, *Why Big Fierce Animals Are Rare: An Ecologist's Perspective* (Princeton: Princeton University Press, 1978), 18–31.

29. Ibid., 212.

30. *Vermont State Papers*, vol. 40, "Wolf Certificates," in the Archives of the Secretary of State, Montpelier. "Wolf-Scalp Payment Certificates (1811–1828)," in Ashtabula County, Ohio, records, 1811–70, Western Reserve Historical Society, Cleveland. Handel M. Shumway, Collector, Wolf Scalp Certificates, 1810–18, Cuyahoga County, Ohio, Western Reserve Historical Society, Cleveland.

31. For an overview of wolf population densities see Mech, *The Wolf*, 65–67.

32. For a quick introduction to wildlife population swings see Botkin, *Discordant Harmonies*, 27–49. For carrying capacity see Colinvaux, *Why Big Fierce Animals Are Rare*, 13; and Durward L. Allen, *Our Wildlife Legacy* (New York: Funk and Wagnalls, 1954), 44–60.

33. For seasonal travels and denning see Mech, *The Wolf*, 55–56.

34. Bounty laws often distinguished puppies or whelps from grown wolves. In 1736 Worcester, Massachusetts, adopted a bounty of four pounds for "any grown wolf within the [town] bounds" and of twenty shillings "for a wolf's whelp other than such as shall be taken out of the belly of a bitch wolf." *Early Records of the Town of Worcester*, book 1, 1722–39 (Worcester: Worcester Society of Antiquity, 1879), 101. For whelp fraud see John Russell Bartlett, ed., *Records of the Colony of Rhode Island and Providence Plantations in New England* (Providence: A. Crawford Greene, 1856), 4: 574.

35. Abby Maria Hemenway, *The Vermont Historical Gazetteer*, vol. 5 (Claremont, N.H.: Claremont Manufacturing Company, 1877), 444–45.

36. Sources for bounty recipients' military service include Carleton E. Fisher and Sue G. Fisher, *Vermont Soldiers, Sailors, and Patriots of the Revolutionary War* (Rockport: Picton, 1998); and Adjutant General's Office, *Roster of Ohio Soldiers in the War of 1812* (Columbus, Ohio: Edward T. Miller, 1916). For military wolf hunt drills see Bruce Hampton, *The Great American Wolf* (New York: Henry Holt, 1997), 74. Hubbardton fight witness Lieutenant William Digby quoted in Richard M. Ketchum, *Saratoga: Turning Point of America's Revolutionary War* (New York: Henry Holt, 1997), 213.

37. Phyllis Brown Miller, ed., *Index to the Grave Records of Servicemen of the War of 1812, State of Ohio* (Columbus: Ohio Society United States Daughters of 1812, 1988). For northern Ohio in the War of 1812 see Donald R. Hickey, *The War of 1812: A Forgotten Conflict* (Urbana: University of Illinois Press, 1989), 85.

38. For examples of bounties placed on wildcats and crow-billed blackbirds see *Copy of the Old Records of the Town of Duxbury, Mass., from 1642 to 1770* (Plymouth, Mass.: Avery and Doten, 1893), 241, 249; for rattlesnakes see *Concord Town Records, 1732–1820* (Concord, N.H.: Republican Press Association, 1894), 16, 18, 31; for foxes see *Watertown Records* (Watertown, Mass.: Fred G. Barker, 1894), 16.

39. *History of Medina County and Ohio*, 635.

40. Ibid., 635–36.

41. Redfield's nose twisting ibid., 490. Lindholdt, ed., *John Josselyn*, 60; Scott Russell Sanders, ed., *Audubon Reader: The Best Writings of John James Audubon* (Bloomington: Indiana University Press, 1986), 51. Thomas Morton, *New English Canaan* (1637; Boston: The Prince Society, 1883), 208. Story of Ohio wolves running from boy in *History of Medina County and Ohio*, 571.

42. *Pioneer and General History of Geauga County* (Burton, Ohio: Historical Society of Geauga County, 1880), 110.

43. *History of Medina County*, 418.

44. For howling behavior see Fred H. Harrington and L. David Mech, "Wolf Howling and Its Role in Territory Maintenance," *Behaviour* 68 (1979): 207–48.

5. SURROUNDED

1. The story of the Ohio travelers feeding their children to the wolves is retold in Thomas A. Knight, "Did Wolves Ever Attack a Human Being?" unpublished manuscript, Western Reserve Historical Society, 4–5.

2. For an assessment of record of wolf predation on humans see L. David Mech, *The Wolf: The Ecology and Behavior of an Endangered Species* (Minneapolis: University of Minnesota Press, 1970), 291; and R. J. Rutter and D. H. Pimlott, *The World of the Wolf* (Philadelphia: J. B. Lippincott, 1968), 202.

3. For examples of the type of local histories that often contained wolf legends see A. M. Gaverly, *History of the Town of Pittsford, Vt.* (Rutland: Tuttle, 1872); *A History of the First Century of the Town of Parsonsfield, Maine* (Portland: Brown Thurston, 1888); and George Kuhn Clarke, *History of Needham, Massachusetts, 1711–1911* (Needham: privately printed, 1912).

4. Knight, "Did Wolves Ever . . . ?" 4.

5. "Ivan Ivanovich," in *Poems and Plays of Robert Browning* (New York: Modern Library, 1934), 1057–64. Willa Cather, *My Antonia* (Boston: Houghton Mifflin, 1926), 63–67.

6. For a discussion of faulty folklore see Richard Dorson, *Folklore and Fakelore: Essays Toward a Discipline of Folk Studies* (Cambridge: Harvard University Press, 1976).

7. Richard Slotkin, *Regeneration Through Violence: The Mythology of the American Frontier, 1600–1860* (Middletown, Conn.: Wesleyan University Press, 1973); Richard Slotkin, *The Fatal Environment: The Myth of the Frontier in the Age of Industrialization* (Middletown, Conn.: Wesleyan University Press, 1985); Richard Slotkin, *Gunfighter Nation: The Myth of the Frontier in Twentieth-Century America* (New York: HarperPerennial, 1998).

8. David Humphreys, *An Essay on the Life of . . . Israel Putnam* (Middletown, Conn.: Hudson and Goodwin, 1794), 21.

9. Ibid., 21–22.

10. Ibid., 23–24.

11. Ibid., iii–iv.

12. For republican virtue see Gordon S. Wood, *The Radicalism of the American Revolution* (New York: Vintage, 1991), 104–9.

13. Marsh story in *History of Medina County and Ohio* (Chicago: Baskin and Battey, 1881), 560.

14. Michael Jay Katz, *Buckeye Legends: Folktales and Lore from Ohio* (Ann Arbor: University of Michigan Press, 1994), 162.

15. "A Night Among the Wolves," *Harper's New Monthly Magazine*, May 1853, 810–12.

16. Fish-flinging story and sawyer's escape in George Wheeler and Henry Wheeler, *History of Brunswick, Topsham, and Harpswell, Maine* (Boston: Alfred Mudge, 1878), 88–89. Sam Hill anecdote in Elsie H. Pool, "Sam Hill!" *Vermont History* 22 (1954): 145.

17. Lost-in-the-woods stories in James Hosmer, ed., *Winthrop's Journal*, vol. 1 (New York: Scribner's, 1908), 98, 135, 142.

18. Lost-child story in Charles Bronson, *The Bronson Book: Accounts of the Establishment and Early Settlement of the Connecticut Western Reserve as Written and Collected from the Writings of the Early Pioneers* (Stow, Ohio: Stow Public Library, 1945), 69.

19. Anecdotes in L. H. Everts, *Combination Atlas Map of Medina County* (Chicago, 1874), 203–4, 221–24.

20. For wolves' daily activity patterns see C. Vila, V. Urios, and J. Castroviejo, "Observations on the Daily Activity Patterns in the Iberian Wolf," in L. N. Carbyn, S. H. Fritts, and D. R. Seip, eds., *Ecology and Conservation of Wolves in a Changing World* (Edmonton: Canadian Circumpolar Institute, 1995), 335–40.

21. Distance of wolf howls in Mech, *The Wolf*, 100.

22. Walter R. Nelson, *History of Goshen, New Hampshire* (Concord, N.H.: Evans, 1957), 140.

23. Aquidneck hunt in Samuel Greene Arnold, *History of the State of Rhode Island*, vol. 1 (Providence: Preston and Rounds, 1894), 154. For examples of New England circle hunts see John B. Hill, *History of the Town of Mason, New Hampshire, from the First Grant to 1858* (Boston: Lucius A. Elliot, 1858), 46; William H. Gifford, *Colebrook: A Place Up Back of New Hampshire* (Colebrook: News and Sentinel, 1970), 173–74; John Langdon Sibley, *A History of the Town of Union, in the County of Lincoln, Maine* (Boston: Benjamin B. Mussey, 1851), 407; Francis Manwaring Caulkins, *History of New London, Connecticut, from First Survey of the Coast in 1612 to 1860* (New London: H. D. Utley, 1895), 404. Essex county hunt in Alonzo Lewis, *History of Lynn, Essex County, Massachusetts: Including Lynnfield, Saugus, Swampscott, and Nahant, 1629–1864* (Lynn: George C. Herbert, 1864), 329. Lyman Simpson Hayes, *History of the Town of Rockingham, Vermont,*

1753–1907 (Billows Falls, Vt.: by the town, 1907), 104–5. *The History of the Town of Amherst, Massachusetts* (Amherst: Carpenter and Morehouse, 1896), 31. Chittenden hunt in Amy Belding, "Bound to No Sect," *Vermont History,* October 1965, 454. Nelson, *History of Goshen,* 140.

24. Abby Maria Hemenway, "The Great Wolf Hunt on Irish Hill," in *The Vermont Historical Gazetteer: A Local History of All the Towns in the State,* vol. 4 (Montpelier: Vermont Watchman and State Journal, 1882), 70–72.

25. Rufus Smith's barn raising in *History of Medina County,* 379.

26. For examples of bear attack see Lewis, *History of Lynn,* 135–36. Mother and the balls of fur in Wilson Waters, *History of Chelmsford, Massachusetts* (Lowell, Mass.: Courier-Citizen, 1917), 427.

27. William Wood, *New England's Prospect* (London: John Bellamie, 1634), 19.

28. Bugbee and Abbott stories in Henry Hubart Vail, *Pomfret, Vermont,* vol. 1 (Boston, 1930), 145–47. Butterfield's adventure in W. R. Chochrane, *History of Francestown, New Hampshire* (Francestown: George K. Wood, 1895), 439–40. Woman and infant in Waters, *History of Chelmsford,* 427. Farnsworths in Martha Frizzell, *Second History of Charlestown, New Hampshire: The Old Number Four* (Littleton: Courier, 1955), 311.

29. Levi W. Leonard, *The History of Dublin, New Hampshire* (Dublin: published by the Town of Dublin, 1920), 280.

30. *History of Medina County,* 628.

31. Ohio road story ibid. Chochrane, *History of Francestown,* 187.

32. Stowell anecdote in William H. Child, *History of the Town of Cornish, New Hampshire, 1763–1910,* vol. 1 (Concord: Rumford, 1910, rpt. 1963), 37–38.

33. Bear trap story ibid., 35–36.

34. Vail, *Pomfret, Vermont,* 148.

6. METAPHORS OF SLAUGHTER

1. Several accounts of the Great Hinckley Hunt exist. See Milton P. Peirce, "The Great Hinckley Hunt," *American Field,* January 4, 1890, 1–3; Richard H. Dillon, "The Great Ohio Wolf Hunt," *Midwest Folklore* 3 (Spring 1953): 29–34; and N. B. Northrop, *Pioneer History of Medina County* (Medina, Ohio: George Redway, 1861): 110–21. Quotation from Peirce, "The Great Hinckley Hunt," 2.

2. Peirce, "The Great Hinckley Hunt," 2, 3.

3. Judge Hinckley's name is mentioned in Dillon, "The Great Ohio Wolf Hunt," 29.

4. Travelers' accounts are the best sources on the physical and social landscape of the Western Reserve. See Henry Leavitt Elsworth, *A Tour of Connecticut in 1811,* ed. Philip Shriver (Cleveland: Western Reserve Historical Society, 1985); and D. Griffiths, *Two Years Residence in the New Settlements of Ohio, North America: With Directions to Emigrants* (London: Westley and Davis, 1835). Connecticut Colony's royal charter quoted in Harlan Hatcher, *The Western Reserve: The Story of New Connecticut,* 3d ed. (Kent, Ohio: Kent State University Press, 1991), 3–15.

5. For the Connecticut Land Company see W. W. Williams, *History of the Fire Lands*

Comprising Huron and Erie Counties, Ohio, with Illustrations and Biographical Sketches of Some Prominent Men and Pioneers (Cleveland: Leader, 1879).

6. See Brian Harte, "Land in the Old Northwest: A Study in Speculation, Sales, and Settlement on the Connecticut Western Reserve," *Ohio History* 101 (Summer–Autumn 1992): 115–39.

7. For the living conditions in the Western Reserve see Zerah Hawley, *A Journal of a Tour Through Connecticut* (New Haven: S. Converse, 1822), 27, 31, 44, 34, 63. The immigrant Margaret Dwight on roads quoted in R. Douglas Hurt, *The Ohio Frontier: Crucible of the Old Northwest, 1720–1830* (Bloomington: Indiana University Press, 1996), 202.

8. See Harte, "Land in the Old Northwest," 132–33.

9. Wild lands mentioned in Harte, "Land in the Old Northwest," 129.

10. Hawley, *A Journal of a Tour Through Connecticut*, 44.

11. Ibid., 63.

12. Harte, "Land in the Old Northwest," 129, 133.

13. "Hunts," *Cleveland Register,* January 19, 1819, 2. "Ashtabula County Hunt," ibid.

14. "Hunts." For agrarian protest see Thomas P. Slaughter, *The Whiskey Rebellion: Frontier Epilogue to the American Revolution* (New York: Oxford University Press, 1986); and Edward Countryman, *The American Revolution* (New York: Hill and Wang, 1985), 74–104.

15. William Cogswell, "The Great Hinckley Hunt," in Northrop, *Pioneer History of Medina County,* 110–14.

16. Ibid., 111.

17. Ibid., 113. Cogswell was lucky to escape alive; in 1821 a stray bullet killed a seventeen-year-old hunter during a circle hunt in Medina County. See "Fatal Accident," *Cleveland Herald,* June 12, 1821, 2.

18. Cogswell, "The Great Hinckley Hunt," 114.

19. Wilford Woodruff, *Leaves from My Journal,* 2d ed. (Salt Lake City: Juvenile Instruction Office, 1882), 11.

20. Ibid., 11, 12.

21. The migration path, for example, of Joseph Smith's family from southern New England to Vermont, upstate New York, and northern Ohio follows the geographic movement of this study exactly. See Richard Anderson, *Joseph Smith's New England Heritage: Influences of Grandfathers Solomon Mack and Asael Smith* (Salt Lake City: Deseret, 1971).

22. For early persecutions see Leonard J. Arrington and David Bitton, *The Mormon Experience: A History of the Latter-day Saints,* 2d ed. (Urbana: University of Illinois Press, 1992), 44–64.

23. Lucy Smith, *Biographical Sketches of Joseph Smith the Prophet* (Liverpool, England: S. W. Richards, 1853), 250. For the events surrounding Joseph Smith's death see Arrington and Bitton, *The Mormon Experience,* 81–82.

24. *Times and Seasons* 5, no. 23 (December 15, 1844): 741–42.

25. *Journal History of the Church of Jesus Christ of Latter-day Saints* (hereafter *JH*), Church Archives, Salt Lake City, 42, August 18, 1844.

26. Ibid.

27. Bounty notice in *Times and Seasons* 2, no. 23 (September 28, 1841): 566. Sources on the Nauvoo wolf hunt include Brigham H. Roberts, *History of the Church of Jesus Christ of Latter-day Saints*, vol. 7 (Salt Lake City: Deseret, 1932), 45; Thomas L. Ford, *History of Illinois* (Chicago, 1854), 406.

28. Ford quoted in *JH* 42, September 27, 1844.

29. For a summary of the anti-Mormon critique of LDS social bonds see Arrington and Bitton, *The Mormon Experience*, 49–51.

30. For examples of mudslinging from both sides see *Times and Seasons* 2, no. 12 (April 1, 1841): 317; 5, no. 1 (January 1, 1844): 388; 6, no. 13 (July 15, 1854): 969; for a sampling of anti-Mormon vitriol see Eber D. Howe, *Mormonism Unveiled* (Painesville, Ohio: by author, 1834).

31. For Illinois party politics see Ford, *History of Illinois*, 406. Ford's advice in *JH*, 42, September 8, 1844.

7. A WEALTH OF CANINES

1. Will Bagley, ed., *The Pioneer Camp of the Saints: The 1846 and 1847 Mormon Trail Journals of Thomas Bullock* (Logan: Utah State University Press, 1997), 132.

2. Ibid., 168–69, 254, 152, 161. Joseph Smith, *Teachings of the Prophet Joseph Smith*, compiled by Joseph Fielding Smith (Salt Lake City: Deseret, c. 1938, rpt. 1974), 71.

3. See Jan Shipps, *Mormonism: The Story of a New Religious Tradition* (Urbana: University of Illinois Press, 1985), 57–58.

4. For determinism see Virginia Scharff, "Man and Nature! Sex Secrets of Environmental History," in John P. Herron and Andrew G. Kirk, eds., *Human/Nature: Biology Culture and Environment* (Albuquerque: University of New Mexico Press, 1999): 31–48. For the history of evolution and social theories see Carl N. Degler, *In Search of Human Nature: The Decline and Revival of Darwinism in American Social Thought* (New York: Oxford University Press, 1991). For evolutionary explanations of social or cultural phenomena see Richard Dawkins, *The Selfish Gene* (New York: Oxford University Press, 1976); Matt Ridley, *The Red Queen: Sex and the Evolution of Human Nature* (New York: Viking, 1993); Daniel C. Dennett, *Freedom Evolves* (New York: Viking, 2003).

5. For cute body proportions and breeding for juvenile characteristics see James Serpell, *In the Company of Animals* (New York: Cambridge University Press, 1986), 75–76, 81. See also Stephen Jay Gould, "Mickey Mouse Meets Konrad Lorenz," *Natural History* 88 (May 1979): 30–36.

6. For the evolution of culture see Edward O. Wilson, *Sociobiology: The New Synthesis*, 25th anniversary ed. (Cambridge: Belknap Press of Harvard University Press, 2000), 559–62; Daniel C. Dennett, *Darwin's Dangerous Idea: Evolution and the Meanings of Life* (New York: Touchstone, 1995), 338–40; and Ernst Mayr, *This Is Biology: The Science of the Living World* (Cambridge: Belknap Press of Harvard University Press, 1997), 241–43. For a discussion of the concept of fitness see Diane Paul, "Fitness: Historical Perspectives," in Evelyn Fox Keller and Elisabeth A. Lloyd, eds., *Keywords in Evolutionary Biology* (Cambridge:

Harvard University Press, 1992), 112–14, and John Beatty, "Fitness: Theoretical Contexts," ibid., 115–19.

7. Wilson places culture on the slow end of "environmental tracking devices." I argue that culture combines quick and slow responses (as does Wilson), and when compared with the glacial pace of evolutionary adaptation, culture is rather fast. See Wilson, *Sociobiology*, 560.

8. M. W. Fox, "Ontogeny of Prey-Killing Behavior in Canidae," *Behaviour* 35 (1969): 259–72.

9. For socialization and play see Marc Bekoff, "The Development of Social Interaction, Play, and Metacommunication in Mammals: An Ethological Perspective," *Quarterly Review of Biology* 47 (December 1972): 412–34; L. David Mech, *The Wolf: The Ecology and Behavior of an Endangered Species* (Minneapolis: University of Minnesota Press, 1970), 48–49, 75, 81, 127–28, 136, 142, 148, 288. See Mech also for dominance and play, *The Wolf*, 69, 128, 134.

10. Mech, *The Wolf*, 59–64.

11. Ibid., 114–16.

12. Thomas J. Meier et al., "Pack Structure and the Genetic Relatedness Among Wolf Packs in a Naturally-Regulated Population," in L. N. Carbyn, S. H. Fritts, and D. R. Seip, eds., *Ecology and Conservation of Wolves in a Changing World* (Edmonton: Canadian Circumpolar Institute, 1995), 293–302. For a discussion of wolf incest as well as new evidence that refutes the incest theory see D. Smith et al., "Is Incest Common in Gray Wolf Packs?" *Behavioral Ecology* 8 (1997): 384–91.

13. For the relationship between predators and prey and the wild rides these two populations often take together see Michael E. Nelson and L. David Mech, "Deer Social Organization and Wolf Predation in Northeastern Minnesota," *Wildlife Monographs* 77 (July 1981): 6–59; William C. Gasaway et al., "Interrelationships of Wolves, Prey, and Man in Interior Alaska," *Wildlife Monographs* 84 (July 1983): 1–50; and A. T. Bergerud and W. B. Ballard, "Wolf Predation on Caribou: The Nelchina Herd Case History, A Different Interpretation," *Journal of Wildlife Management* 52, no. 2 (1988): 344–57.

14. See Charles S. Elton, *Animal Ecology* (New York: Macmillan, 1927). For a discussion of predator and prey size, Elton's energy pyramid, and the species that finesse the numbers see Paul Colinvaux, *Why Big Fierce Animals Are Rare: An Ecologist's Perspective* (Princeton: Princeton University Press, 1978), 18–31. Pyramid of numbers in Elton, *Animal Ecology*, 209. Baleen whale example taken from Colinvaux, *Why Big Fierce Animals Are Rare*, 29.

15. The demands of hunting do not determine the size of wolf packs. Food supply seems to be the primary regulator. Many packs retain a coterie of freeloaders. These animals eat from communal kills, but they rarely help bring the prey down. As long as calories remain plentiful, the hunting minority (usually the dominant members of the pack with the physical vigor and life experience to kill without being killed) indulge hangers-on that may be too young, infirm, or passive to participate. When food resources tighten, however, pack numbers

will drop through death and dispersal. In either case, it is the amount of food, not the acquisition of it, that determines pack size. See L. David Mech and Luigi Boitani, *Wolves: Behavior, Ecology, and Conservation* (University of Chicago Press, 2003), 10–11.

16. For a brief summary of altruism debate see Evelyn Fox Keller and Elisabeth A. Lloyd, eds., *Keywords in Evolutionary Biology* (Cambridge: Harvard University Press, 1992), 19–33. Definition and examples of altruism in Wilson, *Sociobiology*, 117, 121–28.

17. See Charles Darwin, *The Descent of Man and Selection in Relation to Sex* (London: John Murray, 1871), 87; and W. D. Hamilton, "The Genetical Evolution of Social Behaviour I. and II.," *Journal of Theoretical Biology* 7 (1964): 1–52.

18. R. L. Trivers, "The Evolution of Reciprocal Altruism," *Quarterly Review of Biology* 46 (1971): 35–57.

19. For a thoughtful discussion of the effects of the altruism metaphor see Alexander Rosenberg, "Altruism: Theoretical Contexts," in Keller and Lloyd, *Keywords in Evolutionary Biology*, 19–33.

20. Lois Crisler, *Arctic Wild* (New York: Harper Perennial, 1973; orig. pub. 1953); Lois Crisler, *Captive Wild: One Woman's Adventure Living with Wolves* (New York: Lyons, 2000; orig. pub. 1968).

21. Actually, Herb tried to discipline the wolves once and Lois scolded him. Crisler, *Captive Wild*, 104–5. For examples of the couple's imitative behavior see *Arctic Wild*, 121, 158, 268.

22. For loving see *Captive Wild*, 184. Crisler lists wolves' qualities in *Arctic Wild*, 288–90. For bullying episodes see *Captive Wild*, 147–48, 184, 189.

23. For a sampling of the Crislers' views on humanity see *Arctic Wild*, 179, 289–90.

24. Paul D. Riley, ed., "A Winter of the Plains, 1870–1871: The Memoirs of Lawson Cooke," *Kansas Historical Quarterly* 37, no. 1 (Spring 1971): 36. G. S. McCain, "A Trip from Atchison, Kansas, to Laurette, Colorado: Diary of G. S. McCain," *Colorado Magazine* 27, no. 2 (April 1950): 98.

25. "Journal of Mosiah Lyman Hancock," in Daughters of Utah Pioneers, *Chronicles of Courage*, vol. 6 (Salt Lake City: International Society of Daughters of Utah Pioneers, 1995), 209–11.

26. Lewis H. Garrard, "Wah-To-Yah and the Taos Trail," in Ralph P. Beiber, ed., *Southwest Historical Series*, vol. 6 (Glendale, Ariz.: Arthur H. Clark, 1938), 12. Calvin Perry Clark, *Diary (1859): From Plano, Illinois, to Pikes Peak*, April 3, Western History Collections, Denver Public Library. For canid names see Thomas D. Sanders, "Reminiscence," Western History Collections, Denver Public Library; Frank M. Stahl, *One-Way Ticket to Kansas: The Autobiography of Frank M. Stahl*, as told to Margaret Whittemore (Lawrence: University of Kansas Press, 1959), 49; and Alfred Barnits, *Papers*, September 15, 1867, Beinecke Library, Yale University, New Haven, Connecticut. For wolf numbers see Clark, *Diary*, April 3, 1859; Louise Barry, "The Ranch at Walnut Creek Crossing," *Kansas Historical Quarterly* 37, no. 2 (Summer 1971): 124. Huge pack in Garrard, "Wah-To-Yah and the Taos Trail," 81.

27. For human and animal adaptations on the plains see Andrew C. Isenberg, *The Destruction of the Bison: An Environmental History, 1750–1920* (Cambridge: Cambridge University Press, 2000); and Dale F. Lott, *American Bison: A Natural History* (Berkeley: California University Press, 2002), 99–104.

28. For wolves running to gunshots see Bruce Hampton, *The Great American Wolf* (New York: Henry Holt, 1997), 107–8; and Isenberg, *The Destruction of the Bison,* 159.

29. Barry, "The Ranch at Walnut Creek Crossing," 134. George Simpson, interview, 1926, Bison Range Collection, J. Evetts Haley Library, Midland, Texas. Justus L. Conzad, "Reminiscence," Nebraska State Historical Society, Lincoln. L. C. Fouquet, "Buffalo Days," *Kansas State Historical Society Collections* 16 (1923–25): 344.

30. *JH,* 67, May 8, 1848.

31. Pawnee incident in Bagley, *The Pioneer Camp of the Saints,* 134.

32. For Euro-American and Plains Indian relations see Robert M. Utley, *The Indian Frontier of the American West, 1846–1890* (Albuquerque: University of New Mexico Press, 1984); Richard White, "The Winning of the West: The Expansion of the Western Sioux in the Eighteenth and Nineteenth Centuries," *Journal of American History* 65 (September 1978): 319–43.

33. For an example of shot buffaloes left to the wolves see *JH,* 70, September 24, 1848. Wolf encounters in Bagley, *The Pioneer Camp of the Saints,* 311, 304, 143.

34. Livestock losses in *JH,* 69, August 28, 1848. Edwin Bryant, *Rocky Mountain Adventures* (New York: Worthington Company, 1887), 131. Burton quotation in *JH,* 70, September 24, 1848. Mangled ox described *JH,* 70, September 5, 1848.

35. *Missouri Republican* quoted in *JH,* 66, March 14, 1848. Esther Emily Ogden Bosworth, "A Difficult Journey," in *Unpublished Pioneer Stories,* Daughters of Utah Pioneers, Lessons for December 1976, Special Collections, Utah State University, 201. "A Sketch of the Life of Mrs. Sarah Burbank," University of Utah, Special Collections, unpublished manuscript, 3.

36. Heber C. Kimball, "Remarks at the Funeral of President Jedediah M. Grant," Great Salt Lake City, December 4, 1856, in *Journal of Discourses,* vol. 4 (Liverpool, England: F. D. and S. W. Richards, 1856), 136–37.

8. CALL IT A COYOTE

1. Austin Fife and Alta Fife, *Saints of Sage and Saddle: Folklore Among the Mormons* (Bloomington: Indiana University Press, 1956), 278–79.

2. Ibid., 280.

3. For wolves in nineteenth-century New England local histories see John Langdon Sibley, *A History of the Town of Union, in the County of Lincoln, Maine* (Boston: Benjamin B. Mussey, 1851), 406–7; Charles Brooks, *History of the Town of Medford* (Boston: Rand, Franklin, 1886), 35; and John B. Hill, *History of the Town of Mason, New Hampshire* (Boston: Lucius A. Elliot, 1858), 46.

4. The Latter-day Saints' attitudes toward and treatment of the Great Basin environment have stirred a debate among environmental historians. On the critical side, Dan Flores argues that the Mormons behaved like typical Euro-American

invaders, cutting down, tearing up, and otherwise exploiting the eco-region. See Dan L. Flores. "Zion in Eden: Phases of the Environmental History of Utah," *Environmental Review* 7 (Winter 1983): 325–44. Thomas G. Alexander offers a more positive "stewardship" vision of Mormons' relationship with the land. For his view, see Thomas G. Alexander, "Stewardship and Enterprise: The LDS Church and the Wasatch Oasis Environment, 1847–1930," *Western Historical Quarterly* 25 (Autumn 1994): 341–64. Other voices falling on either side of the debate include Donald Worster, "Expanding Our Moral Vision Beyond the Human Community," in John S. McCormick and John R. Stillito, eds., *A World We Thought We Knew: Readings in Utah History* (Salt Lake City: University of Utah Press, 1995): 411–21; Richard H. Jackson, "Righteousness and Environmental Change: The Mormons and the Environment," in Thomas G. Alexander, ed., *Essays on the American West, 1973–1974,* Charles Redd Monographs in Western History, no. 5 (Provo, Utah: Brigham Young University Press, 1975): 20–42; Jeanne Kay and Craig J. Brown, "Mormon Beliefs About Land and Natural Resources, 1847–1877," *Journal of Historical Geography* 11 (July 1985): 235–67.

5. Orson Hyde, "Common Salvation," September 24, 1853, in *Journal of Discourses,* vol. 2 (Liverpool, England: F. D. and S. W. Richards, 1856), 114. Kimball quotation in *Journal of Discourses* 3 (1856): 55. Claude T. Barnes, *The Grim Years* (Salt Lake City: Ralton, 1949), 12. Margaret McNeil Ballard in Joel Ricks, "Memories of Early Days," *Journal* (Logan, Utah), February 9, 1924, 12; "History of Daniel Leigh Walters, 1843–1917," unpublished manuscript, Special Collections, Utah State University, Logan, 2.

6. For the handcart episode see Leonard J. Arrington and Davis Bitton, *The Mormon Experience: A History of the Latter-day Saints* (Urbana: University of Illinois Press, 1979; 1992 2d ed.), 133–34.

7. Naomi M. Cottam, ed., "The Scouts at Devil's Gate (from Dan Jones' Diary)," in Daughters of Utah Pioneers, *Chronicles of Courage,* vol. 2 (Salt Lake City: International Society of Daughters of Utah Pioneers, 1991), 276, 280–81.

8. Edwin Bryant, *Rocky Mountain Adventures* (New York: Worthington, 1887), 162.

9. Howls in *JH,* 72, November 27, 1848. Livestock depredations in *JH,* 66, March 6, 1848. Cricket infestation in *JH,* 68, June 4, 1848.

10. *JH,* 68, June 9, 1848.

11. *JH,* 72, December 7, 1848. For a detailed account of the hunt's arrangements see Victor Sorensen, "The Wasters and Destroyers: Community-Sponsored Predator Control in Early Utah Territory," *Utah Historical Quarterly* 62 (Winter 1994): 26–41.

12. Tally in Edith Jenkens Romney, ed., "Thomas Bullock Diaries," March 1, 1848, LDS Church Archives, Salt Lake City; Sorensen, "The Wasters and Destroyers," 31. Second count in *JH,* 73, March 5, 1849.

13. Ute raid in *JH,* 73, February 28, 1849. Young's opinion of California in *JH,* 73, February 24, 1849.

14. Song in J. Marinus Jenson, *History of Provo, Utah* (Provo: by author, 1924), 169. *Salt Lake City Herald,* June 14, 1870, 3.

15. "Ordinances of the State of Deseret," *Utah Historical Society* 8 (April, July, October 1940): 175–76. *Auditor's Report of Public Accounts,* January 2, 1852, microfilm, Utah State Archives, Salt Lake City, 174. *Journal of Joint Sessions of the Legislative Assembly of Utah Territory,* September 23, 1851, microfilm, Utah State Archives, Salt Lake City, 106.

16. For coyotes and wolves see Rolf O. Peterson, "Wolves as Interspecific Competitors in Canid Ecology," in L. N. Carbyn, S. H. Fritts, and D. R. Seip, eds., *Ecology and Conservation of Wolves in a Changing World* (Edmonton: Canadian Circumpolar Institute, 1995), 315–23.

17. For coyote name see Gerry Parker, *Eastern Coyote: The Story of Its Success* (Halifax, Nova Scotia: Nimbus, 1995), 4.

18. Ibid., 43. John B. Theberge and Mary T. Theberge, *Wolf Country: Eleven Years Tracking the Algonquin Wolves* (Toronto: McClelland and Stewart, 1998), 253.

19. *Utah Office of the State Auditor,* 1852–98, microfilm, series 514, Utah State Archives, Salt Lake City. Cache County Records, "Bounty Records," Utah State University Library, Special Collections, Logan; Wasatch County, Bounty Records, 1911–31, microfilm, series 84150, Utah State Archives, Salt Lake City.

20. *Utah State Auditor,* 1852–98. Wasatch County 1911–31; Cache County Records, "Bounty Records," Utah State University Library, Special Collections, Logan.

21. "Reminiscences of Pioneer Childhood," in Daughters of Utah Pioneers, *Chronicles of Courage,* vol. 6 (Salt Lake City: International Society of Daughters of Utah Pioneers, 1995), 147.

22. Ibid., 144.

23. Thomas Irvine in Joel Ricks, "Memories of Early Days," *Journal* (Logan, Utah), January 19, 1924, Utah State University Library, Special Collections, Logan, 9.

24. John Smith, Great Salt Lake City, to George A. Smith, Pottawattamie Lands, March 5, 1848, in *JH* 66, March 5, 1848.

9. ANNIHILATION AND ENLIGHTENMENT

1. Aldo Leopold, *A Sand County Almanac* (New York: Ballantine, 1949; reissue 1986), 138–39.

2. J. Franklin Jameson, ed., *Johnson's Wonder-Working Providence* (New York: Barnes and Noble, 1910), 110. Timothy Dwight, *Travels in New England and New York,* ed. Barbara Miller Solomon (Cambridge: Harvard University Press, 1969; orig. pub. 1821), 33.

3. Henry David Thoreau, *The Journal of Henry D. Thoreau,* ed. Bradford Torrey and Francis H. Allen, 2 vols. (New York: Dover, 1962; orig. pub., 1906), 220–21. William Cronon, *Changes in the Land: Indians, Colonists, and the Ecology of New England* (New York: Hill and Wang, 1983), 4.

4. The last wolves have become popular literary subjects. See Barry Holstun Lopez, *Of Wolves and Men* (New York: Simon and Schuster, 1978), 191–94; Bruce Hampton, *The Great American Wolf* (New York: Henry Holt, 1997), 1–14; and Rick McIntyre, *A Society of Wolves: National Parks and the Battle over the Wolf* (Stillwater, Minn.: Voyageur, 1993), 70–73.

5. For a history of the relationship of colonization and extinction see Peter Matthiessen, *Wildlife in America* (New York: Viking, 1959).

6. For a quick overview of taxonomic debates over species definition see Peter F. Stevens, "Species: Historical Perspectives," in Evelyn Fox Keller and Elisabeth A. Lloyd, eds., *Keywords in Evolutionary Biology* (Cambridge: Harvard University Press, 1992), 302–11. For an introduction to the development of biological classification schemes see Ernst Mayr, *This Is Biology: The Science of the Living World* (Cambridge: Harvard University Press, 1997), 124–50.

7. For a summary of the evolutionary history of wolves see L. David Mech, *The Wolf: The Ecology and Behavior of an Endangered Species* (Minneapolis: University of Minnesota Press, 1970), 19–20; and John B. Theberge and Mary T. Theberge, *Wolf Country: Eleven Years Tracking the Algonquin Wolves* (Toronto: McClelland and Stewart, 1998), 240–41.

8. See W. G. Brewster and S. H. Fritts, "Taxonomy and Genetics of the Gray Wolf in Western North America: A Review," in L. N. Carbyn, S. H. Fritts, and D. R. Seip, eds., *Ecology and Conservation of Wolves in a Changing World* (Edmonton: Canadian Circumpolar Institute, 1995), 353–73. For an example of subspecies categories see Edward E. Goldman, *The Wolves of North America*, part 2, *Classification of Wolves* (Washington: American Wildlife Institute, 1944), 404–7. For lycaon subspecies see Ronald M. Nowak, "Another Look at Wolf Taxonomy," in Carbyn, Fritts, and Seip, *Ecology and Conservation of Wolves*, 395–96.

9. The classic work in biogeography is Robert H. MacCarthur and Edward O. Wilson, *The Theory of Island Biogeography* (Princeton: Princeton University Press, 2001; orig. pub. 1967); for a popular treatment of the subject see David Quammen, *The Song of the Dodo: Island Biogeography in an Age of Extinctions* (New York: Scribner's, 1996). Peter Steinhart quotes geneticist Robert Wayne: "A wolf can disperse five hundred miles; one researcher estimates the zone of hybridization . . . is fifty times the dispersal distance, so that means wolves have a hybridization zone almost as big as a continent." Peter Steinhart, *The Company of Wolves* (New York: Vintage, 1995), 185.

10. See Peter F. Stevens, "Species: Historical Perspectives," in Keller and Lloyd, *Keywords*, 302–11. Jonathan Weiner, *The Beak of the Finch: A Story of Evolution in Our Time* (New York: Vintage, 1995), 122–23.

11. For the importance of genetic diversity to small and isolated wolf populations see Pär K. Ingvarsson, "Conservation Biology: Lone Wolf to the Rescue," *Nature* 420 (5 December 2002): 472.

12. The molecular classification of wolves started in the early 1990s. See Brewster and Fritts, "Taxonomy and Genetics of the Gray Wolf," 368–70.

13. See Robert K. Wayne, Niles Lehman, and Todd K. Fuller, "Conservation Genetics of the Gray Wolf," in Carbyn, Fritts, and Seip, *Ecology and Conservation of Wolves*, 400–403.

14. Theberge, *Wolf Country*, 256. For coyote expansion see Parker, *Eastern Coyote*. The relationship between coyotes and wolves has received new attention as reintroduced wolves have entered coyotes' territory in the Rocky Mountains.

See Wendy M. Arjo and Daniel H. Pletscher, "Behavioral Responses of Coyotes to Wolf Recolonization in Northwestern Montana," *Canadian Journal of Zoology* 77 (1999): 1919–27; Eric Gese and Scott Grothe, "Analysis of Coyote Predation on Deer and Elk During Winter in Yellowstone National Park, Wyoming," *American Midland Naturalist* 133 (January 1, 1995): 36–43; and Wendy M. Arjo, Daniel H. Pletscher, and Robert R. Ream, "Dietary Overlap Between Wolves and Coyotes in Northwestern Montana," *Journal of Mammalogy* 83 (August 1, 2002): 754–66.

15. For the debates over hybridization see L. David Mech and Luigi Boitani, eds., *Wolves: Behavior, Ecology, and Conservation* (Chicago: University of Chicago Press, 2003), 236–38. Coyotes' somewhat increased popularity has been due in part to the introduction of Native American trickster folktales into popular culture. See Jeanne Campbell Reesman, ed., *Trickster Lives: Culture and Myth in American Fiction* (Athens: University of Georgia Press, 2001).

16. For animals and cognitive development see Paul Shepard, *The Others: How Animals Made Us Human* (Washington: Island/Shearwater, 1996), 43–57.

17. For anxieties about mixing categories see Mary Douglas, *Purity and Danger: An Analysis of the Concepts of Pollution and Taboo* (New York: Routledge, 1966), 55–58. Elizabeth Atwood Lawrence, "The Sacred Bee, the Filthy Pig, and the Bat Out of Hell: Animal Symbolism as Cognitive Biophilia," in Stephen R. Kellert and Edward O. Wilson, eds., *The Biophilia Hypothesis* (Washington: Shearwater, 1993), 326, 318–19.

18. For a summary of Young's career see "Some Highlights Regarding the Official Life of Stanley P. Young," unpublished manuscript, Stanley Paul Young Papers, box 1: 100, Correspondence 1958–59, Western History Collections, Denver Public Library.

19. See Stanley Paul Young, "Bibliography of Stanley P. Young," privately published, 1956, ibid., box 1: 101.

20. Arthur H. Carhart and Stanley P. Young, *The Last Stand of the Pack* (New York: J. H. Sears, 1929). One need only look at the book's dedication to experience the purple haze of Carhart's prose: "They are the heirs of the Mountain Men. They are the followers of the last frontiers. They are the friends of all animals; the compassionate, regretful executioners of the animal renegades . . . to these men, the predatory animal hunters of the U.S. Biological Survey, this book is dedicated."

21. Ernest Thompson Seton, "Lobo: The King of Currumpaw," rpt. in Rick McIntyre, ed., *War Against the Wolf: America's Campaign to Exterminate the Wolf* (Stillwater, Minn.: Voyageur, 1995), 219, 227, 229.

22. For nature-faker debate see Thomas R. Dunlap, *Saving America's Wildlife: Ecology and the American Mind, 1850–1990* (Princeton: Princeton University Press, 1988), 27–31. Seton, "Lobo," 223–26.

23. Seton, "Lobo," 226–29.

24. For examples of modern folklore see Jan H. Brunvand, *Curses! Broiled Again! The Hottest Urban Legends Going* (New York: Norton, 1990); and Jan H.

Brunvand, *The Choking Doberman and Other "New" Urban Legends* (New York: Norton, 1986).

25. For examples of Young's reports see Stanley Young, "Financial Statement, February 1921"; "Narrative Report April, 1922"; and "Narrative Report of Work Accomplished for July, 1923," in Stanley Young Papers, box 2: 102, manuscripts: *The Last Stand of the Pack*.

26. Young's reports for June 1923 and December 1923 show 162 coyotes and 3 wolves killed in June and 133 coyotes and 2 wolves killed in December. Stanley P. Young, "Narrative Reports," June 1923 and December 1923, ibid. Bigfoot, member of a pack outside of Grand Junction, Colorado, reportedly had a $500 bounty on his head. See Carhart and Young, *The Last Stand of the Pack*, 137.

27. For problems with bounties see Monroe Bros. and Henderson, Thatcher, Colorado, to Stanley P. Young, predatory animal inspector, Denver, Colorado, June 10, 1923, Stanley Young Papers, box 2: 102, manuscripts: *The Last Stand of the Pack;* and R. J. Currier Jr., Grand Junction, Colorado, to Stanley P. Young, predatory animal inspector, Denver, Colorado, May 11, 1922, ibid. For the practice of den hunting see Stanley P. Young, *The Last of the Loners* (London: Macmillan, 1970), 51.

28. Stanley P. Young, "Old Lefty of Burns Hole," 3, unpublished manuscript, Stanley Young Papers, box 2: 102, manuscripts: *The Last Stand of the Pack*, 7–8.

29. For an example of wolves being educated by encounters with traps and baits see H. A. Roberts, government hunter, Burns, Colorado, to L. B. Crawford, predatory animal inspector, Denver, Colorado, January 29, 1921, transcript in the hand of Stanley Young, ibid.

30. Stanley P. Young, "Three Toes of the Apishapa," 1, unpublished manuscript, ibid. Stanley P. Young, "Unaweep," 6, unpublished manuscript, ibid. Carhart and Young, *The Last Stand of the Pack*, 125.

31. Stanley P. Young, "Old Whitey of Bear Springs Mesa, Colorado," 10, unpublished manuscript, Stanley Young Papers, box 2: 102, manuscripts: *The Last Stand of the Pack*, 11.

32. Ibid.

33. For examples of publicity see "Terror Slain: Bigfoot, Wolf Cattle Killer, Meets Fate," *Denver Express*, October 14, 1921, clipping in Stanley Young Papers, box 2: 102, manuscripts: *The Last Stand of the Pack*, WHC, DPL; and "Big Lefty: Noted Wolf, Is Captured After Eight Years," *Denver Express*, undated, clipping ibid. Old Lefty mentioned in The Stockmen of the Castle Peak Ranges, Burns Hole, Colorado, to the U.S. Biological Survey, Denver, Colorado, March 2, 1921, transcript in the hands of Stanley Young, ibid. Young outlines the goals of cooperative control in Stanley P. Young, "Our Federal Cooperative Control Work," unpublished manuscript, 1938, ibid., misc. fragments.

34. Carhart and Young, *The Last Stand of the Pack*, 289.

35. Frederick Jackson Turner, "The Significance of the Frontier in American History" (1893), in *The Frontier in American History* (Tucson: University of Arizona Press, 1986): 1; Brian W. Dippie, *The Vanishing American: White Attitudes and*

U.S. Indian Policy (Lawrence: University of Kansas Press, 1982), 218–19. James Fenimore Cooper, *The Pioneers*, ed. Leon Howard (New York: Holt, Rinehart, and Winston, Rinehart Editions, 1959); and Edward Abbey, *Desert Solitaire: A Season in the Wilderness* (New York: Ballantine, 1968; reissue ed. 1991).

36. Carhart and Young, *The Last Stand of the Pack*, 104, 200, 32, 163–64, 286–77.

37. Ibid., 168.

38. Arthur H. Carhart, Denver, Colorado, to Stanley P. Young, Washington, D.C., January 19, 1932, Stanley Young Papers, box 1: 100, correspondence, 1930–33.

39. Arthur H. Carhart, Denver, Colorado, to Stanley P. Young, Washington, D.C., February 23, 1932, ibid. For window display see Arthur Carhart, Denver, Colorado, to Stanley Young, Washington, D.C., September 20, 1929, ibid., correspondence 1928–29.

40. A. E. Gray, Oklahoma City, to Stanley P. Young, Washington, D.C., April 10, 1930, ibid., correspondence, 1930–33. Arthur H. Carhart, Denver, Colorado, to Stanley P. Young, Washington, D.C., July 8, 1927, ibid., correspondence, April–December 1927. Macon Miller, associate editor, *True Western Stories*, New York City, to Stanley P. Young, Denver, Colorado, March 24, 1926, ibid., correspondence, January–April 1927.

41. For the place of the wolf story in Leopold's biography see Curt Meine, *Aldo Leopold: His Life and Work* (Madison: University of Wisconsin Press, 1988), 458–59. Scholars intrigued by Leopold's philosophy include Mary Lorbiecki, *Aldo Leopold: A Fierce Green Fire* (New York: Oxford University Press, 1999); A. L. Herman, *Community, Violence, and Peace: Aldo Leopold, Mohandas K. Gandhi, Martin Luther King, Jr., and Gautama the Buddha in the Twenty-First Century* (Albany: State University Press of New York, 1998); J. Baird Callicott, ed., *Companion to* A Sand County Almanac: *Interpretive and Critical Essays* (Madison: University of Wisconsin Press, 1991); and Thomas R. Dunlap, *Saving America's Wildlife: Ecology and the American Mind, 1850–1990* (Princeton: Princeton University Press, 1988). For his experiences as a wildlife manager see Susan L. Flader, *Thinking Like a Mountain: Aldo Leopold and the Evolution of an Ecological Attitude Towards Deer, Wolves, and Forests* (Columbia: University of Missouri Press, 1974), 11–12.

42. For a description of the display see D. A. Gilchrist, Phoenix, Arizona, to Stanley P. Young, Washington, D.C., March 8, 1930, Stanley Young Papers, box 1: 100, correspondence, 1930–33.

43. Flader, *Thinking Like a Mountain*, 32. Leopold, *A Sand County Almanac*, 262.

44. The disappearance of the man who had claimed to be the principal author of the stories is an odd development. See Arthur Carhart, Denver, Colorado, to Mr. Williams, editor Sears and Company, New York City, December 17, 1927, transcript in Stanley Young Papers, box 1: 100, correspondence, November–December 1927. The wolf stories in *The Last of the Loners* are verbatim copies of the stories in *The Last Stand of the Pack*.

45. Young, *The Last of the Loners*, jacket. Radio program, "Sportsman's Guide,"

Hal Denton narrator, February 1, 1947, British Columbia, transcript in Stanley
Young Papers, box 2: 102, manuscripts, radio talks, 1931–47.

46. Charles F. Bassett, "Feeding the Weaned Minks," *Wildlife Research and Manage-
ment Leaflet*, BS-60, June 1936, USDA, Washington, D.C.; Robert C. McClana-
han, "Protecting Blueberries from Damage by Herring Gulls," *Wildlife Leaflet*,
BS-141, August 1939, USDA, Washington, D.C.; Ralph B. Nestler, "Common
Salt as Curative for Cannibalism Among Game Birds in Captivity," *Wildlife
Leaflet*, BS-163, June 1940, USDA, Washington, D.C.; USDA Section of Food
Habits, "The American Chameleon and Its Care," *Wildlife Research and
Management Leaflet*, BS-92, May 1937, USDA, Washington, D.C.

47. Sigurd T. Olson, regional director, FWS, Juneau, Alaska, to Stanley P. Young,
April 6, 1955, transcript in Stanley Young Papers, box 1: 100, correspondence:
1953–57. For predation myths see Young, *The Last of the Loners*, 180–81. Death
warrant comment ibid., 222.

48. Young, *Last of the Loners*, 308.

REINTRODUCTION

1. See Thomas McNamee, "The Killing of Number Ten," *Outside Magazine*
(May 1997) http://www.outsidemag.com/magazine/0597/9705wolf.html, 1–14;
Thomas McNamee, *The Return of the Wolf to Yellowstone* (New York: Henry Holt,
1998).

2. McNamee, *The Return of the Wolf*, 301.

3. For wolf recovery in the Rocky Mountains see Michael A. Nie, *Beyond Wolves:
The Politics of Wolf Recovery and Management* (Minneapolis: University of Min-
nesota Press, 2003); Karen R. Jones, *Wolf Mountains: A History of Wolves Along
the Great Divide* (Calgary, Alberta: University of Calgary Press, 2002); Renée
Askins, *Shadow Mountain: A Memoir of Wolves, a Woman, and the Wild* (New
York: Doubleday, 2002); Gary Ferguson, *The Yellowstone Wolves: The First Year*
(Helena: Falcon, 1996); Rick McIntyre, *A Society of Wolves: National Parks and
the Battle over the Wolf* (Stillwater, Minn.: Voyageur, 1993); and Hank Fischer,
Wolf Wars: The Remarkable Inside Story of the Restoration of Wolves to Yellowstone
(Helena: Falcon, 1995). For the restoration of red wolves in North Carolina,
Mexican wolves in the American Southwest, and plans for the species' return
to the Northeast, see Roland Smith, *Journey of the Red Wolf* (New York: Penguin,
1996); Rick Bass, *The New Wolves: The Return of the Mexican Wolf to the American Southwest* (New York: Lyons, 1998); and John Elder, ed., *The Return of
the Wolf: Reflections of the Future of Wolves in the Northeast* (Hanover: University
Press of New England, 2000). EIS comment numbers in McNamee, *The
Return of the Wolf*, 45.

4. Population numbers in McNamee, *The Return of the Wolf*, 25.

5. For a modern cow's life see Michael Pollan, "Power Steer," *New York Times
Magazine*, March 31, 2002, 44–77.

6. For Red Riding Hood and the wolf in the twentieth century see Catherine
Orenstein, *Little Red Riding Hood Uncloaked: Sex, Morality, and the Evolution of*

a Fairy Tale (New York: Basic, 2002). Wolf numbers for 2003 in Bruce Barcott, "Back in the Crosshairs," *Outside Magazine,* October 2003, 20–21. For delisting and management plans see Todd Wilkinson, "Call of the Wild Echoes in West as Wolf Recovery Succeeds," *Christian Science Monitor,* May 1, 2003; and "Fremont County Resolution Declares Wolves Predators," *Associated Press Newswire,* January 25, 2003.

7. Stockgrowers report quoted in Barcott, "Back in the Crosshairs."

Adaptation: and affective bonds, 152; and culture, 151–53; and fitness, 153, 159; human refusal to, 162, 171–72, 179, 230; persistence through, 105, 230–31, 239n10; speed and mistakes, 165–66; wolves, 6–7

Algonquians, Southern New England: and black wolves, 47, 50, 53, 64; called animals, 32, 42–43, 62; called wolves, 32, 42, 59, 62; encouraged to kill wolves, 52–53, 60–61; hunting taboos, 48; and Mohawk raiders, 43–44, 49–50; Narragansetts, 46, 48, 60; reciprocal justice, 49–50; use of wolf and sheep metaphors, 43–44, 50; wolf trapping, 45, 48, 59–61

Altruism, 157–59

Animals and history, ix

Aquidneck Island, 60

Ashtabula County, Ohio, 83, 87

Audubon, John James, 1–2, 4, 14, 70, 214

Bears: Algonquians' wrestling of, 34; brutality towards, 117–18; compared to wolf legends, 121–22; danger of, 117, 121–22; inversion in stories about, 118, 120–22; killed with axes, 95–96, 118; as sources of humor, 117–21

Biology, and cruelty, 74; timescale of, x, 4–5, 7, 14. *See also* Evolution

Bison, 164–65

Bounties: to encourage skilled trappers, 57–58; fraud, 61, 89; as historical sources, 83–87; Ipswich, Mass., experiments with, 56; last paid in New England, 55; and Native Americans, 52, 60–61; professionals' disapproval of, 194, 211; restrictions on payment, 60; seasonality of, 87

Browning, Robert, 103

Bureaucratization of wolf killing: bureaucrats as folk group, 12, 194–95, 209; government hunters, 194; last wolves, 194–95; partnership with livestock associations, 12, 192, 214; role of nostalgia in, 13, 195, 224; role of publicity in, 193, 195, 209, 215–18, 221; utilitarian mission, 220–22

Cape Cod, skirmish on, 19–22, 29

Carrying capacity, 85

Cogswell, William, 95–97, 131–33

Colonization: colonists' sense of victimization, 10, 142, 229–30; and extinction, 196; and human territoriality, 35; and time, 9

Communal hunts: booze in, 116, 125; conservatism of, 134, 139, 142–43; as folklore, 116, 131, 133; inversion in, 114, 126, 141, 229; Irish Hill hunt, 115–16; in New England, 115–16; as rite of passage, 131–33

Communication, animal vs. human, 20–21, 23, 29, 34; dominance displays, 31–32, 35; humans using animal signals, 22, 29; miscommunication, 21, 36; and territory, 19–23, 35–36, 64; writing, 22, 32. *See also* Howling

Coyotes, 183–87, 200–202, 211

Crisler, Lois, 159–61

Cuyahoga County, Ohio, 83–84, 87, 91

Denali National Park, 25

Dogs: and hunting, 37, 55, 75; as intermediaries between cultures and species, 34, 45, 100; mastiffs, 32–33, 52, 55–56, 69; mentioned in bounties, 52, 55, 61

Ecological Imperialism, 8, 92, 184

Eliot, John, 43

Elton, Charles, 156

Endangered Species Act, 13, 225, 228

Evolution: absence of motives, 7, 158–59; and culture, 231; and determinism, 149–50; and history, 8–9, 150; natural selection, 6–7, 9; and predator coexistence, 7–8; wolf and human social compatibility, 99, 150–52

"Experimental-nonessential Population," 14, 225

Extinction: cultural, 195, 216, 223–24

Farmers, as predators, 86–87, 89, 92

Folklore: and colonization, 5, 10–11, 72, 105, 230; compared to history, x, 38–39; and cruelty, 107; importance of historical context, 38, 46, 105, 110, 116–17; innovation and repetition in, 108–10; problems of inheritance, 38–40; timescale of, x, 4–5, 14; winnowing of, 38, 41

Ford, Thomas, 139–41

Goshutes and Paiutes, cricket eating among, 179

Grant, Jedediah, 170–71

Great Hinckley Hunt: body count, 125; described, 123–24; inspires more hunts; 130; killing of "monster bear," 132–33; as protest, 129–30, 134, 142–43; and speculators, 125–26

Great Plains: ecological transformation, 164–65; extermination of bison, 165–66; innovation on, 162; multiplicity of wild canines on, 164; open sightlines, 164

Hamstringing: by humans, 1; by wolves, 75

Harrington, Frederick, 28

Hawley, Zerah, 128–29

History: anachronism and cruelty, 4; timescale of, x, 4

Hosmer, Henry, 74–75

Howling: anti-Mormon mobs, 137; on Great Plains, 163–64, 169; group howls, 28; humans sounding like wolves, 19–20; misinterpretation of, xi, 98, 113; role in territory maintenance, x–xi, 28–29, 98, 155; in Utah, 180, 185–86; Wadsworth, Ohio, 98–99

Humphreys, David, 107–10

Hybridization: and evolution, 199–200; threat to wolves as symbols, 202; wolves and coyotes, 199, 200–202

Isle Royale National Park, 77–78, 81

Josselyn, John, 55, 69–70, 97, 100, 214, 228

King Philip's War, 32, 62–64

Last Stand of the Pack: death in, 216–17; fate and progress in, 210, 215–17; as historical sources, 211; and last wolf legends, 209–10; literary merit of, 205; poor sales of, 217–20

Last wolves: damaged bodies, 211–14; as doomed, 12, 195, 208, 222; intelligence, 12, 194, 212; *Lobo, King of the*

Currumpaw, as model for, 205–8; names, 194–95; nostalgia in, 213; Old Whitey, 213–14

Latter-day Saints: anti-Mormon mobs, 134–35, 137–38; and coyotes, 175–76, 183–85; crickets and gulls, 179–83; Devil's Gate fort, 178–79; folklore into history, 175; handcart immigrants, 178; hungry in Utah, 177–79; as hunters, 168–69, 183; livestock, importance to, 149, 167–69; Nauvoo "wolf hunt," 124–25, 139–43, 167; overland trail, privation on, 169; pioneer day celebrations, 181–82; pioneer hardship legends, 176–77, 185–77; recapitulation, 148–49; redefining wolves as coyotes, 175, 183–86; Salt Lake City vermin hunt, 180–81; whelp killing, 148; wolf bounties, 139, 184–85; wolf and sheep metaphors, 138–39, 148; wolves consigned to history, 174–75; wolves scavenging graves on Great Plains, 148, 169–71. *See also* Joseph Smith Jr.

Legends: inversion in, 111–12, 122, 229; lost in woods stories, 112–13; man kills bear with ramrod, 119–20; man steps in bear trap, 120; March, John surrounded, 110; Ohio couple feeds children to wolves, 102–3; Old Dick fiddles for life, 111; Patterson, Theodocia, surrounded, 110–11; sacrifices in, 112; Saint Edmund's head, 39; Uncle Tom fiddles for life, 173–74; wolf and Indian trapped together, 52; Woodruff, Wilford, surrounded, 134–35

Leopold, Aldo, 191–92, 195, 203, 220–21, 224

Livestock: as cause of conflicts, 11, 36, 166–69; and colonization, 9–10, 11; conquest of time, 5–6, Euro-American herding practices, 10, 54; mobility, 5; owners' identification with, 42, 50, 232–33; as territory, 54; in twenty-first century, 203, 232–33

Lopez, Barry, 2–3

Mather, Cotton, 42

McKittrick, Chad, 225–28, 234–35

Mech, L. David, 3, 23, 26, 77–79

Metacomet, 62–64. *See also* King Philip's War

Morton, Thomas, 9, 47, 97

Murie, Adolph, 76, 81

Mutation, xi

Nauvoo, Illinois, 124, 136–42. *See also* Latter-day Saints

New England: expansion of, 72; hunting in, 57, 59; islands as havens for domestic animals, 55; livestock thriving in, 54; patchwork landscape, 53, 56–57, 59; skulls and power, 63–64; swamps, 59; wars in, 62

Northeastern Woodlands: circle hunts in, 87; nimrods, 89–92; shameless hunting stories, 94–96, 100; spread of wolf lore, 104, 109

Panthers, 96

Peterson, Rolf O., 77–78, 81

Pincheon, William, 55

Poutrincourt, Jean Biencourt de, 31–32, 35

Predation: caution displayed by wolves, 77–78, 81–82; on Dall sheep, 73–74, 76; "dance of death," 75, 77–78; on deer, 75, 77–80; and evolution, 80; humans as predators, 6, 82–83, 97 (*see also* Farmers, as predators); humans as prey, 106, 170; misreading of kill sites, 75–77; on moose, 73, 77–78, 81; prey vulnerability, 73–74, 76, 79, 81–82, 100–101, 229–30; surplus killing, 80; as unequal relationship, 73, 80–81, 100, 156

Pring, Martin, 33–34

Putnam, Israel, 106–10, 133

Regeneration through violence, 106, 141–42, 229

Reproduction: cultural, 106, 109, 136; cultural vs. natural, 6, 11, 230; as weapon, 93

Rigdon, Sidney, 135, 138–39, 148

R-10, 225–28

Seton, Ernest Thompson, 205–9
Slotkin, Richard, 100, 229
Smith, Joseph Jr., 125, 135–37; instructions against killing animals, 147–48, 163, 166
Species classification: and cultural values, 196–97, 201; and evolution, 196–97, 202; humans' desire for clear boundaries, 202–3; meaningful variance, 198; and wolves, 197–203
Stoddard, Solomon, 43

Theberge, John B., 201
"Thinking Like a Mountain," 191, 220, 224
Top predators: avoidance and sociality, 94, 96–97; coexistence among, 36, 65; at mercy of environment, 156; niche, 6–7, 21, 74, 157, 229; struggles as prey, 74, 93–94, 100–101, 229
Transcendence, biological and cultural, 5–6, 142, 172, 230–31

Vermin, 93
Vermont, 83, 86–87, 89–92
Verrazano, Giovanni de, 29–30

Waymouth, George, 33
Western Reserve, 83, 102, 126–29, 162, 229
Williams, Roger, 46–49, 60, 63–64
Wolf heads: as disputed symbols, 45, 53, 63–65; and Indian skulls, 63; public display, x, 62; tributes, 45, 62–63
Wolf killing: agricultural context of, 58–59, 92, 95, 100; assorted methods, 52, 55–56, 99; baiting with dogs, 1–2, 5, 69–70; brutality of, 1–4, 69–72, 100, 106, 142, 206–7, 228; denning, 70, 211; federal takeover, 12, 70; pit traps, 1–2, 88, 99; set guns, 58; strychnine, 12, 136; wolf bullets, 52, 55; wolf hooks, 52, 56

Wolf lore: in Bible, 41–42; cures, 70; European legacy, 37, 40–41; Native American, 45–46; werewolves, absence of, 37, 42
Wolf place names, 52–53
Wolf Reintroduction, 13–14, 225–29, 233–35
Wolves: attacks on humans, 3; avoidance of humans, 9; and bison hunters, 164–66; changes in American attitudes towards, 2, 5, 12, 203, 218–19, 224–25, 233–34; chase response, 153–54; color, 47; criminalization of, 42, 45, 48, 62; dispersal, 23–25, 27, 155; dominance hierarchy, 7, 25–27, 154–56, 161; evolutionary history, 7; facial expressions, 25; genetic isolation, 200–201; importance of packs, 24, 156–57; intraspecific strife, 25; life speed, 162; as metaphor for human groups, 140; passivity, 1–2, 5, 37, 69, 97, 99–100, 214; as scavengers in wartime, 91; scent marking, 27–28; shared responsibility for raising young, 154–55; in sheep's clothing, 41, 50–51; social attachments, 7, 26–27, 159, 161–62; taxonomy, 198–99; territoriality, 24; as vermin, 93, 95; as whelps, 26, 154. See also Predation; Howling

Yellowstone National Park, 225
Young, Brigham, 137–41, 147, 167, 181, 186
Young, Stanley Paul, career in Bureau of Biological Survey, 203–4, 214, 222; Carhart, Arthur, 204, 216–20; views of wolves, 222–24; Wolves of North America, 205; as writer, 204